\
a
a
re
are

LES
Hud

DAN
Unive

CAMBRIDGE TEXTBOOKS IN LINGUISTICS

General editors: P. AUSTIN, J. BRESNAN, B. COMRIE, S. CRAIN,
W. DRESSLER, C. EWEN, R. LASS, D. LIGHTFOOT, K. RICE,
I. ROBERTS, S. ROMAINE, N. V. SMITH

Stylistics

In this series:

Stylistics

LESLEY JEFFRIES AND DAN MCINTYRE

University of Huddersfield

CAMBRIDGE UNIVERSITY PRESS
Cambridge, New York, Melbourne, Madrid, Cape Town, Singapore,
São Paulo, Delhi, Mexico City

Cambridge University Press
The Edinburgh Building, Cambridge CB2 8RU, UK

Published in the United States of America by Cambridge University Press, New York

www.cambridge.org
Information on this title: www.cambridge.org/9780521728690

First published 2010
Reprinted 2012

Printed at MPG Books Group, UK

A catalogue record for this publication is available from the British Library

Library of Congress Cataloguing in Publication data
Jeffries, Lesley, 1956–
Stylistics / Lesley Jeffries and Dan McIntyre.
    p.   cm. – (Cambridge textbooks in linguistics)
Includes bibliographical references and index.
ISBN 978-0-521-40564-5 (hardback)
1. English language – Style.   2. English language – Discourse analysis.
3. Style, Literary.   I. McIntyre, Dan, 1975–   II. Title.   III. Series.
PE1421.J447   2010
808 – dc22   2010020577

ISBN 978-0-521-40564-5 Hardback
ISBN 978-0-521-72869-0 Paperback

Additional resources for this publication at www.cambridge.org/jeffries-mcintyre

To the memory of our friend and fellow stylistician,
Mary Ellen Ryder

Contents

Acknowledgements

'Tailpiece' ('*italic*') by Roger McGough from *Gig* (© Roger McGough 1973) is printed by permission of United Agents (www.unitedagents.co.uk) on behalf of Roger McGough.

'Vinegar' by Roger McGough from *The Mersey Sound* (© Roger McGough 1967) is printed by permission of United Agents (www.unitedagents.co.uk) on behalf of Roger McGough.

'A Small Slaughter', from *The Collected Poems of Audre Lorde* by Audre Lorde. Copyright 1997 by The Audre Lorde Estate. Used by permission of W.W. Norton & Company, Inc.

'Up on the Moors with Keeper', 'Foreign Correspondent', and 'Dancing at Oakmead Road' by Maura Dooley from *Sound Barrier: Poems 1982–2002* (Bloodaxe Books, 2002). Used by permission of Bloodaxe Books.

'Privacy of Rain', by Helen Dunmore, from *Out of the Blue: Poems 1975–2001* (Bloodaxe Books, 2001). Used by permission of Bloodaxe Books.

'Doorsteps' by Pamela Gillilan from *Sixty Women Poets* (ed. Linda France) (Bloodaxe Books, 1993). Courtesy of Pamela Gillilan's estate (www.pamelagillilan.co.uk).

'Ironing' from *The Handless Maiden* by Vicki Feaver, published by Jonathan Cape. Used by permission of The Random House Group Ltd.

'Favela' from *In a Rare Time of Rain* by Milner Place, published by Jonathan Cape. Used by permission of The Random House Group Ltd.

'The Front Bedroom' by Allan E. Baker published in *Smiths Knoll* issue No. 30 (© Allan E. Baker 2003). Used by permission of the author.

'Pain Tells You What to Wear' by Medbh McGuckian by kind permission of the author and The Gallery Press, Loughcrew, Oldcastle, Ireland from *Selected Poems* (1997).

The extract from 'true lovers in each happening of their hearts' is reprinted from *Complete Poems 1904–62*, by E. E. Cummings, edited by George J. Firmage, by permission of W.W. Norton & Company. Copyright © 1991 by the Trustees for the E. E. Cummings Trust and George James Firmage.

'Thoughts After Ruskin' by Elma Mitchell first appearing in *The Poor Man in the Flesh* (Peterloo, 1976), now appearing in *People Etcetera: Poems New & Selected* (Peterloo, 1987). Used by permission of Harry Chambers, Literary Executor.

'If It Happens' by Philip A. Nicholson (© Philip A. Nicholson 1990) from *How To Be Well-Versed in Poetry* (ed. E. O. Parrott). Used by permission of Campbell Thomson and McLaughlin Ltd on behalf of Philip A. Nicholson.

'Song of the Non-existent' by Carol Rumens from *Best China Sky* (Bloodaxe, 1995), reprinted in *Poems, 1968–2004* (Bloodaxe, 2004) by kind permission of the author.

'Spring Sunshine' by Louis MacNeice from *Selected Poems of Louis MacNeice* (ed. W. H. Auden) (Faber and Faber, 1964). Used by permission of David Higham Associates Ltd.

'Long Distance' by Tony Harrison from *Selected Poems* (Penguin, 1984) and *Collected Poems* (Penguin, 2007). Used by permission of Gordon Dickerson, literary agent, on behalf of Tony Harrison.

'The Queen's English' by Tony Harrison from *Selected Poems* (Penguin, 1984) and *Collected Poems* (Penguin, 2007). Used by permission of Gordon Dickerson, literary agent, on behalf of Tony Harrison.

'Prayer' is taken from *Mean Time* by Carol Ann Duffy (Anvil Press Poetry, 1993).

'Robbing Myself' by Ted Hughes from *Birthday Letters* (Faber and Faber, 1998). Used by permission of Faber and Faber Ltd.

'Poem' by Simon Armitage from *Kid* (Faber and Faber, 1999). Used by permission of Faber and Faber Ltd.

'Home is so Sad' and 'The Importance of Elsewhere' by Philip Larkin from *Whitsun Weddings* (Faber and Faber, 1964). Used by permission of Faber and Faber Ltd.

'Harvest Bow' by Seamus Heaney from *Field Work* (Faber and Faber, 1979). Used by permission of Faber and Faber Ltd.

'The Kaleidoscope' by Douglas Dunn from *Elegies* (Faber and Faber, 1985). Used by permission of Faber and Faber Ltd.

While every effort has been made, it has not always been possible to identify the sources of all material used, or to trace all copyright holders. If any omissions are brought to our notice, we will be happy to include the appropriate acknowledgements on reprinting.

Preface

This book, in the 'red' series, is one that we are very proud to have been given the opportunity to write. We have both been teaching stylistics courses at different levels of University education for a number of years, and have found that the sheer variety and diversity of practice that it encompasses causes problems in introducing the field to students for the first time. Equally, this diversity is part of its attraction as a discipline which can interest students from all areas of English Studies, from English Language through Literature to Creative Writing, as well as those coming to text analysis from a Linguistics background.

There are very many excellent books on stylistics already in existence of course, and we pay tribute to these in the pages of this book. Many of these books have been written by significant figures in the Poetics and Linguistics Association (PALA), which has been an extremely important player in the development of the field. Most of these books are the product of a particular personal view (of the author) or represent a particular stage in the development of the field, and for this reason, we felt there was room for another, more eclectic book, which would try to sum up the state of the art as it reaches approximately its centenary.

In planning the book, we felt that it was important to engage readers early, but that this could not come before we had set out some of the principles of the field as we see them. We therefore open with a chapter which approaches theoretical questions about the nature and scope of the subject via some of the questions that we thought new researchers might ask. Equally, though we knew it was important to introduce readers to some of the methodological issues in the practice of stylistics, we saw that it was difficult to introduce these until readers had some sense of the subject through seeing it in practice. We therefore return to these more practical questions in Chapter 7, by which time we anticipate that readers will be in a better position to apply the advice to their work.

Between these two extremes, Chapters 2–6 are concerned with the range of activity that we felt currently represents the field of stylistics. There are many ways in which we could have sub-divided the field, but in the end we judged that a reader who is new to this type of work would benefit most from learning about the origins of stylistics, and then reading about how it has branched out and developed from these beginnings. This is not a strict history of the subject, since many of the early forms of stylistics still co-exist with more recent approaches. However, in terms of the ways in which stylistics has exploited the insights, theories and models of linguistics and other related disciplines, there is a broadly developmental structure to this book.

One of the most significant developments in the field is probably the move from being concerned solely with literary texts to seeing all text as having the potential for stylistic (if not aesthetic) effect. Many stylisticians through-out the world are still motivated largely by wanting to explain how literary effects are achieved linguistically, but there is a large and growing number who do not have this motivation as their sole focus and whose interest has increasingly been on the process of reading, the interaction of text and reader to produce meaning, and the effects of this process, whatever they may be. Such effects will differ according to text, context and reader, so that they may include literary effect, but can also include other more practical and/or ideological effects.

Finally, we hope that this book will work on a number of levels. It ought to work as an introductory text book, and the extent to which it is used straightforwardly in this way will depend on the tutor, the students and the context. In addition, we hope that it will serve as a statement of a field reaching maturity in the early part of the twenty-first century, and that this will not be a limiting, but an enabling statement which will encourage future researchers to continue developing a rich field which has come so far since the Russian formalist school of early last century.

1   Language and style

1.1   What is stylistics?

Stylistics has been defined as a sub-discipline of linguistics that is concerned with the systematic analysis of style in language and how this can vary according to such factors as, for example, genre, context, historical period and author (Crystal and Davy 1969: 9 and Leech 2008: 54). For instance, there is the individual style that distinguishes one writer from another, the styles associated with particular genres (e.g. 'newspaper language' or the gothic novel), or the characteristics of what might constitute 'literary' style. In this sense, analysing style means looking systematically at the formal features of a text and determining their functional significance for the interpretation of the text in question (Wales 1989: 438). In fact, the growth of stylistics over the last twenty or so years has meant that this definition no longer captures every aspect of stylistics, and part of our aim in this book will be to outline the remit of stylistics as it stands today. For example, during the 1980s interest began to grow in the role of the reader in interpreting texts (see, for example, Alderson and Short 1989 and Short and van Peer 1989), and recently there has been a surge of interest in the cognitive aspects of text comprehension (see Stockwell 2002a and Gavins and Steen 2003). The connection between stylistics and linguistics is that stylistics uses models of language, analytical techniques and methodologies from linguistics to facilitate the study of style in its widest sense. With some notable exceptions (e.g. Crystal and Davy 1969, Enkvist 1973, McIntyre *et al.* 2004, Jeffries 2007) stylistics has tended to concentrate on the analysis of literary texts, though there is in fact no reason why this should necessarily be the case. In this book we will concentrate our attention on both literary and non-literary texts.

Stylistics has its roots in the formalist school of literary criticism that emerged in Russia in the early years of the twentieth century, though the term 'style' goes back to classical rhetoric and poetics. The prime exponents of Russian formalism were Roman Jakobson, Victor Shklovskii and Boris Tomashevskii, and the aims of the movement were to isolate the properties and characteristics of literary language (notice the predilection for literary texts), and to explore how the concept of **defamiliarisation**[1] in both art and literature was at the root of the intrinsic aesthetic value of the work in question. At the heart of Russian formalism was the belief that the purpose of all art was to defamiliarise the familiar in order to generate for the viewer or reader a new perspective on the topic of the piece of work under consideration.

As a movement, Russian formalism was hugely influential for a large part of the early twentieth century, though its prime tenets were to prove unsustainable (see Simpson 1996: 7–19). The notion that it should be possible to delineate the formal (i.e. linguistic) features which figure in 'literary' as opposed to 'non-literary' language was eventually shown to be misconstrued. Indeed, as we shall show throughout this book, features of what we might intuitively think of as 'literary language' are equally common in non-literary genres, and stylistics nowadays tends to see 'literariness' as a point on a cline (see Carter and Nash 1990: 34) rather than as an absolute. Literariness in this sense is not a quality of a text, rather it is a concept belonging to a specific genre. Similarly, the contextual (social and cultural) aspects of what makes a text literary have been increasingly recognised in stylistics as elsewhere. Nevertheless, the impact of Russian formalism on the development of stylistics was of immense importance, and its influence is seen particularly in the psychological concept of **foregrounding** (see Mukařovsky 1964, Leech 1969: 56–72, van Peer 1980, 1986, Fowler 1986: 71 and Douthwaite 2000), which we will be concerned with in Chapter 2.

The predominance of literary texts as the focus of study within stylistics is reflected in some of the alternative names that stylistics sometimes goes by. These include **literary linguistics**, **critical linguistics**, **literary semantics**, **literary pragmatics** and **poetics**, and are mostly an attempt to find a term for the full range of activities practised by modern stylisticians, as well as an attempt to acknowledge that stylistics is not simply concerned with identifying formal features of style in language.[2] The predilection among some stylisticians for the analysis of literature also leads to a number of potentially confusing names for particular approaches to stylistics. These include **literary stylistics** and **linguistic stylistics**, and it is worth clarifying here the slight differences in focus of these two approaches. Sometimes, a distinction is made between literary and non-literary stylistics, and such a distinction usually refers to the kind of texts commonly studied. Hence, literary stylistics in this sense is concerned with the analysis of literature whereas non-literary stylistics is concerned with the analysis of non-literary texts. However, where the term *literary stylistics* is used in contrast to *linguistic stylistics*, the distinction is not between the kinds of texts studied, but between the objectives behind such analysis. Literary stylistics in this case is concerned with using linguistic techniques to assist in the interpretation of texts, whereas linguistic stylistics is about doing stylistic analysis in order to test or refine a linguistic model (Wales 1989: 438) – in effect, to contribute to linguistic theory. Most stylisticians would argue that what they do is a combination of both of these things, and this is the approach that we take in this book.

1.2   The need for stylistics

Stylistics has a firm place within linguistics, providing theories of language and interpretation which complement context-free theories[3] generated within other areas of language study. Nevertheless, the suggestion that stylistics is concerned with literature more than linguistics is a common criticism from theoretical linguists, though it is countered here by the corpus linguist, John Sinclair, who emphasises the importance of (literary) stylistics for the study of language when he says:

> no systematic apparatus can claim to describe a language if it does not embrace the literature also; and not as a freakish development, but as a natural specialization of categories which are required in other parts of the descriptive system.   (Sinclair 2004: 51)

The alternative criticism – that stylistics is concerned too much with language and not enough with literary concerns – might characterise the censure of stylistics from a literary direction. Our response to these criticisms is to say that whilst literary texts are, typically, the data upon which stylistic theories are developed, tested and applied, in the same way that, for example, spoken conversation tends to be the data used by sociolinguists, nevertheless, the stylistic features we will discuss in the book are not exclusive to any one genre, and stylistic techniques can be applied equally to non-literary texts. In discussing particular stylistic features we will draw on texts that best exhibit the features under discussion, and we will take examples from both literary and non-literary texts to illustrate analytical techniques. In addition, we will demonstrate that the value of a stylistic approach, whether from a literary or a non-literary viewpoint, is the precision and detail with which we can describe the textual effects of literature, whether our focus is the text itself, the reader's contribution or even some notion of authorial meaning. Stylistics has no settled view of the relationship between author, text and reader, but constantly evolves new theories and models of this dynamic relationship, in order to elucidate ever more clearly the processes by which meaning comes about.

Stylistics draws upon theories and models from other fields more frequently than it develops its own unique theories. This is because it is at a point of confluence of many sub-disciplines of linguistics, and other disciplines, such as literary studies and psychology, drawing upon these (sub-)disciplines but not seeking to duplicate or replace them. This versatility of approach and open-mindedness are, of course, characteristic of the humanities in general. Instead, it takes a particular view of the process of communication which places the text at the centre of its concerns, whilst being interested in the relationship between writer and text, and reader and text, as well as the wider contexts of production and reception of texts.

So, as well as drawing upon the descriptive apparatus of context-free linguistics, such as the formal descriptions supplied by structuralists, generativists and other twentieth-century linguistic movements, stylistics also takes into account the concerns of pragmatics on the one hand and sociolinguistics on the other, though these latter two sub-disciplines of linguistics have tended to be more interested in spoken than written language whereas stylistics has traditionally been concerned more with written than spoken texts. In other ways, stylistics also shares boundaries with cognitivist approaches to language, and, increasingly, with corpus linguistics. If what is described in the remainder of this book at times sounds rather similar to pragmatic, sociolinguistic, cognitive or corpus-linguistic accounts of language phenomena, this will be no more than we expect, as stylistics shares many concerns and theories of language and meaning with these fields, sometimes with only slight differences of emphasis. (For readers new to the terminology in this paragraph, we would reassure you that such terms as are needed to understand this book will be introduced and explained as they arise.)

In general terms, then, we have claimed that we need stylistics to provide an angle on language study which places the text at the centre of its concern. But what, in particular, might we expect stylistics to provide in relation to individual texts?

1.2.1   Literary explanations

The first and driving impulse of stylistics was to use the growing field of linguistics to explicate the textual effects that literary scholars may have agreed upon, but had neither the terminology to explain nor in many cases the wish to do so, being interested instead in other approaches to the study of literature which were less concerned with the language and more with the ideas encompassed by literary texts. Though some aspects of classical rhetoric could still be used to analyse the language of literature, this tended to be less appropriate to use with contemporary writing, whose authors were not trained in classical rhetoric and whose goal in writing works of fiction and poetry was not self-consciously rhetorical. Rhetorical analysis also worked at a more general level than the emerging linguistic analysis, the latter suggesting that it would become possible to explain in more detail the workings of the literary text and its rhetorical or other effects. Thus, for the first time, there was the opportunity to explain linguistically a range of literary features including the musical effects in poetry and the narrative complexities of modernist novels.

We will demonstrate the stylistic analysis of such different text-types throughout the rest of the book, but for now, let us consider one illustrative example of how linguistics might inform literary analysis. A principle that all stylisticians subscribe to is that meaning in language comes about through the linguistic choices that a writer makes (either consciously or unconsciously).[4] The following short extract from James Fenton's poem 'A German Requiem' illustrates this:

(1)   How comforting it is, once or twice a year,
        To get together and forget the old times.
                ('A German Requiem', Fenton 1980)

The second line of this extract stands out because of Fenton's use of the verb 'forget', which seems unusual in this context. Prototypically, we might expect 'remember' in its place. This is because the phrase 'old times' has a positive **semantic prosody** – that is, it collocates most often with positive concepts. We will discuss the concepts of collocation and semantic prosody in Chapter 7, but briefly, **collocation** refers to the fact that particular words frequently occur within close proximity to a restricted set of words, and semantic prosody refers to the meanings that delexicalised (i.e. relatively 'empty') words take on as a result of collocational patterns. Since 'old times' has a positive semantic prosody, it therefore seems appropriate for people to want to get together and *remember* rather than forget them. Moreover, 'forgetting' is not normally considered to be a conscious act, so it is odd to imagine a situation where a group of people would gather together in order to collectively and actively forget something – on the face of it a logical impossibility. We might describe the verb, technically, as changing its **transitivity** pattern, being used to describe an *intentional* action instead of an *unintentional* one, or **supervention**. (Transitivity will also be discussed more fully in Chapter 3.)

The word 'forget', then, is foregrounded – it stands out as not being what we would normally expect. Fenton is essentially playing with our preconceptions and the effect is to focus our attention on the absurdity of actively trying to forget something – an action which takes on a much greater significance when we realise that 'A German Requiem' is a poem about post-war Germany and its efforts to come to terms with its immediate past. The surface-level interpretation here is something that would no doubt be picked up on by a careful 'literary' reading, but the linguistic detail added by a stylistic analysis enables us to see more clearly where the literary effect is coming from.

Further evidence of how a linguistic approach can explicate an interpretation of a literary text can be seen if we consider Fowler's (1977) notion of **mind style**. Basically, mind style refers to the idiosyncratic world view of a character or narrator, exhibited through the linguistic structure of a text. Leech and Short (1981, 2007) explain the concept through an extract from Faulkner's *The Sound and the Fury*. The narrator of the extract below is Benjy, a young man with the mental age of a child, whose unusual view of the world is reflected through the linguistic choices he makes when describing the game of golf he is watching:

(2)   Through the fence between the curling flower spaces, I could see them hitting. They were coming toward where the flag was and I went along the fence. Luster was hunting in the grass by the flower tree. They took the flag out, and they were hitting. Then they put the flag back and they went to the table, and he hit and the other hit.   (Faulkner 1987: 3)

We can notice, for example, that Benjy does not use any of the lexical items associated with the game of golf; for instance, he uses *table* rather than *tee*. Furthermore, he uses the transitive verb *hit*, which we would normally expect to have an object, as though it is intransitive and does not need an object. This, according to Leech and Short (2007: 166), reflects Benjy's lack of understanding of the concept of cause and effect. The hitting that he witnesses is, for him, to no purpose; there is, literally, no object to the men's activity.

The reasons why such explanations of literary effects appealed to early stylisticians were various. It meant that some attention could be given to the question of whether 'literariness' was indeed a linguistic phenomenon, and to what extent features that were to be found in poetry were also to be found in other texts, such as advertisements, sermons, speeches of all kinds and so on. For example, foregrounding, of the sort described in example 1, can also be found in adverts and other kinds of non-literary writing. Example 3 is from a retirement announcement in a Huddersfield University staff newsletter. The final word has been blanked out here, and it is probably fair to say that most people, if asked, would guess that this last word is likely to be 'family' or 'children' or such like.

(3)   Stephen intends to spend more time with his wife and _____.

The reason that most people would choose a noun relating to family members to fit the blank slot in example 3 is again because of common collocational patterns. There is a restricted set of words that we would normally expect to follow 'wife and'. In actual fact, the word in the original announcement was 'caravan', giving rise to a humorous effect,[5] largely because the word 'caravan' is foregrounded as a result of not conforming to our expectations for this frame. This deviant collocation appears to put 'caravan' on a par with children and other family members, leading us to make inferences about the sort of person who would care as much for a caravan as for members of his family (depending on the cultural schemata of the reader, the word 'caravan' may also be imbued with certain negative connotations, perhaps deriving from long-remembered childhood holidays . . .). It turns out, then, that the kinds of features common to literary texts turn up just as much in non-literary texts too, though one thing we have not done here is to consider the literary merit or value of such language use. Such questions of aesthetics have normally not been the main concern of stylisticians, but it is not completely unknown for linguistic definitions of literary value to be debated too (see, for example van Peer *et al.* in press).

Much recent work in literary stylistics has been concerned with the reader's role in the creation of textual meaning, and this has led to an explosion of cognitive approaches which have taken the view that stylistics can help to explain the ways in which readers put together a meaning from a text. Some of these approaches have contributed to our understanding of how readers conceptualise the world described by a literary text, and this has led to the development of **text world theory** (described fully in Chapter 6) into a rich account of this process of imagining hypothetical situations and events in reaction to textual triggers. Hoover (2004a), for example, shows how changing just one or two of the words in a piece of writing can radically affect our interpretation of that text. In example 4, the words *Mr* and *Miss* are the only additions to this extract from William Golding's novel about prehistoric man, *The Inheritors*:

(4)   Mr Lok was running as fast as he could. His head was down and he carried his thorn bush horizontally for balance and smacked the drifts of vivid buds aside with his free hand. Miss Liku rode him, laughing . . .

                                                                            (Hoover 2004a: 102)

Hoover makes the point that adding these honorifics to the text greatly restricts the way in which the reader can form an image of the text world. *Mr* and *Miss* are titles which have no place in a prehistoric world, and their presence in the text therefore prevents the reader from generating the kind of text world that is triggered in the original text. Instead, Hoover suggests, the titles are likely to trigger the reader to generate an image of a foreign or colonial fictional world (note that this is especially likely if the reader has a Western European background). The full account of text world creation that stylistics can provide is a further indication of the value of stylistics for contributing to our understanding of how readers make sense of texts.

Other stylistic approaches which take a cognitive view have included the use of **schema theory** (from psychology) to explain certain kinds of responses to literary (and other) works. Some researchers (e.g. Cook 1994) have claimed that one of the distinctive features of literary works relates to the effect that they have on the perceptions of the reader. To the extent that they change the reader's 'schemata' – or standard ways of understanding the world – they are more or less 'literary' in effect. This viewpoint has been debated (see, for example, Jeffries 2001 and Semino 2001), but it points to one of the useful and productive features of stylistic study, which is the ability to advance thinking about literary value as well as processes of reading and negotiating meaning.

1.2.2   Language, rhetoric and power

The explanatory power of stylistics can also help us to understand in more depth the ways in which the style of texts can help to influence the perceptions of readers in more everyday situations, such as listening to political speeches, responding to advertisements and so on. One example, from a teenage magazine (*Jump*), is discussed in Jeffries (2007b):

(5)   Nor am I the kind of guy who only goes for earthy types (you know, girls who prefer eco-terrorism to experiencing life and refuse to, like, shave and stuff).   (quoted in Jeffries 2007b: 113)

Here, the writer of the article manages to create a 'new' semantic opposition which is a more specific version of the superordinate opposition between *normal* and *abnormal*, ubiquitous in such magazines and likely to have a strong influence on the young girls who read them. Jeffries comments on the structure which makes this ideology possible:

> This distancing from abnormality is achieved by the negation of a case which is pumped up by a hyperbolic and negative description of *earthy types*. The constructed opposite of the normal male (who doesn't like such women) and the abnormal male who does is compounded by the constructed opposition between *experiencing life* and *eco-terrorism*, the latter in some sense being a lack of living in the terms of this writer.   (Jeffries 2007b: 114)

Stylistics has evolved a detailed linguistic account of the kinds of persuasive techniques which are more generally covered by classical rhetoric. The use of stylistics for these purposes enables scholars to approach the explicitly persuasive aspects of style as linguistic phenomena, with the similarities between these rhetorical techniques and literary style also constituting comparative data for each other, since the tools available for the analysis of both these effects are essentially the same.

In addition to providing a more technical account, then, of persuasive textual features, stylistics, aided by insights from other fields such as pragmatics and discourse analysis, may also provide us with an account of the more implicitly manipulative uses of language. The development of **critical discourse analysis**, though not a product of stylistics alone, can nevertheless be seen as one of the sub-disciplines that has a family resemblance to stylistics, particularly in its positioning of the text at the centre of its concerns. This field is concerned with how the texts that surround us may subtly and sometimes even deliberately influence our political, social and even consumerist outlooks. For instance, Fairclough (1992), in an analysis of an extract from a university prospectus, shows how the language of the text constructs students as consumers and higher education as a commodity to be advertised in the same way as any other marketable product. In relation to his chosen text, he makes the point that the phrase 'You will need', which precedes a graphical representation of the university's entry requirements, shifts the emphasis away from the university as an authoritative gatekeeper, and instead constructs the student as a powerful consumer rather than a powerless applicant. This shift in emphasis is also realised through the university's entry requirements being outlined in a graphic, which, according to Fairclough, marginalises the entry conditions so that they are 'construed as matter of fact which no-one is responsible for' (Fairclough 1992: 214). Thus, the linguistic structure of Fairclough's example text reflects the increasing 'marketisation' of higher education.

The 'exposing' of such potentially insidious uses of language has been one of the most radical uses of the techniques of stylistic and critical discourse analysis, though it is instructive to see that it is at the level of interpretation, in context, that these more political considerations enter the discussion. The analytical techniques, varied as they are, are all available to the stylistician (see, for example, Simpson's 1993 use of CDA techniques for literary analysis), whatever the main purpose of the research project in question.

In summary, then, we need stylistics because much of our lives is negotiated through language, and though this language is well-described in structural terms by descriptive linguistics, and in contextual terms by such disciplines as discourse analysis and pragmatics, there remain insights about textual meaning that are addressed more effectively by a discipline which arose from literary studies, took on the apparatus of linguistics, and with the text at its core, became a powerful discipline in its own right. How, for instance, do we understand the hypothetical world in a sci-fi novel? Why does a particular line of poetry seem to move not only one reader, but a number of readers? Is there something subtly persuasive about Tony Blair's speeches, and how do insurance companies attract (and keep) our attention? All of these questions can be addressed through stylistic analysis.

1.3   The scope of stylistics

This section will introduce some of the parameters of stylistics which define its scope. In some cases, the topics explored here will be discussed in more detail later in the book. The following sub-sections, therefore, will delineate the boundaries of stylistics with reference to the kind of texts that it studies, the theories that it draws upon and the methodologies that are available to those working in this field.

1.3.1   Range of texts

In section 1.1 we made a distinction between literary and non-literary texts, both of which are studied by stylisticians. Though the origins of stylistics are in the literary field, and many stylisticians even today consider literature their field of study, it rapidly became clear that the techniques of analysis being developed in this hybrid discipline were as applicable to non-literary texts as to literary ones.

There is, therefore, in principle, no restriction whatsoever on the kinds of text that may be subjected to stylistic analysis. However, there are both historical and also practical reasons why there has been more emphasis on the literary aspects of style in the past, and also on the written language in preference to the spoken. Now that recording techniques have made the capture and transcription of spoken texts more accessible, we may find that stylistics concerns itself with the full range of linguistic usage. Certainly, there have been recent examples of stylisticians turning their hand to look at the language of spoken conversation (McIntyre *et al.* 2004), advertisements (Short and Wen Zhong 1997, Jeffries 2007b), humour (Simpson 2004) and film (Simpson and Montgomery 1995).

This latter development in the direction of multimodality, of course, is not restricted to stylistics, but is also reflected in the move from literary theory to 'cultural theory' and the increasing interest that all such commentators are taking in not only linguistic, but also visual communication of all kinds.

1.3.2   Range of theories

Stylistics, as we shall see throughout this book, is eclectic in its use of theory, though it originated in literary theories of formalism and took on the theory of structuralism as developed by Saussure (1959 [1916]) in the early twentieth century. What these theories together provided was the descriptive apparatus (such as grammatical and lexical terminology and categories) which would enable scholars to pinpoint the precise techniques of construction that writers were using in order to demonstrate the linguistic basis of well-known literary effects, particularly those which were foregrounded. The focus on the actual language of the text which is epitomised by these theories is still present in some stylistic practice, and demonstrates that stylistics does not originate from an author-based view of textual meaning in the same way that, for example, some areas of literary studies did.

In time, stylistics responded to the developing of new theories of language, based more on contextual factors in the case of pragmatics and discourse analysis and on cognitive factors in the case of generative grammar and cognitive linguistics. With the ever-present aim of explaining textual meaning and effects, it was able to use the insights provided by all of these theories to support new analytical processes and provide new insights into the style of texts and their reception by a range of potential audiences. Thus, there are now stylisticians working alongside psychologists (see, for example, Sanford *et al.* 2004 and Schram and Steen 2001) to establish some of the processes by which readers respond to linguistic style. There are stylisticians working in critical discourse analysis (e.g. Fowler 1991, Mullany 2004), with theories of social exploitation and manipulation at the heart of their approach. There are also those working with computational and statistical theories (e.g. Culpeper 2002, Hoover 2004b), who draw literary and linguistic conclusions from the computer analysis of large quantities of data.

A recent set of developments in cognitive stylistics have also drawn on theories that are seen by some as beyond the scope of linguistics, such as psychology and philosophy, but have provided useful insights and models for analysing what is going on in the processing of texts by readers. These theories include schema theory, possible worlds theory and theories of figure and ground. Chapters 5 and 6 examine the interface between the analysis of style and such theories of the human mind, and exemplify theories of how texts can build up mental pictures of their topics in the mind of the reader.

1.3.3   Range of methods

In addition to drawing upon a wide range of theories about the nature of language and particularly the nature of reading, stylistics is eclectic in its use of methodologies. It would be true to say that theories, such as those mentioned above, produce possible models of what the language or text is like, and that these models also tend to dictate the methods to be used to analyse them. However, there is normally some choice of method to be made, even when a theory and a model have already been chosen. For example, if a stylistician wanted to find out whether the vocabulary of Shakespeare is really much wider than the vocabulary of Ben Jonson, the model of a vocabulary range as the number of different lexemes used by each of the authors will dictate a corpus-based (probably computerised) methodology in which statistical analysis will be paramount. It would be possible, in theory, to choose a different model for measuring vocabulary, such as the range of different senses of common words that are used, but it is still likely that the results would be statistical.

This brings us to the most important methodological distinction in all research, that of the difference between qualitative and quantitative methods. Traditionally, most stylistics has been qualitative, though some slightly separate offshoots, such as stylometrics[6] (the study of authorship attribution), have been more quantitative in method. In recent years, with the development of easily accessible and powerful computer software, there has been renewed interest in quantitative study in stylistics; indeed, there is even a developing sub-discipline increasingly referred to as corpus stylistics.

It is probably relatively easy to recognise what we mean by quantitative study, since it clearly involves the statistical analysis of elements from large quantities of data, in order to test the significance of numerical findings. Thus, one might compare the incidence of high-frequency function words (such as pronouns and determiners) by different characters in Jane Austen's novels, as Burrows (1987) does, and discover that Austen's characters have their own unique stylistic 'fingerprint'. Once statistically significant differences are found, the literary and stylistic questions of what these differences mean can be discussed.

The question of what constitutes qualitative study is less easy to define. There are as many ways of carrying out qualitative study as there are people and texts, though we will see in section 1.6 that there are certain guiding principles of stylistics which constrain the range of possibilities a little. For now, we need to consider a few examples of what might be included under the heading of qualitative study. An analysis of a single poem, for the sake of analysing that poem alone, might well be qualitative, particularly if the poem is fairly short. It would make no claims about texts other than the poem itself, though it may well indicate potentially fruitful directions for future study. It would be possible to count the features of a short poem, but no statistical significance is likely to be provable with so few cases.

The advantage of qualitative study is that there is the possibility of taking many more of the contextual factors into account, and this means that one is likely to use a different range of tools. Take, for example, the reporting of the so-called 'war on terror' which has been a regular feature of news reporting since 11 September 2001. Whilst it would be possible to collect every single occurrence of this phrase in news reporting since that date and subject these to computer-based analysis, it is also possible to choose, for example, a few texts, possibly reflecting different attitudes or concentrating on a single incident, and scrutinise them in detail, using some tools of analysis which may not be amenable to automatic searching (see, for example, Montgomery 2004). The result of this analysis would be some insights into the texts themselves and, depending on how they were chosen (e.g. random or structured selection), may also have implications for data beyond the data analysed, which could be tested by others or at a future date.

1.4   Aims of stylistic analysis

The aims of stylistic analysis are varied and reflect the rich range of approaches taken to all sorts of text-types and genres. This means that it is not easy to narrowly define what the aims of all stylistic analysis will be. However, in order for the reader to grasp some of this range, we will attempt here to rationalise the practice of stylistic research under two main headings, reflecting the distinction between what is sometimes called 'bottom-up' versus 'top-down' approaches. Before we look at these two broad approaches in detail, it should be made clear that this distinction cuts across the one made in the last section, between quantitative and qualitative research. There is a tendency for quantitative research to be more inductive (bottom-up) and for qualitative research to align with deductive (top-down) approaches, but this is no more than a tendency and the researcher embarking on a project should consider carefully the particular combination of approaches that s/he will take.

1.4.1   Starting with data

The task that stylisticians often set themselves is to analyse texts and draw from their analysis any patterning or features that they find there, without necessarily wanting to generalise these findings beyond their data. This 'inductive' approach (see section 1.6) suits the material of stylistics very well, and has perhaps been more widespread in the past than the alternative (see 1.4.2).

It is probably worth pointing out that for many stylisticians, individual examples of various features (such as a particular metaphor or symbolic use of grammatical structure) will be all the results that are needed to fulfil the research aim of her/his project. Thus, a scholar might wish to use a stylistic approach to discovering some of the techniques that Wordsworth's Prelude seems to make use of in conjuring up the mountains of the Lake District or the excitement of skating on a frozen lake in winter. This will require a close analysis of the passages concerned, followed by an interpretation of the technical features that are discovered there.

To take a different scale of example, let us consider a hypothetical study of the style of a contemporary novelist, such as Margaret Atwood or Julian Barnes. Depending on the precise research questions being posed, we may want to consider the whole of the author's output, or a section of it (according to dates maybe) or possibly to sample it either randomly or with some structured sample in mind (see section 1.5). Whatever the precise focus of the research, the impetus is to find out from the data what patterns or features of language make it distinctive or make it work in particular ways for the reader. This could involve a computer-based search for lexical or grammatical features, or informant-testing for reader reactions, or a qualitative close analysis of selected passages. Whatever the decisions about the precise data set and the method of analysis, the data sits at the centre of the research project.

Readers will be able to imagine many other research projects of this nature, dealing with all kinds of data, and using different methodologies. Some examples to demonstrate the range of work that could still be considered to be data-driven include Jeffries's (2000) analysis of deictic positioning in Carol Ann Duffy's poetry, Semino's (2002) study of linguistic variation in poetry and McIntyre's (2005) investigation of mind style in Alan Bennett's play *The Lady in the Van*. Note that underlying this type of analysis there are assumptions about the nature of language and theories that help to explain it. The outcomes of such research, too, might well include some development of the theories and models of language, in response to the analysis. However, in general terms, we may still wish to characterise some stylistic research as fundamentally asking questions about the data. This was called 'literary stylistics' in section 1.1, but we can now see that the data-driven type of stylistics may also be asking questions of non-literary data.

1.4.2   Starting with theories

Whilst many stylistic research projects are concerned with questions about texts, using theories and models developed in other fields as convenient, there are also approaches which might be seen as more deductive (see section 1.6) and theory-driven than these. Such a 'top-down' approach would probably involve asking general questions about the nature of textual meaning, possibly including questions about the process of reading, and the reader's role in negotiating textual meaning. The part that textual data plays in this kind of project is secondary, and serves the general aim of pushing forward the theoretical view of how language works. For example, a stylistician may be interested in how metaphor works in literature from the point of view of the reader, and decide to do some informant-testing with particular examples of metaphors from literary sources, to establish how they are received by readers (see Steen 1994 for an example of this kind of study). The aim of the research, in this case, is to find out more about how language works in general, though incidentally there will also be some outcomes which shed light on the workings of particular metaphors. Note that the amounts of data (see section 1.5) are relatively small for this kind of project, but this is not necessarily the case in theory-driven projects, which can necessitate large amounts of data where the research aim requires it. It would, therefore, be possible to devise a theory-based project whose aim was to demonstrate that, for example, words which regularly collocate with certain other kinds of words may carry with them an association with that collocational tendency. This idea is at the root of Louw's work on semantic prosodies (Louw 1993) for instance, and he uses examples from the poetry of Philip Larkin to demonstrate the theory in action. Thus, he is able to show, for instance, that the poem by Larkin which begins 'Days are where we live' evokes a kind of negativity because, perhaps surprisingly, the words 'days are' tend to collocate with negative words in a significant majority of cases found in large computer corpora.

What is important to note here is that ultimately it is not necessarily the case that stylistic research is *only* either data-driven or theory-driven. Though many studies will begin from one of these positions, it is very often the case that both impulses are served by a single piece of research.

1.5   Data in stylistics

It may sound like a truism, but we should start by establishing that stylistics cannot happen without some language to analyse, or 'data'. The reason that this is important is that some sub-disciplines in linguistics, and particularly (but not only) general and theoretical linguistics, can at times function without any particular collection of data upon which to carry out analysis. Thus, the developments of some grammatical theories, approaches to language acquisition and so on, have progressed at times with only the smallest number of illustrative examples, and these may even be invented by the researcher, rather than being in any sense 'naturally occurring data'. This is not to criticise such endeavours, since they have often produced very large steps forward in our thinking about language, and the kinds of 'thought experiments' carried out by philosophers of language in particular produced theories of language which underpin much of linguistics as we know it today.[7]

However, stylistics is different. It is fundamentally attached to data in a way that other branches of linguistics are not. The central concern of stylistics is with the style of particular texts, whether they are representative of a genre, an author, or themselves alone. The context in which they are produced and received cannot be ignored, as we shall see, as this affects their 'meaning' in a range of subtle ways. But the unavoidable basis of all stylistics remains the text itself, and the linguistic choices that have been made (albeit unconsciously) to arrive at a particular form of words.

If data is at the heart of stylistics, then, we need to establish what kind of data, and make other decisions about the range and scope of the kinds of texts that this sub-discipline can encompass. This section addresses some of the important questions that stylisticians need to answer. This is intended to delineate the fundamentals of stylistics enough for students to be able to begin to do stylistic analysis of the kind outlined in Chapters 2 to 5. We will then revisit some of these methodological considerations in Chapter 7, when the aims and methods of stylistics are investigated in more detail.

1.5.1   Literary and non-literary texts

In part, we have already considered (see section 1.1) one of the most important questions for stylistics, this being the extent to which stylistics is concerned with only literary texts. The simple answer, as we have stated already, is that it isn't, though there are many stylisticians who only work with literary texts, and a few who think stylistics *ought* to be so restricted, in the tradition of classical rhetoric and poetics. In the main, though, there is a recognition that however we might try to define literature as distinct in some way from 'ordinary' language, the same kinds of stylistic phenomena turn up in all sorts of text, and it is thus difficult to make a clear distinction on linguistic grounds. Whilst there may be no absolute linguistic distinction between literary and non-literary works, there is clearly a functional and social difference between, for example, a novel and a gas bill, or, to make the texts more obviously similar, between a short story and a 'real-life' story told by one neighbour to another. Some stylisticians are particularly interested, for good reasons, in the linguistic detail of literary works, because their findings may inform a literary response to the work by, for example, giving some indication of why readers may respond in some way to particular effects, or how well-known effects are actually achieved in linguistic terms. We have already seen some examples of this, and will see more in later chapters.

Whilst we are considering the literary end of stylistics, we should address the question of what is sometimes labelled 'high' literature, in other words 'great' literature, versus the popular end of the spectrum. These two kinds of literary work are often thought of as being situated at either end of some kind of cline on which can be found the more elite, statusful, canonical novels, plays and poetry and the popular, low-status work of fiction, drama or verse. It is not necessarily as simple as a single range, of course, since much of the division of literature into such categories depends more on social judgements than linguistic ones, and there may be different opinions about where on the scale a particular work belongs in relation to others. Does, for example, a novel by Stephen King or a poem by Dorothy Parker belong on the popular end of the range compared with a 'chick-lit' novel like *Bridget Jones's Diary* (Fielding 1999) or the poetry of Wendy Cope or Pam Ayres? The latter example is particularly interesting, given that Cope's poetry is funny, formal (rhyming and metrical) and deals with everyday subject-matter. Parker's and Ayres's verse is, likewise, light-hearted, formal, metrical and funny. Cope is published by what might be considered a 'serious' poetry publisher (Faber and Faber) whereas Ayres is seen more as an entertainer and a comedian, as evidenced by the fact that her verse is published by the BBC.

The last paragraph implies that there is no real difference between the work of writers who have very different status in literary circles. However, we have not analysed the poems of Cope and Ayres stylistically, and have only the most superficial impression of their similarities in subject-matter and form. Were we to do so, we may find that there are indeed some stylistic differences which may account for their different status, but it may also be that there is no linguistic difference, and only a difference of presentation and context that accounts for their respective reputations. The way that a stylistician may approach questions of high versus popular literature, then, might be to take texts from genres and authors which have different social values, and consider to what extent there is indeed some linguistic indication of the differences between them. This valuing of a certain aesthetic would be context-bound, in the sense that it would have its origins in the society in which it accrues such aesthetic value, and there is one type of stylistics that is indeed interested in charting the linguistic aspects of different aesthetic judgements in this way. However, stylisticians are not only interested in what might be seen as 'great literature' in certain societies. They are also interested in popular literature for its own sake, and might, for example, be found investigating what it is that makes popular romance novels, such as those published by Mills and Boon, so distinctive in their style that they form a sub-genre on linguistic grounds, as well as on the grounds of plot, characterisation and so on.

We have established, then, that the data considered by stylisticians may be 'literature' in very broad terms, including popular fiction as well as canonical and high-status works. We have also suggested that non-literary texts may be of as much interest to stylistics as literary ones. One simple reason why this is the case is related to stylistic techniques themselves. When early stylisticians attempted to define literature in linguistic terms (see, for example, Havránek 1964 and Mukařovský 1964), it became clear that, on the one hand, many of the so-called literary 'devices' (such as punning or metaphor) were present in other, non-literary, texts such as advertisements and that, on the other hand, any style of language could occur in literary works, depending on the subject-matter. For instance, cognitive metaphor theory (discussed fully in Chapter 5) has shown how metaphor is present in all discourse types since metaphor is one of the primary ways in which we conceptualise our experience of the world around us. As an example, the conceptual metaphor LIFE IS A JOURNEY is a structuring device that underlies our experiences of daily life and the way in which we talk about these. Common phrases that make use of this conceptual metaphor include 'I feel like I'm going nowhere', 'I'm at a crossroads in my life' and 'I don't know which path to take'. The underlying conceptual metaphor, then, is one which is found in many different kinds of texts and spoken language, and is clearly not restricted to literary texts.

This is not to say that the presence of certain conceptual metaphors (for example, novel metaphors) wouldn't have potentially different effects in literary contexts, something which we will come to, but it certainly belies any notion that the actual words of literary texts are in any sense different from other texts. The question of the effects of texts is one that stylistics has recently begun to grapple with in many different ways, as we shall demonstrate in later chapters. Here, it is worth pointing out that the stylistic analysis of non-literary texts may use the same tools, but may be concerned with a different set of questions in terms of the effect or interpretation of the texts themselves. Thus, critical discourse analysis and other stylistic approaches in a similar vein may be ultimately concerned with the persuasive or manipulative effect of advertisements, newspaper reports or political speeches, whereas a literary stylistic analysis may be concerned with the literary value or interpretative effect of a literary work. This will not prevent them from using similar basic tools of analysis.

So far, we have discussed – and rejected – the possible narrowing of stylistic data to 'high literary' texts and have also rejected the notion of stylistics being only concerned with literary works in general. We also need to consider, given this opening up of data to all texts, whether spoken as well as written data might be the subject of stylistic analysis. Increasingly, this is the case (see for example Lambrou 2003). It may be worth pointing out first of all that the question of spoken or written medium cuts across the literary/non-literary division, since much 'literature' may be spoken, most obviously in the performance element of drama, but also in performance poetry, or even broadcast fiction on radio or television. Likewise, of course, much non-literary text is written, though there is also a great deal of spoken language in our everyday lives.

In principle, then, the question of whether texts are spoken or written does not affect their eligibility for stylistic analysis. In practice, much stylistic analysis has tended to concentrate on the written language, or a transcribed version of the spoken language, so that the same kinds of issues (lexis, grammar etc.) are normally considered more than, for example, intonational or other spoken phenomena.

1.5.2   Defining the data

Having established that there is, in principle, no restriction on the kinds of linguistic data that can be subjected to stylistic analysis, we have to consider what kinds of decisions need to be made when embarking on stylistic study. As we will see in section 1.5.4, these questions of defining the data for analysis arise out of the research questions that we might wish to ask, and also from the methods and theories that underlie our approach. Nevertheless, there are some issues of data definition that can be addressed in general and separately from the particular study or analysis.

The first question to consider is 'How much data is needed?' This question may be answered fairly automatically if, for example, the analysis is pre-determined as relating to a single poem or a pair of contrasting poems. Beyond such minimal data sets, there will always be questions of amount to be answered. If we consider the case of a single novel – for example, *Great Expectations* by Charles Dickens – any researcher setting out to study this novel stylistically would need to make a decision about whether every word in the novel was to be analysed, and if so whether this would involve a computer-based analysis. An example of such an approach would be Hardy's (2003, 2004, 2005) stylistic analyses of the work of Flannery O'Connor. An alternative, using more traditional and qualitative methods, would be to choose a set of extracts to analyse. This could be a randomly-selected set, to represent the novel as a whole, or it might rather be a set of selected extracts that are expected to contrast in some way, perhaps reflecting the different phases of Pip's life or relationships.

The decisions taken about how much data to analyse are likely to be in response to, and also to limit, the kinds of analysis that will be possible. A large-scale study, involving many thousands of words, makes for more statistical data and less contextually-based analysis. At different times these different approaches may serve the overall purpose equally well. What is most important, in all stylistic research, is to be clear about the data to be included, and to be clear about why this data set is appropriate. Thus, we may be aiming to find out why all of Alan Bennett's writing is recognisable as having been written by him, whether it is a play, a diary or a lecture. We will therefore need to make sure that the data includes some of each of these genres, and also that there is enough data to see any overall stylistic patterns that may be present. This means that the quantity of data is large, and will necessitate an approach that can cope with large numbers of words, such as corpus stylistics. Alternatively, extracts from across Bennett's works could be randomly selected and analysed in more detail and with regard to context. Whichever of these approaches is taken, the important thing is to define the process of deciding how much data to analyse, how it is selected and what it consists of. This is mainly so that the stylistic analysis that results can, if required, be checked against the data by other scholars, or compared with other studies of a similar nature or with similar aims.

If the data for study is not already well-defined (e.g. a whole poem), then the question of selection involves making decisions that are often relatively arbitrary. Nevertheless, it is important to try to use some kind of rationale to guide these decisions. For example, the choice of advertisements to study may involve a single day's (twenty-four hours') worth of TV advertising, to investigate style in TV advertising generally and at a single point in time (see, for instance,

Leech's seminal 1966 book on the stylistics of advertising). Alternatively, one might choose to concentrate on the advertising of particular products, for example cars versus make-up, which may reflect stereotypically gendered approaches to selling. If one is studying a novel, the choice of whether to choose ten 1,000-word extracts or two 500-word extracts may depend on the tools to be used and the purpose for which this analysis is to be carried out. The more different tools of analysis that will be applied to a text, the longer it will take to complete the analysis and the longer the written-up account of the analysis will be. Depending on whether the analysis is an undergraduate essay, a PhD thesis or a journal article, the amount of data and length of extracts will vary. This practical aspect of data definition is unavoidable, and not problematic, as long as there are clear reasons given for the choices made in relation to the research questions that are being asked.

1.5.3   Authorial versus genre style

In discussing the choosing of data, we have already mentioned in passing the question of exactly which 'style' the researcher is trying to analyse. This question relates, of course, to the main aim of the research and the research questions it produces, as we shall see in section 1.5.4. Here, we will simply exemplify the kinds of different style which could be the focus of stylistic study.

Clearly, the style of a single text (advertisement, letter, poem, novel, play) may be of interest in itself, or we may wish to look at a particular phase in an author's output (e.g. by poetry collection or groups of fictional works by date). Broadening out, we may wish to consider the whole output of an author, or the works of a group of writers who have some common theme or other connection, for example, absurdist writers, Romantic poets or writers of instruction manuals. In all cases, of course, we may wish not only to analyse a set of data for its patterns of similarity, but we may wish to construct a data set with inbuilt contrasts, to compare the sub-sets with each other.

Beyond the individual writer, and groups of writers, we may wish to consider the analysis of a whole genre, such as contemporary poetry in general or the style of Acts of Parliament. As the potential pool of data gets larger, questions of sampling become more significant. It is probably also the case that there is a sense in which the most common, and possibly also the most successful, stylistic analysis to date has looked at relatively limited and homogeneous sets of data. This position may well be changing in the light of recent developments in corpus stylistics, though it remains the case that the larger the data set, the less one is able to conclude in terms of distinctive style. With non-literary works (e.g. a gas bill) it is likely that the research will be looking for patterns across the whole of that text-type. Staying with the non-literary, then, we may wish to study the whole of a particular genre, such as begging letters, or planning objections and so on. In attempting to draw out the common stylistic factors in such genres, we will need to decide how to sample the available material, and this will take us back to considerations of quantity that were discussed earlier.

In addition to the genre and text-type approach to data selection, one may also have a different kind of focus, relating more to the topic of the texts than their genre. Thus, we may ask the question of what, if any, stylistic tendencies there are in texts on the internet relating to Christianity, or we may ask how a current political question (such as the proper funding of political parties) is treated across a range of text-types, including news reporting and political speeches. This will have an effect on the range, quantity and type of texts that make up the data for a particular study (see Chapter 7 for examples of this kind of work).

Finally, the focus of a stylistic study may be more theoretical than any that we have mentioned so far. This focus could be, for example, the question of how widespread the use of metaphors is in literary and other works, and whether these metaphors can be categorised in certain ways, irrespective of their context. Similarly, there could be a focus on opposition-creation across a range of text-types, including literary and non-literary texts, to see what general case can be made for contextual construction of new and unconventional opposites. Another example may be the development of the theory of mind style, and the use of a range of texts to provide a broad set of data from which to draw generalisations about how mind style is reflected in language (see, for example, Baker and McEnery 2005, Gregoriou 2006). In practice, stylistic studies are often a combination of these approaches, and may well provide evidence for a general theory at the same time as focusing on a topic or theme, and limiting the data to a particular genre or other set of texts.

1.5.4   Matching data to research questions

We have seen already that the question of what data to choose is related to the questions that you wish to ask. Most research projects have an overall aim, which is made more specific as a set of research questions to be answered. This set of questions will in some sense determine what data is needed. Let us take, for example, the question of the rather unusual style of the Irish poet Mebdh McGuckian. One possible way of approaching the question of what makes her style distinctive is to start with a single poem, and consider what foregrounded stylistic features occur in this text. The analysis could be followed up by a series of similar analyses, using the findings of the first analysis to inform the tools to be used in subsequent analyses. This process is rather like a set of ever-widening nets that catch ever more of McGuckian's poetry and, consequently, style. In theory the process would not be complete until all of her poems had been considered, though in practice some kind of sample might suffice. The question of whether such analysis truly captures McGuckian's uniqueness is harder to establish, since the task of comparing her with all known poets in terms of the particular combination of stylistic features that have been found would be unmanageable, and, indeed, unnecessary, since questions of evaluation are not necessarily the purview of stylistics.

At a different level, the stylistician may wish to try to define linguistically the stream-of-consciousness style often attributed to Virginia Woolf, among others. In this case, one might decide to narrow down the set of analytical tools one is using, to focus on this research question, but it will also be important to define the range of material that will be analysed. Woolf's novels could be randomly searched for 500-word extracts, to give a representative sample, but one might also justify choosing particular passages where the effects of changing consciousnesses are particularly striking, in order to analyse an impressionistically 'typical' set of data, and to produce a description of the range of techniques being used (free indirect style, for example – see Fludernik 1993), before testing these findings on further data.

As we have seen, the questions that arise when a stylistician chooses her/his data are many and varied. As we shall attempt to make clear in the next section, the underlying principles of the discipline may provide a guiding hand in answering them.

1.6   Principles of stylistics

As we have described, stylistics evolved out of the literary and linguistic developments of the twentieth century and it has developed so many strands and sub-fields that the sheer variety and exuberance of the discipline as a whole is hard to pin down to a set of procedures, theories or methodologies. Some fields of linguistics have developed a very clear and agreed set of standard practices, based on a consensus about current theories and models; the field of conversation analysis would be one such example. This has not so far happened with stylistics, perhaps mainly because of the enormous range of practices which seem to shelter under the label. Nevertheless, there are certain principles by which most, if not all, stylistics operates, and these will be the subject of this section.

1.6.1   Stylistics as text-based

As we saw in section 1.5, stylistics is very much based on textual data (though, arguably, the notion of what constitutes a text is becoming ever broader; see, for example, Fairclough's 1992 definition of a text as the written or spoken 'product' of discourse). In a sense, there can be no such thing as stylistics unless texts are being analysed, and although some recent developments in cognitive stylistics have hypothesised principally about the processes that a reader engages in when s/he is reading a text, ultimately the task of the stylistician remains that of working out what effect is achieved by *particular* texts, whether the research aims are phrased as a cognitive, a linguistic or a literary question.

This adherence to the centrality of the text has earned stylistics some criticism, not least from literary theorists (for example, Fish 1981) who have claimed that it is only a slightly more technical version of 'close reading', which is less fashionable than it used to be, because it seems to imply that literary works have single meanings, and that these can be 'teased out' by a set of analytical procedures. In fact, though early stylistics did indeed claim to provide a more rigorous set of tools for analysing literary language in detail, there has not been a time since the early twentieth century when stylistics wasn't changing and responding to new linguistic and literary theories and models. Thus, in the early twenty-first century, we have a range of practices subsumed under stylistics, including cognitive stylistics and corpus stylistics as well as stylistics based on functional and discourse-analytical approaches to language. At their most extreme, they vary considerably, but it is probably fair to say that they all remain text-based in the sense that they are trying to explain something about the operation and effect of particular texts.

1.6.2   Objectivity and empiricism

The second set of principles, which stylistics shares with other subdisciplines in linguistics, derives from principles in the natural sciences, which have been variously taken on board by the human and social sciences as evidence of their status as reputable academic disciplines. Whilst literary studies has never made any attempt to be recognised as comparable with the sciences, linguistics certainly started out as a reaction against the notion that human communication couldn't be studied in a scientific way. There had, of course, been other attempts to be objective about studying literature, most notably I. A. Richards's argument that literary criticism is essentially a branch of psychology, dealing with the states of mind induced by art (Richards 2001 [1924]; see also West forthcoming). It was on this scientific basis that Richards created a new school of practical criticism devoid of subjective emotionalism. This approach led to many developments in our understanding of how language works, and though stylistics itself straddles both literary and linguistic attitudes to scientific principles, it nevertheless owes a great deal to linguistics.

The first principle that we should consider is the importance of **rigour** in stylistic analysis. Probably the most general of the scientific principles, rigour refers to the way that research is carried out and written up, so that, whilst they may not share the same conclusions, other scholars can easily see the consistency and clarity in the work that has been done. To give an example, stylistic research which takes samples from larger bodies of data must be clear about the way in which the sampling was done, and why. This is the only basis upon which later commentators or reviewers can comment upon the sampling that has been done. Similarly, analytical tools must be clearly stated, whether or not they are a generally agreed set, and even if they are controversially applied in a new or different way. The important thing is to be transparent about what has been done, what methods have been used, and why. Whether quantitative or qualitative, it is vital that analytical tools are applied consistently, to alleviate the risk of bias or unconscious slanting of the analysis toward favoured outcomes.

This latter point, the reason for consistency, leads us to the question of **objectivity** and **replicability** in stylistics. Stylistics has on occasion been criticised over its claims to analytical objectivity (see Fish 1981 and MacKay 1996, for example). Whilst it is true that stylistics aims to avoid purely subjective commentary on texts, objectivity in stylistic analysis needs some discussion, since the notion of objectivity as a concept is often misunderstood (see Short *et al.*'s 1998 response to MacKay 1996 for a discussion of this). Objectivity in stylistic analysis does not mean making impassive comments on the meaning of a text without regard to context or ideology. As Simpson (1993: 3) points out, few stylisticians would claim to do this. Short and van Peer (1999) outline what being an objective analyst means when they explain that:

> In trying to be objective, one tries to be (a) clear, detailed and open (so that one's position is unambiguous), and (b) ready to change one's mind if the evidence or a subsequent counter-argument demands it.
>
> (Short and van Peer 1999: 273)

The aim, then, is to be as objective as possible, given the constraints of the subject-matter and the difficulties of distinguishing the analyst from the subjective reader. There are, of course, techniques for minimising the effect of the personal subjectivity of the individual analyst. These include the replicating of research by other analysts, and this can be built into projects so that more than one researcher applies the analytical tools to any single piece of data.[8] At one extreme, there are tools which can employ computer-based techniques for making the analysis and these rely on the surface form of the text. Such corpus studies are perhaps the most clearly 'objective' in their operation, though as in any analytical procedure, the choice of categories and models may influence certain outcomes of the analysis. What corpus studies demonstrate most clearly is something that is true of all stylistic study, and this is the separation, in principle if not in practice, of the analytical and interpretative processes. As we will explain in section 1.6.4, interpretation is another of the important principles of stylistics. Here it is worth noting that objectivity is easier to approximate to at the analytical than the interpretative stage, though both are vital to stylistics.

The penultimate principle that we will discuss in this section, and which is also a scientific principle, is that of **empiricism**. The requirement of an empirical approach to study is that all claims should be based on observation or experience. In other words, the strictly empirical approach would insist upon an inductive method (see section 1.4.1) of working whereby the patterns observed in large quantities of data would be the only available outcomes of the study and no generalisations or predictions beyond these outcomes would be permissible. In practice, some branches of stylistics are more inductive (e.g. corpus stylistics) and some more deductive (e.g. critical stylistics) in method, and even within these sub-fields, many studies will in fact use both approaches to answering the research questions. Thus, many stylistic projects may analyse a set of texts, or extracts from texts, and describe what is found empirically by this method, whilst also making predictions from this basis about the likely occurrence of similar features and effects in other data. Note that the deductive method represented by these generalisations and predictions leads us to another requirement of research in stylistics, namely that it should be **falsifiable**. This requirement means that any claims must be clear enough to be able to be challenged by other researchers, either by replication of the original work, or by the application of the findings to new data. The requirement for falsifiability, then, takes us back to the need for rigour and objectivity, which together enable other scholars to challenge the findings of the original researcher(s). Chapman (2006) puts it this way:

> What is important to a deductive hypothesis, indeed what makes it a valid scientific statement at all, is not that it can be supported by data, but rather that it can be falsified. That is, the hypothesis must make specific predictions that can be tested against data and that can in principle be proved wrong.   (Chapman 2006: 20)

The notion of falsifiability is important in stylistics (see, for example, van Peer 1980, Hogenraad *et al.* 1997). As we have seen, stylistics models itself on the scientific principles that underpinned the origins of linguistics, but we will also see that the reality of stylistic analysis – and some would argue any linguistic analysis – is that striving to be scientific is limited to some extent by the nature of the data that is being investigated and that eclecticism (see section 1.6.3) is not only necessary but acceptable.

This section has introduced a range of scientific terms which relate to each other in complex ways. One way of seeing the relationship between these concepts is to see the drive towards objectivity as the overriding scientific principle which is (partially) achieved by practical measures such as making sure that stylistic work is replicable and falsifiable. These two guiding principles may be seen as the core values of a rigorous approach to research in any field, including stylistics.

1.6.3   Stylistics as eclectic and open

As we have seen in relation to induction and deduction, stylistics is not a discipline to be constrained to one particular theoretical viewpoint or methodology, though some individual researchers may do so, and some of the sub-disciplines espouse one approach more than others. As a whole, though, stylistics' main strength has been to remain open to new theories of language and literature, and to evolve by incorporating these new insights into its practice. This eclecticism is not only a source of strength, but is a principled position that is taken by many researchers in the field. Though the hard sciences may, in principle, be aiming at the ultimate theory of everything, in practice most scientific theories are recognised as supplying only part of the explanation of how the physical world works. These theories provide models of the data which inevitably concentrate on those aspects of a complex system that are under investigation, and to this extent they simplify the picture for the purposes of understanding and explaining one particular strand of the whole field. Likewise, in most stylistic endeavours, there is a recognition that the act of theorising and modelling textual meaning and effects is bound to be partial (in the non-judgemental sense of 'incomplete'), or simplifying, and that this is not only practically expedient in order to make progress, but methodologically sound too, since no theory that is just as complex as the data it describes will manage to explain anything.

The result of this eclecticism in stylistics is the explosion of new theories and methods in recent years, drawing from cognitive linguistics, corpus linguistics, critical discourse analysis and functional linguistics. In addition, the practice of text analysis still depends extensively on those models of language which developed in the formal linguistics of the early twentieth century and gave us the detailed methods of description and analysis that are exemplified in Chapter 2.

Stylistics, then, takes on the new, but does not necessarily throw out the old in doing so. As Chapman (2006) says:

> Theorists in all fields generally accept that they are unlikely to come up with the definitive account of their subject matter that will be proved to be correct and will be universally accepted.   (Chapman 2006: 22)

One way to think of the question of theory/theories is to realise that we do not abandon theories wholesale when they are proved wrong in some small way. We either adapt them or we add another theory to explain those aspects of the world which our original theory didn't cover. By these means, scientists and social scientists add to human understanding by accretion rather than revolution.

1.6.4   Choice, analysis and interpretation

The final set of principles upon which stylistics depends is more specific to linguistics than some of the general, scientific principles we have been investigating. The principles outlined in this section underlie most of what we would call stylistics, though some stylistic approaches emphasise one or the other more emphatically.

Some of the earliest discussions of stylistics emphasised that the choices available to writers (or, in our case, speakers too) were evidence that there was something we could call 'style' which was separate and separable from the normal concerns of linguistics (morphology, syntax, lexis and so on):

> the idea of style implies that words on a page might have been different, or differently arranged, without a corresponding difference in substance. Another writer would have said *it* another *way*.   (Ohmann 1970: 264)

Thus, it was argued that there are many different ways of saying essentially the same thing, and that this element of choice over *how* to say something was the proper subject of study for stylistics.

Developments in our understanding of human language have made this apparently straightforward claim seem rather naive in recent years. It is, for example, not clear that in a very formal situation, such as a job interview, we have any clear choice in ways of expressing ourselves. So, although in some abstract sense saying 'I'm bleeding ecstatic about this job' is semantically equivalent to saying 'I'm very enthusiastic about this job', there is only a theoretical choice, since the former would have quite an adverse effect on one's chance of being appointed. Stylistics, as we shall see in the following chapters, has grown, with other linguistic sub-disciplines, into a contextualising discipline, with the awareness of social and other factors that characterise all actual uses of language. Nevertheless, at its core there remains a consciousness of the importance of linguistic choice (see Leech and Short 2007: 9–31), though one constrained by all sorts of non-linguistic factors.

The other principle, which is perhaps more generally applicable across the social sciences, and linguistics in particular, is the importance of the duality inherent in the relationship between analysis and interpretation. Whilst even the hard sciences would probably agree that one can distinguish the results of, say, an experiment into the efficacy of a particular drug from its interpretation as a contributor to human health in the future, the distinction between analysis and interpretation in stylistics is both vital and yet not as complete a separation as in some endeavours. The choice of what data to study, which tools of analysis to use and what research questions we are trying to answer is often dictated by our overall desire to explain something about interpretation, whether that be the literary effect of a poem or the manipulative effect of political rhetoric. These motivations for our research may help us to choose which analytical methods to use, but once the analysis is embarked upon, the techniques should not differ, whatever the larger motivation. For example, one might use the same analysis of modality in a passage of a novel as in a newspaper article, and the results will be presented in similar ways. However, the research is not satisfactorily completed until we draw some conclusions from these results which relate to the meaning of the text in its context. Thus, a novel showing little sign of modality may well be interpreted as demonstrating the typical style of the hard-bitten detective novel, whilst the lack of modality in a news report may be interpreted as over-confidence in the details and sources of a news story. It is the combination of rigorous analysis and contextual interpretation that makes stylistics the very rich field that it is.

1.7   The structure of the book

This book is structured in part to reflect the historical development of stylistics as a discipline. Chapter 2 focuses on the structural properties of language and how these can be manipulated to produce foregrounding effects. Here we concentrate on the psychological principles underpinning foregrounding theory, in many ways the cornerstone of stylistic analysis, and how this begins to take account of the ways in which readers engage with texts. In Chapters 3 and 4 we focus on the notions of discourse and context, and the frameworks that have been developed in order to take account of these concepts in stylistic analysis. Such approaches were developed as attempts to counter the limitations of those purely structural approaches to style that were common in the early days of stylistics. Chapters 5 and 6 concentrate on the relatively recent abundance of work in the area of text cognition. Here we outline the development of cognitive approaches to stylistic analysis, and explain how such approaches can complement those frameworks described in Chapters 2, 3 and 4. Following these chapters, in Chapter 7 we return to issues of methodology in stylistics, and outline, by exemplifying with particular stylistic studies, the variety of methodological approaches that can be adopted in stylistic analysis, and the contexts in which these might be employed. Finally, in the light of what we have outlined throughout the book, in Chapter 8 we consider the place of stylistics within the discipline of linguistics, and how stylistics might develop in the future.

Exercises

In this introductory chapter we have attempted to sketch out the main aims and principles of stylistics, along with a flavour of its historical development and some indicative analyses. We have not, at this stage, fully introduced the linguistic tools with which to go about doing stylistics, and so it would be rather unfair of us to set some analytical exercises here. Nevertheless, there are a number of questions that it would be worthwhile to consider at this stage. Keep your responses to these questions in mind as you continue through the book.

Exercise 1.1

We have emphasised in this chapter the interdisciplinary nature of stylistics. If you are approaching stylistics with a background in literature, consider the following questions:

- How do you currently go about carrying out an analysis of a literary text? Write down the stages you go through, and as you continue reading this book, see if what you currently do differs in any way from what is common within stylistics.
- Is the kind of analysis you currently do satisfactory? (i.e. Does it answer all the questions you might have about your text?)
- Is there anything that you find difficult about the study of literature? Make a note of any issues in order to see later on whether stylistics can assist with addressing these.

If, on the other hand, you are approaching stylistics from a background in language study, think about the questions below:

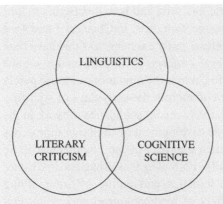

Figure 1.1 *Stylistics and the intersection of other disciplines*

- What constitutes data in the area of language study that you are most used to? (For example, is it spoken language, written text, intuitive examples? Why is this?)
- How do you proceed when investigating a particular issue in the area of language study with which you are most familiar? (e.g. What comes first – research question or data?)
- Which of the questions that arise in the study of the data you most frequently use do you find difficult to answer?

If your background is in another discipline, think about what specifically has prompted you to read this book. What 'answers' are you looking for and how do you envisage that stylistics might help?

Exercise 1.2

Stylistics, as we have said, is by its nature interdisciplinary. As you progress through this book, think about what particular aspects of the various disciplines that stylistics has been influenced by intersect. One way of thinking about this is to consider the overlap between stylistics and other disciplines as being represented in a Venn diagram (Venn 1880), as in figure 1.1.

Stylistics might be seen as incorporating the overlapping elements of numerous disciplines. What specifically are these overlapping elements?

Further reading

John Douthwaite's *Towards a Linguistic Theory of Foregrounding* (Edizioni dell'Orso, 2000) incorporates a detailed history of stylistics in its introduction, which is useful for setting the practice of stylistic analysis in its historical context. Some of the key texts from the early days of stylistics are the edited collections, *Style in Language* (Sebeok 1960), *Essays on Style in Language* (Fowler 1966) and *Linguistics and Literary Style* (Freeman 1970). Roman Jakobson's (1960) paper, 'Closing statement: linguistics and poetics', is considered a seminal work in terms of defining the remit of stylistics and can be found in Sebeok's (1960) collection. It is worth returning to these texts once you have read more of this book. The more you learn about the practical aspects of stylistics, the easier it will be to follow the arguments outlined in the texts listed above.

2 Text and style

2.1 What is style?

The previous chapter was a general introduction to stylistics, and many of its topics will be explored in more detail in later chapters. Here, we will introduce some of the core activities of stylistics by considering the beginnings of stylistics as it arose from a combination of some of the principles of Russian formalism and the emerging descriptive techniques of linguistics. Though the remainder of this book will demonstrate that stylistics has developed a rich array of further techniques and principles since this starting point, the principles and techniques with which it began are still very much in evidence in contemporary stylistics, and remain relevant for the close study of literary – and non-literary – language. We will draw the majority of our examples in this chapter from literary works, and especially poems, since these were the principal objects of study of early stylistics. Nonetheless, all of the techniques described in this chapter are applicable to non-literary texts too.

In section 1.5.3, we considered the question of whether we were interested in the style of an author or a genre, and concluded that stylisticians are interested in all aspects of style, whatever their scope. Here, the question of what constitutes style addresses the assumption in earlier criticism that literary language was somehow set apart from the 'everyday' or elevated above the mundane uses of language in, say, shopping transactions or workplace documents. Though there remains an impetus to try to explain the linguistic aspects of what is considered 'great' writing, it turns out that many of the same linguistic features occur in non-literary genres as well, so that we find our techniques of analysis, which have been greatly improved by the development of linguistics generally, apply equally to all forms of language and do not on their own help us to define literariness.

Later in this chapter (section 2.4), we will consider some of the arguments for and against a linguistic definition of the literary, but first we will look at the roots of stylistics in the still hugely influential theory of **defamiliarisation** (section 2.2) and then consider how linguistic description enabled the important principle of **foregrounding**, derived from defamiliarisation, to be applied to the detailed study of texts (section 2.3).

2.2   Defamiliarisation: foregrounding by deviation and parallelism

As we noted in Chapter 1, stylistics as a linguistic discipline has its roots in Russian formalism, which attempted to isolate the properties and characteristics of literary language in contrast with everyday and non-literary language. This movement produced a label, defamiliarisation, for the process that was thought to be at the heart of literary language, described by Douthwaite (2000: 178) as 'Impeding normal processing by showing the world in an unusual, unexpected or abnormal manner'. Foregrounding was established early on by pioneers in the application of linguistics to literary analysis as the mechanism by which defamiliarisation takes place.

Although the distinctiveness of literary language has been contested during the century or so since the introduction of foregrounding as a concept, and although it is by no means absent in non-literary genres, foregrounding is nevertheless particularly prevalent in literary texts, especially poetry, and as such might be seen as the cornerstone of stylistic analysis and a key feature of poetic style (Leech 1970). This chapter will feature a range of foregrounding examples taken mainly from literary works, thus superficially seeming to support the notion that there is a style of language associated with literature. However, the debate about its distinctiveness will be reviewed in section 2.4, where recent views on style as a feature of language in general will be introduced.

Foregrounding in language was first identified by Mukařovsky (1964 [1958]) and refers to features of the text which in some sense 'stand out' from their surroundings. The term itself is a metaphorical extension of the concept of foregrounding in the visual arts (e.g. painting and photography). Essentially, foregrounding theory suggests that in any text some sounds, words, phrases and/or clauses may be so different from what surrounds them, or from some perceived 'norm' in the language generally, that they are set into relief by this difference and made more prominent as a result. Furthermore, the foregrounded features of a text are often seen as both memorable and highly interpretable. Foregrounding is achieved by either linguistic **deviation** or linguistic **parallelism**.

The notion of linguistic deviation is another concept arising from the Russian formalists, and poetry is the genre that most clearly exemplifies this feature, thus giving support to the notion that there is a distinct language of literature. Deviation is essentially the occurrence of unexpected irregularity in language and results in foregrounding on the basis that the irregularity is surprising to the reader. Deviation may occur at any of the levels of linguistic structure, as we will see below, but here is a classic example to illustrate the general principle of deviation (a full analysis can be found in Leech 1969: 30):

(1)   A grief ago
           ('A grief ago', Thomas 2003)

In example 1, the word 'grief' is semantically deviant as a result of its flouting our expectations that a countable noun[1] related to time will occur in the syntactic frame 'a...ago' ('grief' being, in contrast, an uncountable, or mass, noun of emotion). As a result of this deviation, the title of the poem is foregrounded and consequently, we are invited to look for a significance that goes beyond surface-level understanding. One plausible interpretation might be to see the poem as encapsulating the all-consuming nature of grief, to the extent that the grief in question is so strong that it becomes the measure by which we gauge time.

Example 1 illustrates semantic deviation, though deviation can occur at any linguistic level (see sections 2.3.1–5). Although we tend to think of deviation as a variation from 'normal' usage (however that is judged), which is known as **external deviation**, it is also possible for deviation to be internal to the text as opposed to external (Levin 1965).[2] A good example of **internal deviation** is the poetry of E. E. Cummings. Perhaps the most striking aspect of deviation in much of Cummings's poetry is the use of lowercase letters where we would normally expect capitals. This, though, is typical of Cummings's poetry and so it is difficult to attribute any great significance to it, other than a general desire to break with normal convention. However, one of the effects of this deviation is to foreground any instances where Cummings *does* use capitalisation, such as in the line below from poem 63:

(2)   sing) for it's Spring
         ('63', Cummings 1964)

As a consequence of the internal deviation we can infer that Spring is an important concept in the poem, since 'Spring' is the first word we come across with initial capitalisation. The only other capital letters in the poem come in the final line, where the first letter of each word is a capital, thereby foregrounding the propositional content of the poem's last phrase.

Deviation, then, is a common feature of poetic style, though it is also common in other genres and text-types. Of course, the idea that poetry 'breaks the rules' is not a new one, but the precision offered by stylistics has enabled analysts to accurately map the specific kinds of rule-breaking[3] and innovation to be found in poetry and other texts. We will investigate some examples of poetic and other deviation in later sections of this chapter.

If deviation is unexpected *irregularity* in language, then parallelism is unexpected *regularity*. Parallelism is the other means by which foregrounding effects can be created in texts. In cases of parallelism, the foregrounding effect arises out of a repeated structure, such as in example 3:

(3)   And every week he tipped up half his wage.
         And what he didn't spend each week he saved.
         And praised his wife for every meal she made.
         And once, for laughing, punched her in the face.
                                    ('Poem', Armitage 1999: 29)

As with deviation, parallelism can occur at different levels of linguistic structure. The short extract above from Simon Armitage's 'Poem' contains a number of instances of parallelism. First of all there is the syntactic parallelism of every line beginning with the conjunction *and*. Second, there is the phonological parallelism inherent in the /eɪ/ sound that appears in the final word of each line. Third, there is semantic parallelism in the first three lines, in that each of them details a positively-valued action, in comparison with the negative connotations of the action described in the fourth. This semantic parallelism occurs in each of the poem's three main stanzas (the poem ends with a couplet), thereby extending the parallelism across the whole text (we will deal with the issue of the anomalous fourth line of each stanza in a moment).

With regard to interpreting parallel structures, Leech (1969: 67) explains that every instance of parallelism 'sets up a relationship of equivalence between two or more elements: the elements which are singled out by the pattern as being parallel. Interpreting the parallelism involves appreciating some external connection between these elements' (see also Levin 1962). Essentially, we are invited to look for a connection between each of the lines that are parallel. This is easy to do for the first three lines of the stanza in example 3; the parallelism appears to reinforce the positive evaluation of the propositional content. The fourth line, though, despite being syntactically and phonetically parallel to the three preceding lines, differs greatly in semantic terms, because it contains words with pejorative connotations. Nevertheless, the parallelism invites us to see the action described in the fourth line as being somehow equivalent to those described in the first three lines. The fourth line is also foregrounded additionally because it is semantically deviant when compared to the preceding three lines. This is quite a complex example because of the mix of parallelism and deviation, and the paradoxical interpretation we are forced into as a result of the parallelism is summed up in the final couplet of the poem:

(3a)   Here's how they rated him when they looked back:
         Sometimes he did this, sometimes he did that.

One of the issues raised by the concept of foregrounding is that it begs the question of the status of the large majority of the words in any text, which by definition are not foregrounded. There is a sense in which foregrounding is just one side of the coin, the other side being the 'backgrounded' or 'topographical' features of a text, which may be regular and repetitive, but may nevertheless form a distinctive part of the style of a text. We notice these features sub-consciously as readers when we think that a text 'sounds' like Jane Austen, or Alan Bennett, but can't quite place the individual features that make us recognise their style. This vital relationship between foregrounded features and their surroundings is captured in theories of figure and ground which we explore more fully in section 5.3, while a method for objectively gauging foregrounding is outlined in Chapter 7 in our discussion of corpus stylistics.

While prose and drama are good exemplars of style residing in the back-grounded or topographical features of a text, poetry lends itself more to the study of foregrounded features than to topographical ones, though as the discussion of figure and ground will show, the relationship between foregrounded elements and less prominent features is crucial to our understanding of the language of literature. This is not to say that backgrounded elements of language don't exist in poetry, but they will largely be studied in later chapters, and in relation to texts more typified by repetitive[4] or cumulative features than poems.

The sections that follow will investigate a range of linguistic features of litera-ture and other texts in some detail. All of them can be characterised by reference to one or more of the principles of foregrounding, deviation or parallelism.

2.3   Linguistic levels and stylistic analysis

One of the more straightforward applications of linguistic analysis to literary texts is a product of the linguistics of the early-to-mid-twentieth century when a great deal of progress was made in the description of languages following the structuralist developments arising from de Saussure's work (Saussure 1959 [1916]). One of the approaches that arose, building on such new insights, was to apply the 'levels' model of language to the language of literature and investigate, in turn, everything from the phonology to the semantics of literary texts.[5] This 'levels' model remains a large part of the basis of most approaches to linguis-tic description, and is founded upon the notion that human language has more than one level of organisation, being made up of (at least) 'meaningless' units of sound (phonemes or bundles of phonological features) and 'meaningful' units (morphemes and words) which are formed from arrangements of the smaller phonological units. These meaningful units are then, themselves, organised into higher-level structures (phrases, clauses etc.). The levels model might be rep-resented a little like figure 2.1 (with p representing phonemes, m representing morphemes and g representing graphemes).

Clearly, the syntax of languages is more complex than this, but it shows that in each utterance there are a greater number of smaller units and a lower number of the larger units, with each level being made up of units from the levels below. Like other models of language, this one does not fit the facts of language in every particular instance. Specifically, the model does not allow for a 'layer' which represents meaning. Though 'semantics' is often spoken of as another separate layer, meaning is in fact associated with each of the other structural levels, even the phonological one. Early semantics tended to focus on the lexical and morphological types of de-contextualised meaning, though sentence semantics, and later pragmatics, have shown that meaning permeates the whole system.[6]

The other issue raised by the levels model is the theoretical problem which is that the levels are not in fact separate from each other, but each co-exists with the others, so that choosing to focus on one level to the exclusion of others inevitably

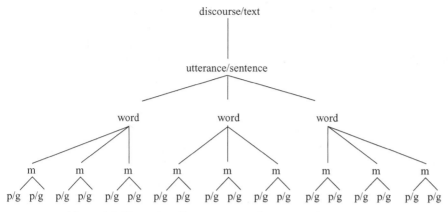

Figure 2.1 *Hierarchy of linguistic units (based on Jeffries 2006: 5)*

ignores all sorts of potentially relevant information. This is less of a problem for those wanting to use the tools of analysis for practical tasks, such as the investigation of literary language. In a sense, though this may be seen as a slight flaw in the model, it is also its strength, since it has enabled linguists to concentrate on parts of the linguistic system at different times, in order to describe them in detail, without having to try to encompass all aspects of language at once. This practical advantage is certainly one that has been exploited in stylistic studies, as the language of a poem or a play can then be explored one level at a time, making the whole project more manageable.

Stylistic analysis based on the levels model is unavoidably detailed because it requires very close scrutiny of the workings of the text at all levels. There are a number of ways of using the model itself, as with most of the analytical tools mentioned in this book, and the reader is referred to Chapter 7 for more discussion of the overall design of research projects in stylistics, which cuts across decisions about which tools to use. For now, we will follow the path taken historically by stylistic researchers, which was to take the theory of foregrounding as its basis and investigate how foregrounding might take place at any and all of the different levels of structure in literary texts. At times, we may also consider some of the less foregrounded, but still relevant, patterning at each level, though the main description will be of foregrounded features.

The detail required in this type of analysis lends itself to the investigation of poetic style, particularly in the contemporary period where poems are relatively short. For this reason, the sub-sections here will frequently be exemplified by poems, though other texts, literary and non-literary, will also figure at times.

2.3.1   Phonology

The sound of poetry is often mentioned as one of its attractions. Sound may also be a significant feature of certain kinds of prose and dramatic literature. The task for stylistics is to break down the phonological features of poetic style, so that they can be studied in detail. Of course, poetry mostly exists in a written form, and this means that any analysis of the sounds that make it up will be partly conjecture (e.g. about the accent in which it could be read). But even in English, which is not a phonetically written language, there are many things that readers will know about the sounds in a poem, without having to hear the poet – or other performer – read it aloud. One of these facts is that many of the patterns that make up the music of poetic style can be deduced from the written text alone. These patterns can be found not only in poems, but also in advertisements, and other genres, such as children's story-books. In most cases, the musical patterns in poetic style are examples of foregrounding, for example, when two words are marked out by alliteration. However, there are also some repetitive patterns, such as rhyme and rhythm, which are primarily backgrounded, or sometimes parallel in nature. And as for phonological deviation, this is most clearly seen in spelling changes intended to indicate a particular articulation of a word. These effects will all be explored in the discussion that follows.

This chapter will use a limited number of full poems to illustrate the effects of poetic style as it is often easier to understand the examples if they can also be seen in context. The first of these full poems describes the Brontë sisters walking on the moors near their home in Haworth with Emily's dog, Keeper. The poem follows:

(4)   *Up on the Moors with Keeper*

Three girls under the sun's rare brilliance
out on the moors, hitching their skirts
over bog-myrtle and bilberry.

They've kicked up their heels at a dull brother
whose keep still can't you? wants to fix
them to canvas. Emily's dog stares at these

three girls under the juggling larks
pausing to catch that song on a hesitant wind,
all wings and faces dipped in light.

What could there be to match this glory?
High summer, a scent of absent rain,
away from the dark house, father and duty.

(Dooley 1991: 66)

Alliteration/consonance and assonance

Alliteration is a pattern based on consonant sounds, and traditionally has been used to refer to adjacent words beginning with the same letter, though the effect is usually a phonological one, rather than visual, and should therefore be more properly defined as a property of phonemes rather than letters. A more appropriate name is therefore **consonance**, though the terms **alliteration** and its adjective, **alliterative**, are often used in this sense and will occur in places interchangeably with consonance in this chapter. Many uses of alliteration are simply playful, particularly in humorous literary texts or in advertising. This, for instance, is the strapline of an advertisement produced by Unite, a public service workers' union in the UK: CAMERON'S CRONIES CASHING IN ON CREDIT CRUNCH. The use of repeated voiceless velar plosive (/k/) sounds is effective in drawing attention to the text, and it might possibly be argued that the sharpness of sounds produced by plosives is some indication of rage on the part of the producers, but the main effect must surely be a simple sound effect with the capacity to entertain and attract. Normally, the use of alliteration in literary texts is less insistent, and in many examples there is a clearer reflection of the meaning encapsulated in the consonance itself. The last line of the first stanza in Dooley's poem, for instance, has a clear example of consonance:

(5)   over bog-myrtle and bilberry

Whilst the /b/ phoneme beginning two adjacent words would be alliterative in any case, the effect is increased because there is a third /b/ phoneme at the beginning of the second syllable of *bilberry*. This demonstrates that we might usefully take note of multiple occurrences of the same phoneme, whatever their position in the word, as having a potentially poetic effect.

It is the development of phonetic description since the early twentieth century that has enabled stylisticians to look beyond the bald definition of alliteration as 'words beginning with the same letter' and to see the more subtle patterns of consonance that can occur in poetic texts. The grouping of consonant sounds according to their *manner* or *place* of articulation is another step forward, allowing the effects of similar, though not identical, consonants to be mapped in any text. Thus, the line discussed above has not only the three bilabial plosive /b/ phonemes, but also the bilabial nasal /m/ of *myrtle*, which adds a further bilabial consonant to the phrase, resulting in something of a tongue-twister, with the proliferation of consonants in a single position in the mouth.

We will look at sound symbolism in more detail later, since it is one of the major forms of direct mimesis in language. Whilst linguistics has rightly argued that most human language is arbitrary in its sounds and structures, there are small ways in which language can directly reflect the world it describes (Bolinger 1949, Genette 1994 [1976], Hinton *et al.* 1994), and these are very well exploited by creative forms of language, particularly in literature.[7] We will return to mimesis, but here it is worth noting that in addition to the musical effect of having a particular clustering of sounds, there may also be meaningful significance in their grouping. In the case of the three Brontë sisters, who are *hitching their skirts*, the articulatory effort involved in pronouncing the four bilabial consonants in the phrase *bog-myrtle and bilberry* may be seen as obliquely mimetic of the difficulty of walking over Yorkshire moors in long, Victorian skirts which catch on the heather and small bushes typical of that landscape.

One of the main phonological characterisations in the poem is of the three girls as having the lightness, optimism and youthful exuberance that their father and brother seem to lack. This can be seen in the alliteration of the /s/ sound in the first line (note that one of the occurrences is in the word brilliance, where the pronunciation is /s/ but the spelling does not contain the letter 's'). This use of the sibilant /s/ sound in association with the girls continues through the poem, most clearly in the line 'High summer, a scent of absent rain'. In other contexts the rushing air of the fricative /s/ sound might be seen as directly sound-symbolic of something more negative, such as secretiveness ('Ssh!') or harsh weather ('whistling wind'). Here, however, in combination with the high vowels (see below) and semantic context (a walk on the moor), it appears to capture the light, airy feeling the girls experience when they are away from the claustrophobic nature of their home life in the valley.

Assonance is another 'traditional' sound effect that benefits from phonetic description as an accurate way of capturing the sounds of language. The vowels of English are particularly complex, as there are only five letters to capture what in many accents of English may be twenty-four or more different vowel sounds, including diphthongs. The visual effect of two or more words with the same vowel in their spelling is therefore very much less interesting and diverse in its effect than the clustering of vowel sounds which share particular acoustic characteristics. The phonetic description of vowels is based on which part of the tongue (front, back or middle) is involved and the height of this part of the tongue (open = low tongue, close = high tongue). The result is that instead of only being able to map the vowels which are identical in pronunciation, we can identify clusters of open, close, back, front or central vowels, and thus make a more accurate estimate of their musical – or meaningful – effect.

Dooley's poem is particularly full of assonantal effects, which appear to be both musical and meaningful. They work in tandem, of course, with consonantal effects, such as the alliteration mentioned above. Here, there is an association of the girls with high, front vowels, such as /ɪ/ and /ɪə/ and the brother with back, open vowels such as /ʌ/ or /ʊ/, depending on the accent of the reader:

(6)   They've kicked up their heels at a dull brother

Here, the girls have /kɪkt/ their /hɪəlz/ in contrast to the /dʊl brʊðə/. At the end of the poem, the long back vowels in /dɑːk haʊs/, /fɑːðə/ and /djuːtiː/ seem appropriate as a representation of the life of drudgery which awaits them when they come down off the moors. These vowels have an intrinsically lower pitch than front or high vowels, and their positioning away from the light and air at the front of the mouth also seems appropriate here.

Rhyme

Consonance (or alliteration) and assonance focus their attention on the clustering of individual sounds, whilst other sound patterns, which tend to have more a musical than a meaningful effect, focus on repeated combinations of sound. Rhyme, the more recognisable of these patterns, most typically occurs when there are two (or more) words which end with a stressed syllable, where the vowel and the final consonant(s) are the same. If we consider the basic structure of the syllable in English, it has a compulsory vowel, a very common initial consonant cluster (up to three consonants) and a less common, but still fairly frequent, final consonant cluster (of up to four consonants). Thus, the most minimal syllable, a vowel, would rhyme with itself (e.g. *I* and *eye*) but because rhyme is not normally considered to occur in cases of complete phonetic identity (another example is *pie* and *pi*), such cases are not used very often for poetic effect. The most frequent, open syllable of initial consonant plus vowel (C + V), which is common in all languages of the world, can rhyme its vowel alone, with different opening consonant clusters (e.g. *star/car*; *try/high*). The other typical rhyme in English is the closed syllable, with differing opening consonant(s) and matching vowel and closing consonant cluster (e.g. *fat/bat*; *thought/fort*). Notice in the Unite advertisement above, the sub-heading (David Cameron: Cheesy and Sleazy) uses a two-syllable rhyme (/iːziː/) to attract attention to the criticisms of the British Conservative Party Leader of the time.

Even where the rhyming in a poem occurs at the ends of lines in couplets, as in the opening to this Elegy by John Donne (example 7), it is not a simple technique:

(7)   *To his mistress going to bed*

Come, madam, come, all rest my powers defy;
Until I labour, I in labour lie.
The foe ofttimes, having the foe in sight,
Is tired with standing, though he never fight.
Off with that girdle, like heaven's zone glittering,
But a far fairer world encompassing.
Unpin that spangled breast-plate, which you wear,
That th' eyes of busy fools may be stopp'd there.
Unlace yourself, for that harmonious chime
Tells me from you that now it is bed-time.
                         (Donne 1896)

Only one of the rhymes here, between *sight* and *fight*, occurs on a straightforward single-syllable word, which has the same spelling and has a clearly stressed vowel. The other single-syllable rhyme is on the differently spelt words *there* and *wear*, and the final rhyme (*chime / bed-time*) is between a single-syllable word and a compound word. The other rhymes in this extract include *defy / lie*, where the rhyme is between the second (stressed) syllable and a single syllable, and *glittering / encompassing*, which has only the final unstressed syllable rhyming, and is therefore a weaker (sometimes called 'feminine') rhyme.

All of these variations on the simplest form of rhyme help to relieve any sense of monotony in the poem. This effect of regularity tempered by variety is more striking still when the grammatical structure cuts across the line breaks, leaving a tension between end-rhymes and the sense. This kind of musical effect, which is more subtle than the strictest form of rhyme scheme, is used to very great effect by some twentieth-/twenty-first-century poets such as Tony Harrison, whose poems sometimes give the initial impression that they are not rhymed, though most usually are.

Another means of varying the potential monotony of strict end-rhymes is the use of **reverse rhyme**, **half-rhyme** and **internal rhyme**. The former is the reverse of conventional rhyme – the first consonant cluster and the vowel match but the final consonant cluster does not (e.g. *slip / slim*). Half-rhyme involves only the final consonants (e.g. *clap / trip*). Seamus Heaney uses half-rhyme at the ends of each couplet in 'The Harvest Bow', some of which are illustrated in the following lines from stanza three:

(8)   And if I spy into its golden loops
       I see us walk between the railway slopes
       Into an evening of long grass and midges,
       Blue smoke straight up, old beds and ploughs in hedges
              (Seamus Heaney, in Morrison and Motion 1982: 36)

Note that the final rhyme, between 'midges' and 'hedges', is both half-rhyme (/mɪdʒ/ and /hɛdʒ/) and also feminine rhyme, since the final syllable (/dʒɪz/) is unstressed. The effect is one of a light musical touch, which marks out the form without intruding on the sense of the poem.

Internal rhyme is conventional rhyme but within the same line of poetry, so that the pattern works independently of any other pattern in the poem, such as metre or verse structure. Thus, in 'Dancing at Oakmead Road' (Dooley 1996: 29), the poet is saying goodbye to a childhood home where she feels her father's presence:

(9)   the resin of the wood would somehow catch
       in patina the pattern of his tread

Here, there are two examples of internal rhyme, one of complete identity through homophonic words with different spellings: *wood* and *would* (/wʊd/) and the other involving an identical first stressed syllable in *patina* and *pattern* (/pæt/). Whilst most internal rhymes have a musical effect which is aesthetically pleasing, but more subtle than end-rhyming, these examples also appear jointly to have a potentially iconic effect, echoing the repetitive nature of the father's footsteps in the house, and her notion that this may be reflected in the resin of the wooden floorboards.

Speech in poetic style

One of the more obvious ways in which literary style tries to emulate the spoken language is by evoking the sounds used by different groups of speakers. There is a balance that writers need to strike if they want their work to be understood by standard English speakers generally, so the use of spelling changes to convey accent is usually patchy, and in some cases has its own conventions. In the case of Yorkshire English, for example, there are some conventions that British English speakers will normally recognise quite readily. Some of these can be seen in the following extract from 'Long Distance' by Tony Harrison where he is quoting his father:

(10)   *Ah've allus liked things sweet! But now ah push*
         food down mi throat! Ah'd sooner do wi'out.
         And t'only reason now for beer 's to flush
         (so t'dietician said) mi kidneys out.
                                  (Harrison 1984: 133)

Here, the reduction of the definite article (*the*) to a glottal stop is conveyed in the standard way using 't'' before the noun concerned. There have been other attempts to convey this sound by using a simple apostrophe – on the grounds that there is nothing like an alveolar plosive being articulated[8] – and by omitting the article completely.[9] However, the convention of using *t'* is quite widespread. Other conventions are to use *ah* to indicate the open front vowel common in much of the north of England for the first person pronoun, 'I'. This sound is most closely represented phonetically by [æ:] and rather different from the long back vowel of southern accents in England: [ɑ:] in words like *bath*. In Yorkshire, there is also a common loss of the interdental fricative /ð/ in *without*, indicated by the loss of 'th' in the spelling (*wi'out*), with the apostrophe to indicate the reduction. Finally, the word *my* becomes effectively /mɪ/ in many accents of British English, and this is indicated by a change of vowel from 'e' to 'i'.

Another common and partly conventionalised accent of English that is evoked in poetic contexts is that deriving from various post-creole forms of English, such as the accents from Jamaica and other Caribbean islands. The following lines from Linton Kwesi Johnson's 'Reggae fi Dada' (Burnett 1986: 77) illustrate some of the common conventions of representing this accent:

(11)   Mi know yu couldn tek it dada
         di anguish an di pain
         di suffahrin di problems di strain

Though the dialect also has lexical words which would be different from standard English, one of the main ways in which a poet like Johnson can communicate in his own variety of English, but without making it difficult for speakers of other varieties to understand, is to represent the common, grammatical words,[10] such as *the*, *and*, *you* in the closest approximation to the pronunciation possible – as *di*, *an*, *yu*. The frequent occurrence of words of these grammatical classes means that the reader will soon become accustomed to the different representation, and comprehension is thereby speeded up.

One of the questions for stylistics, apart from the written conventions by which speech is represented, is what aesthetic effect this may have. Of course, there may be a simple topographical effect, as when Johnson, for example, chooses to write some of his poems wholly in creole. Such a choice may be foregrounded for a reader unfamiliar with this variety of English, but within the poem's own terms, the choice of a non-standard representation is backgrounded. If we return to the main mechanisms of foregrounding, which is achieved by deviation and parallelism, we find examples of speech representation which perform in the first two of these ways, though less often within a parallel device. In a sense, any direct representation of speech in the written language is externally deviant by the rules of the standard language, so that it often falls to the graphology or spelling of the language to indicate its deviant form. We have already seen examples, in Yorkshire and Jamaican creole dialects, of such deviant forms in poetry. Tony Harrison's poems about his parents usually mark out the accented extracts of their speech in italics, with a foregrounding effect in contrast to their son's own, educated speech:

(12)   *Too posh for me!* he said (though he dressed well)
          If you weren't wi' me now ah'd nivver dare!
                              (Harrison 1984: 136)

The effect of foregrounding, however it is achieved, is to mark out a section for attention. The precise effect will depend on the subject-matter and the linguistic context. In the case of Harrison's poetry, where it concerns his relationship with his parents, the contrast highlights the theme of many of his poems – that of his alienation from his working-class roots as a result of his education.

Sound symbolism

We have already touched on some of the potential of the phonology of literary – and in particular poetic – language not only to provide musical effects, but also to symbolise directly the meaning it represents. The most iconic of such effects is normally referred to as onomatopoeia, and concerns the direct echoing of the sounds being described in the phonology of the words used to describe them. Whilst human languages usually have a small number of generally onomatopoeic words (e.g. *clap*, *snip*, *baa*), the potential of individual sounds to be onomatopoeic in certain contexts is a much more exciting and well-used resource for the poetic writer. In all cases, the general poetic effect being called upon is that of foregrounding.

In 'Privacy of Rain', Helen Dunmore uses a combination of conventional onomatopoeic words (*splash*) and further sibilant consonant sounds (/s/, /z/ and /ʃ/) to directly represent the sound of rain, both as it falls in individual drops (*A plump splash / on tense, bare skin*) and also as the rain sets in and becomes a continuous fricative sound, as in the regularly spaced and frequent sibilants[11] in the following extract:

(13)   white
          downpours shudder   /z/, /ʃ/
          like curtains, rinsing   /z/, /s/
          tight hairdos to innocence. /z/, /s/, /s/
                              (France 1993: 118)

Other forms of onomatopoeia also relate to whole categories of sound more often than to individual phonemes themselves. Thus, as well as representing the sound of rain, sibilants can be used to conjure up wind, sighing, breathlessness etc. Plosives, particularly the voiceless ones (/p/ /t/ /k/), being short, sharp sounds, can be used for gunfire and other short sounds such as a knock on the door or a clap of thunder – or applause. Nasal sounds are all voiced in English, and are fairly resonant, using, as they do, both the oral and the nasal cavities for their amplification. This makes them ideal for representing resonant sounds like bells, singing and other musical or quasi-musical sounds like the *clang* of an iron gate. The sound-symbolic potential of vowels may also be related to their physical characteristics, and we find, as in Dooley's poem about the Brontë sisters, that the closed and front vowels, being higher pitched, may be used to indicate the higher voices of the girls in comparison with their male relatives whose vowels are open and/or positioned at the back of the mouth, with resultant lower frequencies.

Though not strictly iconic in the sense that onomatopoeia is, the use of sounds to signify concepts is a further aspect of style that is exploited by writers. The signification is normally related to the sound in some way, though not by directly indicating sound. So, for example, the closed vowels which directly reflect higher pitched sounds may also be used to indicate smallness, and the open vowels larger sizes. Similarly, the plosives, which are by their nature short in length, may indicate a short length of time, though not necessarily a *sound* which is short, as in this example from 'The Prelude' where the young Wordsworth panics as he rows across a lake at night when the mountains appear to come after him:

(14)   a huge peak, black and huge,
          As if with voluntary power instinct
          Upreared its head. I struck and struck again,
                              (Wordsworth 1971: 57)

Here, the use of a short word, *struck*, which has a short vowel and ends in a voiceless plosive (/strʊk/), emulates not only the sound of his rowing (each stroke of the oars against the rowlocks), but also the rapid movements of someone trying to move fast through a medium that lends itself more to long, slow strokes.

The length of sounds can provide another form of sound symbolism,[12] and long vowels or diphthongs (which are an equivalent length to long vowels in English) often perform the function of symbolising a slow or long-lasting activity. Wilfred Owen's famous 'Anthem for Doomed Youth' about the dead of World War One ends:

(15)   And each slow dusk a drawing-down of blinds.
                        (Silkin 1979: 183)

The underlined vowels here are long vowels or diphthongs (/iː/, /əʊ/, /ɔː/, /aʊ/, /aɪ/) and, unusually for English, there are three stressed vowels in a row (*each slow dusk*). Both of these features make the sound of this line slower and focus the reader's attention on the sad scenes in many British households where the sign of mourning (the covering of windows) was to be seen during the First World War.

2.3.2   Graphology

Graphology is the equivalent in the written language to phonology, and is conveyed through the visual medium rather than the aural. There have been a number of different approaches taken by poets who wish to exploit the substance of the language in visual form (see van Peer 1993), and this section will introduce some of them. There is a sense in which the manipulation of text in this way is only an extension of the concept of poetic form, where lines of poetry are dictated by something other than the width of the page, and the breaks in the structure may be meaningful, as we will see in section 2.3.4. In this section, however, we will be considering the use of text primarily for visual effect, and the different forms that this can take.

Concrete poetry

The term 'concrete poetry' has been used to describe a range of techniques of manipulating text on the page. One of the most obvious is where the poem is set out to mirror one aspect of the poem's meaning, as in the mushroom cloud shape of Philip Nicholson's poem (in example 16).

(16)
                        If it happens
                  SHOULD SOME MADMAN
                PRESS THE BUTTON AND THE
              DREADFUL SIRENS SOUND, I SHALL
              LIKE MANY OTHERS SEEK A REFUGE
            UNDERGROUND, BUT NOT IN ANY BUNKER
          OR SUBTERRANEAN TOMB – I'LL PASS MY FINAL
              HOURS BEFORE INEVITABLE DOOM IN MY
              COMFORTABLE CELLAR STOCKED WITH
              MEMORABLE WINE – THERE IN ROMAN
                        FASHION
                          I'LL
                    LANGOROUSLY
                      RECLINE,
                        DRINK
                THE DIONYSIAC SPRINGS
          COMPLETELY DRY, THEN QUIETLY DIE.
                              (Nicholson 1990: 52)

This technique simply uses the space of the page to allow the outer shapes of the text to draw an outline of something familiar that is connected with the poem's content. A much earlier, but similar, effect was achieved by the metaphysical poet, George Herbert, in his poem 'Easter Wings', where the poem's lines were arranged to make the shape of wings, though these could be seen clearly only if the page was turned sideways.

Stanley Cook, a Yorkshire poet of the twentieth century, was interested in the possibilities of concrete poetry for introducing schoolchildren to creative writing. In his pamphlet, *Seeing your Meaning*, self-published in 1985, he argued that 'The shape of its subject must not be imposed arbitrarily on its words; you would not, for example, make a concrete poem by imposing a saloon shape on a dictionary entry for "car"' (Cook 1985: 9). Cook's definition, then, differs from those, who, like Nicholson, thought that the shape of a poem could be made to echo the meaning directly in this way. Cook explicitly differentiates this 'outline' type of poem, which he calls 'visual poetry', from truly concrete poetry, which he sees as depending on the visual properties of the letters making up the poem's words. Many of the examples he gives are in fact no more than a word long, as in examples (17) and (18), where the letters of the words 'wave' and 'tunnel' are used iconically.

(17)

(18)

As we have seen, foregrounding effects at the linguistic level of graphology are often achieved by extreme graphological deviation. It should be pointed out, though, that some graphological effects are not foregrounded in this extreme way. Some poems, for example, are graphologically structured in such a way as to foreground particular elements. In Carol Ann Duffy's poem 'Poet for Our Times', the first four lines of each stanza are graphologically conventional, and the last two lines of each stanza are written in uppercase letters to represent newspaper headlines; that is until the final stanza of the poem, where the two lines in capital letters occur in the middle of the stanza, with two graphologically conventional lines following. The positioning in the last stanza of the two lines in uppercase letters is *internally* deviant – it deviates from the norm established by the previous stanzas in the poem. As a result of this, the final two lines (which now occupy the place we have come to expect the headlines to be) are foregrounded – and this turns out to have major interpretative consequences (see Semino 2002).

2.3.3   Morphology

One of the contributions of general linguistics to the description of style, and poetic style in particular, is the distinction between a word and the minimal grammatical unit, the morpheme (see Jeffries 2006: 72–82). The scope for foregrounding, deviation and parallelism within word structure has been used extensively by poets and advertising copywriters through the ages. This section will illustrate the effects that can be achieved by 'playing' with morphology.

First, we should consider what makes morphology a particularly useful technique for poetic writers. Although English words may be free morphemes in themselves,[13] they are also often made up of a combination of free and bound morphemes. There are three processes of forming words in this way: inflection, derivation and compounding (see Matthews 1991 and Carstairs-McCarthy 1992). As we shall see, the second and last of these are more frequently used in poetic style, though inflection has scope for writers who wish to push at the boundaries of the language. In general, though, the fact that many languages have this two-tier arrangement of smallest grammatical unit (morpheme) and smallest popularly recognised unit (word) allows for writers to make up new words using familiar affixes, thus giving them both the power to create and invent and also the strategy of allowing readers a relatively easy insight into the meaning of their work.

For example, in 'Tide and time', Roger McGough (1979: 15) invents an aunt who is a *hortihorologist* and who gives her nephew a *floral wristwatch*. Whilst *hortihorologist* is not made up of recognisably English morphemes, the reader may well think of words with similar Latin or Greek roots (*horticulture, horoscope, horologist*) and with the extra hints from *floral wristwatch*, it is a small step to working out that there is a new concept in time measurement being suggested in McGough's fantastic world. This is confirmed by the next line, where the watch is described as *Wormproof and self-weeding*. These inventions are more obviously English-based, and thus more transparent in meaning, since the reader will know other words with the bound morphemes *-proof* (e.g. *waterproof*) and *self-* (e.g. *self-justifying*) and will be aware that even in everyday language use they can be productive (i.e. can be added to 'new' words), as in *squirrelproof, childproof, Daisyproof* and *self-clarifying, self-dusting*. Notice that these inventions are rarely written down, though they are probably re-invented on a regular basis by speakers, and in some cases may enter the written language in due course, when advertising of commercial products finds it useful:

(19)   Childproof locks
            Squirrelproof bird feeders
            Self-dusting bookshelves

These examples were invented initially, but once they are put into believable contexts, such as those above, it appears more likely that at least the first two are in fact already in existence.

Inflection

The most regular process by which words are formed from adding morphemes, inflection, forms the plural and possessive versions of nouns (*dog, dogs, dog's*), the tenses of verbs (*play, played*) and the comparative and superlative versions of adjectives and adverbs (*soon, sooner, soonest*) in English. Its very regularity means that any deviation from the normal process of inflection would be very noticeable and thus foregrounded as highly deviant to the reader. This can happen where there is either a strong requirement for being noticed (e.g. in advertising) or a strong motivation on the part of the writer to explore the limits of what can be done without communication breaking down altogether, as often happens in poetry.

The poet E. E. Cummings, known for his use of lowercase letters, also tried to play with the inflection system of English, though even he was limited by its regularity. In a poem which begins 'if everything happens that can't be done' (his poems have no titles), he adds the regular comparative and superlative suffixes to adjectives that are usually combined with *more* and *most* (*the stupidest teacher*) and in some cases he makes adjectives with absolute meanings (e.g. *right* and *shut*) gradable, though they are not normally treated that way by the language: 'anything's righter / than books / could plan and books are shuter / than books / can be'. The effects of Cummings's experiments with inflection are limited and tend to be repeated, so that a reader of his work will quite quickly become accustomed to the style of language, and begin to read the new comparative and superlative adjectives with less effect of foregrounding than when the first one was encountered. However, this is not necessarily a negative effect. What Cummings achieves is to make us reassess the absolutes in our lives, and question whether more things are gradable than we had previously noted. If the gradability of all qualities referred to by adjectives begins to be **naturalised** as common-sense by his readers, this is an added achievement of his poetics as a whole.[14]

It has already been pointed out that the inflectional morphemes in English are part of the grammatical system of the language, and are therefore quite difficult to deviate from, or foreground, without making nonsense of the text. Even Cummings only really tries to extend the reach of adjectival suffixes, leaving verb and noun endings alone. However, inflectional morphemes can be used in parallelism or indeed as part of the topography of the text, to give an overwhelming impression of a particular kind. The following excerpt from 'Thoughts After Ruskin' by Elma Mitchell (Adcock 1987: 245), for example, uses a large number of progressive (-*ing*) participles in a short space of time to conjure up the frantic and sometimes cruel activity of women in charge of domestic duties, and contrasts these with the more measured, generic present tense of the activities of the husbands who 'lean' and 'manipulate'.

(20)   Their distant husbands <u>lean</u> across mahogany
            And delicately <u>manipulate</u> the market,
            While safe at home, the tender and the gentle
            Are <u>killing</u> tiny mice, dead snap by the neck,
            <u>Asphyxiating</u> flies, <u>evicting</u> spiders,
            <u>Scrubbing</u>, <u>scouring</u> aloud, <u>disturbing</u> cupboards,
            <u>Committing</u> things to dustbins, <u>twisting</u>, <u>wringing</u>,
            Wrists red and knuckles white and fingers puckered,

The progressive participles convey the idea of activity that is ongoing, and are each appended to a single occurrence of *are*, so that the speed and fury of the women's activity is not slowed down by the inclusion of the repeated auxiliary. Any concentration of particular verb forms could theoretically be used in this way, and the effects would vary according to the context and content. For example, the use of unusual numbers of past tense verb phrases, or even of past perfective verb phrases, such as *had finished* and *had left* could emphasise the finality of some meanings and thus have an opposite effect from the '-ing' forms in Mitchell's poem.

Derivation

As already mentioned, the process of derivation is less regular than inflection in English, and as a result it is also more likely to be used for creative purposes in poetic styles of writing. The basic process of derivation in English is the addition of an affix to a free morpheme, normally changing the word class as a result, and sometimes also altering the basic meaning in a way that inflections do not. Thus, for example, the change of *bake* (verb) to *baker* (noun) involves the addition of an -*er* suffix and also the change of meaning from the activity of baking to a person who performs this activity in a commercial setting (i.e. not your mother). The only regular case of derivation not changing word class in English is that of prefixes, usually negative in meaning, such as *unfaithful, discontinue*.

Some poets are known for their inventiveness, but even those who are normally thought of as working within the normal rules of the language find derivation a useful tool. One of the reasons for this is that there is a tendency for speakers to create and recreate new derivations in everyday language, and the reader of poetry will therefore not find the use of a 'new' derivational form so strange that it obstructs meaning. Indeed, it is quite difficult to be sure when an unusual derivation is indeed invented by the poet, because it may well be that others have also, independently, invented the same form. Louis MacNeice, for example, in 'Spring Sunshine', asks:

(21)   If it is worth while really
              To colonise any more the already populous
              Tree of knowledge, to portion and <u>reportion</u>
              Bits of broken knowledge brittle and dead,
                                (MacNeice 1964)

Whilst if we look it up on the internet, the word 'reportion' can indeed be found, the contexts and apparent meanings of the invention in those cases seem to be rather different from MacNeice's own. It is likely, then, that he did what other users of the word have done, and actively added a prefix ('re' meaning 'to do again') to the verb 'portion', which in itself is derived from a noun. Its positioning in a mini parallel structure with 'portion' itself makes the similar phonology of the two words directly symbolic of the repetitive behaviour, adding a sound-symbolic or iconic dimension to the morphological effect.

Compounding

In compound words, two or more free morphemes are joined to create a new word, usually different in meaning from a phrase made up of the same free morphemes, so that, for example, a 'blackboard' is not just any board which is black, but is a culturally recognisable item with a particular use and the word even tends to be used now that most teaching aids of this kind are white. The creation of new compound words is a very useful foregrounding technique for writers who are looking for both economy of expression and new meaning. It therefore suits poets and advertising copywriters, who can take advantage of the fact that the superficial meaning of compound words is relatively transparent because it is easy to see that it is made up of free morphemes and their meanings are normally clear. The additional bonus is that the reader will be aware that compounds often have something additional in their meaning, beyond the combined meanings of the free morphemes, and this causes a conceptual 'gap' in the text which requires filling in by the reader. Depending on context, that process of filling the gaps might be a game or puzzle (often in advertisements) or it might be part of the process of delving into the deeper meaning of a poem.

The meaning of compounds is not normally difficult to work out, as they are often constructed on analogy with existing compounds in the language. Sylvia Plath (1965: 57), for example, describes her foetus in 'You're' as *moon-skulled* and herself in the early days of motherhood in 'Morning Song' (1965: 11) as *cow-heavy*. In each case, we can think of other familiar compounds which allow us to understand these invented ones. So, we may know *ham-fisted* (fists like hams) and *feather-light* (light as a feather) and conclude that the invented compounds mean having a skull like the moon – i.e. round – and heavy like a cow respectively. This does not complete the process of interpretation, of course, as the reader will wish to think about why these descriptions are appropriate in the context. Thus, the visual effect of the large head on a small body of a foetus is captured by *moon-skulled* and we immediately think of the main purpose of cows (in our society) – to produce milk – and conclude that the heaviness she feels is in her breasts as she goes to feed her child.

2.3.4   Syntax

Most of the syntactic techniques used in literary style are examples of foregrounding by internal deviation and some are additionally deviant in relation to Standard English. Noticeable variations on the 'normal' English sentence can take a variety of forms, and these are often exploited in a way that complements the semantics of the text and the constraints of any poetic form that is imposed.

Some of the syntactic exploitation in poetic style is directly symbolic (iconic) of the meaning it encodes. This is the syntactic equivalent of onomatopoeia, where the structure of the text reflects in an iconic manner what is being described semantically by the lexis. This additional layer of meaning, carried by the structure itself, appears to reflect the referents of the text physically, either temporally (e.g. a line break indicating a pause or a long clause element indicating a long period of time) or spatially (e.g. a large clause element referring to a large item). This is a more subtle version of graphological symbolism, and relies on reader expectations of some kind of 'norm' to create a reaction in the reader which may reflect the emotions of the participants in the action of the poem.

Syntax and verse form (end-stopping and run-on lines)

Whilst many poems in recent years have not been based on a strict form, there are examples, from throughout the history of poetry, of poets exploiting the potential tension between syntax and form. Where there is a conjunction of the ends of lines and stanzas with ends of syntactic units, such as sentences and clauses, the poetic structure adds only rhythm to the text. This is to be found in songs and some forms of traditional poetry, and also in some light-hearted verse of recent years. In most poetry, however, the writer is aware of the possibilities of using the occasional run-on line which cuts across the syntactic units, for particular effect. Here, for example, are the opening lines from Andrew Marvell's 'To His Coy Mistress', which illustrate both the general matching of syntax with line-ending, and also the impact of varying this practice:

(22)   Had we but World enough, and Time,
         This coyness Lady were no crime.
         We would sit down, and think which way
         To walk, and pass our long Loves Day.
                     (Marvell 1681)

These first two sentences in the poem end at the end of the second and fourth lines respectively, and this appears to be a regular pattern being set up. The first sentence, indeed, has a grammatical break also at the end of the first line, when the initial subordinate adverbial clause ends. In the context of so much regularity, then, the run-on line 3, which splits another subordinate clause (*which way to walk*), is foregrounded and the reader is led to make an 'asyntactic' pause at the end of the line which echoes the thinking process of the lovers being described at this point in the poem who have the leisure to take time over seemingly trivial decisions about which direction to take in their walk.

In more recent times, the potential for this kind of tension between end-stopped and run-on lines has been exploited still further. Run-on lines are almost always foregrounded, even in free verse where the tension between line endings and syntax is vital to a text's identity as poetry. Larkin uses the run-on line in the following short poem to symbolise the heavy-hearted loss a (personified) home feels without its creators:

(23)   *Home is so Sad*

           Home is so sad. It stays as it was left,
           Shaped to the comfort of the last to go
           As if to win them back. Instead, bereft
           Of anyone to please, it withers so,
           Having no heart to put aside the theft .

           And turn again to what it started as,
           A joyous shot at how things ought to be,
           Long fallen wide. You can see how it was:
           Look at the pictures and the cutlery.
           The music in the piano stool. That vase.
                              (Larkin 1964: 17)

The contrast here is between the wistful line endings of the first stanza where the syntax runs on and the rather duller effect of the second stanza where all the lines end with a punctuation mark. In the first stanza lines 2, 3 and 5 seem to be looking into the distance at *the last to go*, feeling *bereft*, and the extra hesitation with the run-on lines between the stanzas seems to evoke the pause as one gathers one's energies to start all over again. In the second stanza, the second and third lines, indeed, play a trick on the reader, since the *joyous shot*, with the comma ending line two, seems to be an optimistic assessment of what the home was at first, and it is therefore a let-down to read on and find that it has long been a disappointment or failure. In the latter part of stanza two, full stops start to pile up and the final result is an unconnected list of items in the home which have no connection with each other – and implicitly no connection with the owners either.

Minor sentences and timelessness

Another form of echoing of meaning in structure is the use of minor sentences (i.e. sentences or clauses with no main verbal element) in poetic style. The loss of the verbal element of a clause has the effect of placing the remaining words outside any normal time-frame and results in a kind of timelessness which can be exploited in a range of ways. In the following poem, Pamela Gillilan captures the memory of someone dear to her (older relative – mother or grandmother maybe?) and in doing so she manages to stop time in its tracks twice in the minor sentences underlined:

(24)   *Doorsteps*

>   Cutting bread brings her hands back to me –
>   the left, with its thick wedding ring,
>   steadying the loaf. Small plump hands
>   before age shirred and speckled them.
>
>   She would slice not downwards but across
>   with an unserrated ivory-handled carving knife
>   bought from a shop in the Edgware Road,
>   an Aladdin's cave of cast-offs from good houses –
>   earls and countesses were hinted at.
>
>   She used it to pare to an elegant thinness.
>   First she smoothed already-softened butter
>   on the upturned face of the loaf. Always white,
>   Coburg shape. Finely rimmed with crust the soft
>   halfmoon half-slices came to the tea table
>   herringboned across a doylied plate.
>
>   I saw away at stoneground wholemeal.
>   Each slice falling forward into the crumbs
>   to be spread with butter's counterfeit
>   is as thick as three of hers. Doorsteps
>   she'd have called them. And those were white
>   in our street, rubbed with hearthstone
>   so that they glared in the sun
>   like new-dried tennis shoes.
>   (France 1993: 143)

Other aspects of the syntax in this poem will be discussed in later sections, but it is worth noting here that the minor sentences (underlined above) are foregrounded against the finite clauses that surround them:

(25)   Small plump hands
            before age shirred and speckled them.

(26)   Always white,
            Coburg shape.

Combined with the line-breaks, these two minor sentences seem to interrupt the process of setting the tea table as the narrator's hungry younger self sees the process taking a long time and the older self daydreams of the time when the subject's hands were young and of the time when loaves were always white Coburgs.

Iconic structures

One of the subtler iconic effects of syntactic structure is to manipulate elements of structure to represent the meaning of the text directly as well as semantically. In English, the major ways in which this effect can be achieved are through the manipulation of noun phrase and clause structure. In the English clause, it is the norm to expect shorter units of given information in the early part of the clause, which means that the verb element will be reached relatively quickly, and then the longer units containing new information are normally placed towards the end of the clause. Variations on this format are possible, of course, with the addition of optional adverbials at the start of the clause, delaying not only the subject element, but also the verb. Another variation is to extend the subject beyond the normal short noun phrase, with extra modification before and after the head noun.

What these effects have in common is the discomfort that English speakers feel when the arrival at the verbal element is delayed. Until it is clear what process (verbal element) is at the centre of the activity or state being described in a clause, the reader may not know the significance of the early parts of the sentence and a sense of anticipation is created. The following two sentences differ in that the first uses only a pronoun for subject and then arrives very quickly at the verbal element (underlined) and the second extends the subject to a length that leaves the reader experiencing some form of discomfort before finally arriving at the verbal element (underlined):

(27)   She <u>brought</u> the soft halfmoon half-slices finely rimmed with crust to the tea table

(28)   Finely rimmed with crust the soft halfmoon half-slices <u>came</u> to the tea table

In the case of a hungry child waiting for an elaborate tea to be laid out, the emotion that might be evoked in an empathetic reader by such a delay in the verbal element is probably frustration. The level of lovingly remembered detail in the description of how the bread was presented makes boredom or anger seem unlikely, since the effect is more one of her eyes following every movement of her relative bringing the food to the table. In other contexts, of course, different effects might be achieved by a delayed verb, depending on the semantic content of the text. In the same poem, for example, we have another long subject symbolically representing the thickness of the 'modern' slice of stoneground wholemeal bread:

(29)   Each slice falling forward into the crumbs
            to be spread with butter's counterfeit
            is as thick as three of hers.

In this case, the thick slice of bread that the narrator cuts is represented by a long (two line) subject before the verb (*is*), whilst the thin white slices of her memory are represented simply by *hers*. Thus, the length of clause elements can be directly iconic in this way, or more indirectly indicative of the emotional state of the characters in the poem by potentially inducing similar emotions in the reader.

Like many other stylistic analyses, the interpretation of apparently iconic syntax in this way is vulnerable to the accusation that stylistics attempts to 'read off' meanings from linguistic features in some semi-automatic way. The discussion of objectivity and rigour in section 1.6 goes some way to answering this criticism, and Simpson (1993: 111–16) rejects the accusation that this kind of analysis is a version of 'interpretative positivism'. In the example given above, the important ingredients are the *potential* for iconic representation in English syntax combined with the context, in which, for example, a delayed verb represents frustration (in particular, hunger) as opposed to other possible meanings such as waiting, boredom, emptiness and so on.

Ambiguity

There are a number of ways in which the syntax of poetic style is foregrounded through deviation and one of these is the use of the inbuilt potential in language for ambiguity. One of the potentially ambiguous constructions in English arises from the superficial similarity between a list of noun phrases and a set of noun phrases in apposition.[15] The theoretical difference between these two, of course, is one of reference. Lists have a number of different referents, whereas appositive noun phrases are different methods of labelling the *same* referent. The scope for exploiting this ambiguity lies in the fact that both sets of noun phrases may look identical, and both sets fulfil a single grammatical function (e.g. as subject or object of the clause). The following (invented) examples illustrate the difference between these structures:

(30) *List*:   They were all there: Gordon Brown, Peter Mandelson, David
                    Milliband.

(31) *Apposition*: He was there: Gordon Brown, Prime Minister, man of the people.

What can happen in a poetic context is that these two structures may merge where a number of noun phrases occur which are not necessarily connected but which the reader is inclined to read as apposition and make the connections between the different versions of the same referent. In the following example from 'Foreign Correspondent', the opening lines appear to elaborate on the first noun phrase, *a story*:

(32)   We are inventing for ourselves a story.
          The other life. A narrative that frets and stumbles
          yet moves along at such a pace, I'm winded.
                              (Dooley 1996: 35)

Whilst the third phrase, beginning *A narrative* is clearly semantically related to this, the middle one, *The other life*, is less clearly so. The reader is therefore left with an apparent list of noun phrases, each the object of the verb *inventing*, and the link between the first and third implying that the middle one is also co-referential. With this information available we are able to surmise that the correspondents are perhaps not journalists, but lovers, and that the communication has become strained, and possibly less than truthful, in the way that things can be distorted by distance.

Other ambiguities arise in poetic style where punctuation is minimised and the result may be that a phrase could belong to either the previous or the following clause. This occurs in the following poem by Audre Lorde:

(33)   *A Small Slaughter*

Day breaks without thanks or caution
past a night without satisfaction or pain.
My words are blind children I have armed
against the casual insolence of morning
<u>without you</u>
I am scarred and marketed
like a streetcorner in Harlem
a woman
whose face in the tiles
your feet have not yet regarded
I am the stream
past which you will never step
the woman you can not deal with
I am the mouth
of your scorn

(Lorde 1997: 100)

Line 5, *without you*, is a prepositional phrase, and has the potential to function as a postmodifier to the preceding noun phrase – i.e. *morning without you* – or as an adverbial element in the following clause – i.e. *without you I am scarred*. What this example demonstrates is that poetic style has the potential to build in more meaning than texts which are under pressure to be clear. In this case, and many others, it is not a problem for the reader to see two possible meanings built into the structure, particularly as they do not clash in meaning. It is likely that the narrator means both – the missing of a person has both effects.

Vagueness

Although not strictly grammatical, there is a sense in which the vagueness of some contemporary poetry is closely related to the ambiguity discussed in the last section, though it is delivered in a different textual manner. Unlike ambiguity, where there are a limited number of clearly distinct interpretations possible, vagueness is the property of texts which are lacking in **cohesion**, to the extent that the reader is obliged to work quite hard to understand the poem on any level.

The loss of normal levels of cohesion is one way to achieve a particular effect, so that the reader is aware of the superficial meanings of clauses, but not necessarily given clear guidance in the text as to how to make the connections between them. The result is that the reader has to make extra processing effort in analysing the text. The opening to McGuckian's poem 'Pain Tells You What to Wear' illustrates:

(34)   Once you have seen a crocus in the act
              Of giving way to the night, your life
              No longer lives you, from now on
              Your later is too late.
                            (McGuckian 1984: 41)

There are three clauses here:

(35) •   Once you have seen a crocus in the act / Of giving way to the night
     •   your life / No longer lives you
     •   from now on / Your later is too late.

The first is a subordinate adverbial clause and sets the scene for the others, which are both main clauses and seem to be in some kind of appositional relationship to each other.[16] The reader is likely to be influenced by the structure to see the second and third clauses as co-referential in the context of an experience concerned with crocuses. Apart from the structural link made between 'Once' and the following clauses, and the fact that all three clauses are addressed to 'you' (the reader?), there is no sign of conventional cohesion at all. The broken selectional restrictions on 'giving way', which normally requires a human subject, and 'live', which normally has an animate subject and no object, add to the effect of estrangement. The reader is left working quite hard to interpret how crocuses 'give way' and what is meant by 'later' being 'too late'. The trick, of course, is to find out what the two appositional clauses might have in common with the first, contextual one, though the semantic content is quite disparate. Perhaps the main concept they all communicate is urgency. The first main clause appears to indicate the end of someone being at the mercy of events, and by implication, taking control. The link with the final main clause is the notion that life is too short to delay things that you want to do, so no longer will *you* use *later* as a response to things that need doing, since all delay is *too late*. The link with crocuses is, of course, their short life, and the inevitability of them closing at dusk, which might be the trigger to changing the way that you live, to enjoy the present and not to delay on important matters.

McGuckian is known for the apparent complexity of her poetry, but like many poets, she appears to use and re-use certain particular techniques of style, and in her case it is this tendency to make readers work very hard at piecing together the cohesion of her texts. However, once the reader has worked through a few of her poems, this process becomes easier.

Ungrammaticality

Other poets choose a poetic style that favours ungrammaticality over cohesive deficiency. Whilst the structure of poetry may use all the grammatical possibilities at its disposal, including the kinds of repeated phrases, minor sentences and hesitations that are present in speech, the use of deliberate ungrammaticality is rarer and tends to be the preserve of particular poets who are interested in pushing at the boundaries, though the difficulty for readers of interpreting syntactic deviation may put some poets off this course.

Cummings found a number of grammatical techniques for making the reader think hard, but without making his poetry impossible to read. He tends to use the same techniques repeatedly, as in this extract from 'true lovers in each happening of their hearts':

(36)   such a <u>forever</u> is love's any <u>now</u>
         and her each <u>here</u> is such an <u>everywhere</u>

Here, Cummings has used adverbs in the position of nouns, and with modifiers which cause them to act like countable nouns ('a', 'any', 'each', 'an'). This change of word class is one relatively accessible way to challenge preconceptions and make readers think about the meanings of words. If time adverbs can become nouns, particularly countable nouns, then it seems as though time is being compartmentalised and with the addition of possessive modifiers ('love's' and 'her'), there is the sense that time is experienced differently by different people, rather than being a universal, as adverb usage would usually indicate.

As well as changing word classes, Cummings also frequently uses phrases that are familiar, such as 'side by side', and then uses them as a frame, putting different words into the lexical 'slots':

(37)   busy folk buried them side by side
         little by little and was by was
                      (Cummings 1991)

In this example, from 'anyone lived in a pretty how town', the phrasal frame 'x by x' occurs three times, and although the first two look familiar, the second one in fact has a change of word class inherent in it. Although the normal meaning of 'little by little' is 'gradually', it is clear that busy folk would not bury these friendless people slowly. The result is that we are forced to interpret 'little by little' as a phrase containing nominals, labelling them as 'little' (him) and 'little' (her), and this is confirmed by an even stranger version in the third phrase where a verb, 'was', also has to be taken as a nominal, referring to them as people who are no longer alive.

Where ungrammaticality leads to more serious disruption of meaning, the poet may be in danger of losing all but the most committed readers, and therefore few go down this route. Writers who make use of syntactic deviation have a tendency to use the same type of ungrammaticality regularly, with the result that a reader can become accustomed to the 'poetics' of an individual writer with enough exposure to their work.

2.3.5   Semantics

We have been exploring the way in which poetic style exploits all the levels of language structure, but although it doesn't act as a 'level' in its own right, semantics is perhaps the most important of all aspects of poetics. In this section we will take a *lexical* semantic view of what is meant by semantics, because more sentence- and text-based semantics will be covered in other chapters.

All of the **sense relations** that can hold between words in the language can be exploited in interesting ways by poetic language. The sense relations that may occur between different words include lexical field membership, oppositeness, homonymy, polysemy, hyponymy, collocational and selectional restrictions on cooccurrence and connotation. Apart from being typical texts in having a range of these features in the chosen lexis, poems also have the capacity to highlight these features by foregrounding them through deviation and parallelism.

The more obvious uses of semantic foregrounding tend to occur in advertising campaigns, such as a slogan placed on large trucks, 'Trouble Passing?', to advertise a high-fibre breakfast cereal. This exploits the polysemous double meaning of the word 'passing'. Motorists not able to pass because of the size of the truck were presumably intended to be at least entertained by the other meaning, which refers to the body's ability to 'pass' waste food products, which is one of the well-known effects of eating this particular breakfast cereal.

Whilst humorous poems and comedy dramas also draw on this capacity for multiple meanings to result in puns, the more subtle uses of semantic relations are typical of more serious forms of literary works, and can be best illustrated by poetic examples.

The following poem is built, semantically speaking, on a number of lexical fields, some of which are linked by being opposed to each other:

(38)   *Ironing*

I used to iron everything:
my iron flying over sheets and towels
like a sledge chased by wolves over snow,

the flex twisting and crinkling
until the sheath frayed, exposing
wires like nerves. I stood like a horse

with a smoking hoof
inviting anyone who dared
to lie on my silver-padded board,

to be pressed to the thinness
of dolls cut from paper.
I'd have commandeered a crane

> If I could, got the welders at Jarrow
> to heat me an iron the size of a tug
> to flatten the house.
>
> Then for years I ironed nothing.
> I put the iron in a high cupboard.
> I converted to crumpledness.
>
> And now I iron again: shaking
> dark spots of water onto wrinkled
> silk, nosing into sleeves, round
>
> buttons, breathing the sweet heated smell
> hot metal draws from newly washed
> cloth, until my blouse dries
>
> to a shining, creaseless blue,
> an airy shape with room to push
> my arms, breast, lungs, heart into.
>   (Vicki Feaver, in O'Brien 1998)

The main lexical fields in this poem concern parts of the body ('arms', 'breast', 'lungs', 'heart', 'hoof', 'nerves'); domestic linen and clothes ('sheets', 'towels', 'sleeves', 'blouse', 'silk', 'cloth', 'buttons') as opposed to the more masculine field of heavy industry ('iron', 'crane', 'welders', 'Jarrow', 'tug', 'hot metal', 'wires'); and another pair of opposed fields defining the smooth ('pressed', 'thinness', 'creaseless', 'flatten', 'airy', 'shape') and the wrinkled or otherwise untidy ('flex', 'twisting', 'crinkling', 'crumpledness', 'wrinkled', 'frayed').

Probably the most foregrounded fields here are the two pairs of matched lexical fields. The reader might not be expecting a heavy industry theme in a poem about ironing, for example. The poem divides into three parts and the third part resolves the conflict arising in the first two. In the first stage of the narrator's life, she irons everything, including the sheets and towels. In the second stage, she irons nothing at all and in the third stage she irons again – though apparently only her own clothes. This leads us to perceive a split in the domestic linen between things that are hers, and more communally owned items like towels. There is also a split in the 'wrinkled' field – between absolute, almost vicious flatness and 'an airy shape', the latter being three-dimensional and allowing for life to inhabit the cloth, as opposed to the earlier two-dimensional, and by implication, lifeless, pressing. What the semantic structure of this poem does, then, is to set up in its lexical fields an apparently complementary opposition (if fabric is not flat, it must be wrinkled) and then point out that in reality there are other modes for fabric, one of which is three-dimensional, though smooth.

If Feaver's poem depends on lexical fields and oppositeness for its semantic shape, other poems use unusual collocation as a way of creating poetic meaning. The following poem illustrates a number of these semantic features, some using parallelism in addition to unusual collocation:

(39)   *Song of the Non-existent*

This is the hour between dog and wolf, when the first
Anxiety walks across to the polished counter,
And the sky becomes lighter and darker at the same time,
And the moon, if it shows, is a pale, inessential detail

Because this is the hour of glass, the age of souls;
Gold is in every leaf, and to walk in the glow
Between traceries is to be among the angels:
This is the page on which you write the word 'angels'

And the muse, though stern, doesn't flinch: when impotent wings
Of learning stretch to the cloudiest stony hill:
This is the net of desire, where something adrift and homeless
Is caught and pronounces itself a nightingale.

This is the wolf's hour, after all; he turns it between his teeth:
The watery city thickens, blackens: all that the angels leave
Is this: your sudden reluctance to remember
How hard it was, and how beautiful, to live.

(Rumens 1995: 46)

One of the most common effects of collocating words with unusual partners is the creation of metaphor. In the poem above, 'the first / Anxiety walks' breaks the normal pattern of selectional restrictions on the verb 'walk', which requires an animate subject rather than the abstract subject we have here. The result of this collocation is that 'Anxiety' may appear to the reader to be a personification of the emotion, or perhaps more accurately a person becomes identified solely with their most evident emotion. Another metaphorical effect caused by collocation occurs in the clause 'The watery city thickens, blackens', where the city is likened to a liquid, which is the usual subject of the verb 'thicken', and allows the reader to imagine the fading sights of the city in the dusk as though it were a liquid that was getting thicker and darker.

This poem also uses the parallelism of the phrase 'This is the hour' as a kind of refrain, leading to the foregrounding of those phrases that are built upon these words:

(40) •   This is the hour between dog and wolf
  •   this is the hour of glass
  •   This is the page on which you write the word 'angels'
  •   This is the net of desire
  •   This is the wolf's hour, after all

Rather like the examples of vagueness earlier, these phrases appear not to be cohesive, but the parallel structure implies that we should look for some kind of connection between them. The 'dog and wolf' phrase places these nouns in a position where a noun of activity (e.g. *eating, sleeping*) or of time (*afternoon, evening*) might be expected, and we therefore search for some time connection between them. The wolf is known for howling at night, so the conclusion is easily reached that the dog represents daytime and the wolf nighttime. Once we have established that it is dusk that is being described, we can look for the relevance of the 'hour of glass' to dusk – presumably its appearance of fragility and transparency. The following two phrases are harder to pin down to dusk itself, but there is a momentum from the parallelism that may lead us to conclude that the writer sees dusk as a creative time ('the page on which you write the word "angels"') and the time when ideas fall into place by a wish ('the net of desire'). The final phrase indicates that time is moving on and the night is taking over from the day, as the dog no longer features, and the wilder, more frightening time begins.

2.4   Questions of style: literariness revisited

In this chapter we have seen some of the ways in which progress in general linguistic description has enabled us to make more accurate, relatively objective and consistent descriptions of the language of literature, as a way of demonstrating the processes (deviation and parallelism) by which foregrounding – the textual manifestation of defamiliarisation – occurs. Here, we have mostly illustrated these effects in the language of poetry because this is the genre which is most distinct from what we may loosely call 'everyday' language. Such an approach has been challenged from the later part of the twentieth century onwards when it began to be recognised that there was not, or perhaps was no longer, a language of literature distinct in kind from other types of language. The rest of this section will trace the debate about the existence of a language of literature as background to what happened in stylistics following the initial application of linguistic methods and models to literary style as illustrated above. The approach to close stylistic analysis we have seen so far remains an important aspect of stylistic work, though it is no longer connected simply to literary style, and is often used in conjunction with other methods and models, reflecting developing interests amongst stylisticians in cognition, computer analysis and contextually-based studies of discourse.

Prior to the realisation that literary style was not completely distinct, it was common to make assumptions about the difference between literary and other forms of language, as we can see in this quotation from Birch:

> in his article on Larkin, N. F. Blake assumed an understanding of literariness when he talked about the difference between poetic imagery and 'flat' language.   (Birch 1989: 111)

Birch points out that it has been quite normal in stylistic discussion to take for granted that language comes in two rather distinct types. On the one hand there is the everyday, literal and down-to-earth and on the other hand there is the poetic. Amongst other developments, the progress in investigating metaphor in everyday language (see, for example, Lakoff and Johnson 1980 or Lakoff and Turner 1989) and in stylistics more generally made such an approach untenable by the late twentieth and early twenty-first century.

Whilst literature might indeed be the place where much of the most daring linguistic deviation takes place, it is undeniable that on the one hand there are a great many other genres, not least advertising, where linguistic deviation is endemic, and on the other hand many regular forms of language which are stylistically typical of other genres (e.g. legal, medical and religious registers; regional dialect forms; conversational features) but occur within the boundaries of literary works.

So, it has been reasonably well established that literary language is at the very least not a completely separate type of language, but nevertheless some efforts have been made to define literature in some way, as it seems to be important to us socially to recognise its nature. One such definition is in terms of the competence that readers require in order to process literature as distinct from other forms of text. Thus, one requirement of a reader of fiction is that s/he can imagine the fictional world as it emerges, and follow a fictional set of events as they unfold in the text, taking account of any flashbacks or other changes in the temporal (and indeed geographical) flow of the narrative. The reader of poetry will often have to contend with unusual uses of language like those we have been investigating in this chapter where the phonology, morphology, syntax or semantics of the poem stretches – or breaks – the usual rules of combination to create new effects. The viewer of plays and films has to put her/himself in the position of accepting what s/he sees and hears as an alternative world to the one that s/he exists in, and following the trajectory of the narrative in similar ways to the reading of fiction.

If some see literature as a different kind of *reading* experience, then, others have claimed that it is the *function* of literature that marks it out as different to other text-types. One influential proponent of this viewpoint was Roman Jakobson, whose theory defines the functions of language in terms of the relationships between the different 'factors' of a communicative act. These factors are listed by Jakobson as context, addresser, addressee, contact, code and message, and the various functions of language were seen by Jakobson as operating between the message and other factors, so that, for example, the emotive function of language was seen as operating between the addresser and the message (how the speaker feels about what s/he is saying) whereas the poetic function, according to Jakobson, is really only focused on the message for its own sake (Jakobson 1960: 356). The functions in Jakobson's theory are not exclusive, however, so that though the primary function of, say, poetry, would be poetic, Jakobson's system would also allow for some of the other functions, such as the emotive or even the referential functions, to play some part in the communication arising from poems.

Jakobson's theory, then, allows us to demonstrate the main and subsidiary functions of literary texts, without having to define such texts as belonging to a category separate from other communicative acts. Thus poems would be *primarily* concerned with their message, but might also be seen to have an emotive function in allowing the poet to express her/his feelings. We will return to what this means for the characterisation of literature later, but first we should consider another attempt to define literature by reference to its function, this time considering its function in the broader context of society.

Cook (1994) makes a valiant attempt to define what literature is, and he draws on the Russian formalist tradition in suggesting that one of the main functions of literature is to change the way in which readers see the world. Cook's view that what literature does is 'schema-changing' whereas other texts, such as advertising, are 'schema-reinforcing' will be discussed further in Chapter 5, but here we will consider his wider view that since defining literature linguistically has proved difficult, then we should define it by how a particular culture recognises it. So, for example, Western cultures in the twentieth and twenty-first centuries have recognised a category of artefact labelled 'literature' which is made up of three main printed genres, poetry, fiction and drama. Though drama is written for the stage, we could argue that as far as its membership of the category of literature is concerned, it is still in a printed form.

We might additionally propose that this culturally-defined category of literature has a number of features that most members of society would agree upon. These might include, for example, the idea that 'literature' is an elevated form of language-based art, with the capacity to show readers a version of the world (or other imagined worlds) which will cause them to reflect on their own perceptions of 'reality'. At other times, and in other places, we might have added that literature functions as a call to adhere to a higher morality, but this is not true of the present day.

Some might protest that this definition characterises literature in an elitist way, and that they would prefer to include popular fiction, poetry and drama in the definition. This may well be how literature is defined in some circles, including academic ones, at the present time. The point is that there is no clear boundary and what gets included as literature can differ from group to group and over time. Some people might take Cook's evident desire to find a way of defining 'literature' as a sign that he simply wishes to preserve something of literature's prime place as the highest of linguistic arts, and this may be true. Another approach altogether might be to ask why it is that we feel this compulsion to define a prestigious linguistic art at all, and whether we might simply accept that some forms of entertainment are language-based, and that some of these gain prestige in a number of ways, including their acceptance as part of the canon (evidenced by their inclusion in school curricula etc.).

As we saw with Jakobson's theory earlier, one possible way to describe different text-types is to define a set of features (in his case they were functional ones) and then characterise prototypical text-types by reference to their use of these features. This results in the description of literature, say, or other text-types, as a bundle of features each of which may be present or not. Texts may then have some or all of the features of this characterisation of what constitutes 'literature', and those which tick some but not all of the boxes will be seen as peripheral whereas those with all the features will be central to the group. This approach to the definition of what literature is was taken by Carter and Nash (1983) among others. Birch describes their approach by saying that Carter and Nash argue:

> that to polarize language as either literary or non-literary leads to the assigning of values to particular kinds of language, valorizing the literary against the non-literary (Carter and Nash 1983: 123–4). An alternative to this, they suggest, is that language should be seen in terms of a gradation or 'cline', which makes it possible to find elements of literariness in languages which would usually be defined as ordinary/non-literary.   (Birch 1989: 111)

It is easy to see that such an approach does help us demonstrate the overlapping but not identical forms and functions of, for example, biography and advertising with fiction and drama and this approach may demonstrate some of the features of literary works, but not all. The advantage of the prototypical approach to defining literariness is that the features used in defining central cases may vary from the formal to the functional, so that all of the insights of those who have debated this topic over the years are relevant to the case in point. Thus, prototypical literature may have at least the following features, and probably more:

A   Formal distinctiveness and a focus on the language of the text (i.e. foregrounding through deviation and parallelism)
B   Representational distinctiveness (defamiliarisation through fore-grounding)
C   Specific competence of readers in understanding the fictional world of the text
D   High status in the society where it is produced and read
E   A focus on the content (message) for its own sake.

On the other hand, certain types of literature may only have a subset of these features, with A in particular being more typical of poetry than other genres, and a very great deal of popular literature lacking D: the high status that is sometimes accorded to some literary works.

As far as language, and thus stylistics, is concerned, these features are relevant insofar as they relate to linguistic features. This means that, for example, A and C are clearly linguistic features whereas the others are only indirectly linguistic, with B possibly being delivered through unusual uses of language, D often being based on some notion of linguistic refinement and E complementing A by making plain that the more prototypical literary text exists in form and content simply because it exists, and not for any other reason, such as informing, changing social attitudes etc.

Perhaps one of the more obvious reasons why this question of what constitutes literariness has been difficult to answer is that it starts from the wrong perspective.

If, instead of asking what the different kinds of text are from a top-down view-point, we asked instead what features any individual text had, and then compared it with other similar texts, we would begin to find that we have a complex, but accurate, 'map' of the different types of text in a specific culture and/or language and that these would form partly overlapping groupings which, however, differed in detail and may share features with more than one other grouping. This bottom-up approach is particularly suited to making use of the very many stylistic tools of analysis that we are investigating in this book, as they often lend themselves to describing different text-types and would be helpful in demonstrating the overlaps and differences.

2.5   Summary and conclusions

This chapter introduced the theory of foregrounding and the main ways that texts have of producing this effect: deviation and parallelism. Whilst stylistics was founded upon the insight that many features of what has tradition-ally been considered literariness are foregrounded in being distinct from their surrounding text (internal deviation) or from some notional 'normal' version of the language (external deviation), there has recently been a movement towards recognising that another of the aspects of style that readers respond to is what we could call the 'topographical' aspects of style, i.e. those features which occur regularly within a particular text or author's work and which subliminally affect us as a style. These features of style may also be approached by the linguistic descriptive methods examined in section 2.3, but they require a more quantitative methodology than would usually be used on individual lyric poems, and thus lend themselves to the developing field of corpus stylistics which is discussed in section 7.2.2. There is a related field of computer-aided stylometry, which aims to characterise the really backgrounded features of an authorial style, sometimes with the aim of attributing the work to the correct author. This differs in aim from that of stylistics, though some of its methods are very similar.

The tools of analysis in the bulk of this chapter, probably more than in any other, lend themselves to examining the features of texts which fit the most prototypical view of literariness in language. The description of the 'norms' of a language, which is the product of a linguistics of that language, allows us to describe those places where a text deviates from these norms. This happens, as we have seen, in some rather obvious cases of advertisements playing with language, but it is more typical of poetry and poetic types of prose and drama than other texts.

As we shall see, more recent developments in stylistics have taken account of new theories and methods arising from pragmatics, from functional linguistics and from critical discourse analysis. Most of these more recent approaches take the reader's part in meaning-making into account, though stylistics would still consider itself to be fundamentally text-based. None of these recent additions to the range of approaches has, however, supplanted entirely the notion that at least some of what has traditionally been recognised as stylistically significant can be adequately accounted for in terms of foregrounding and by applying the insights of the levels of language to the analysis.

Exercises

Exercise 2.1

Below you will find a poem by Keats and part of a longer poem by Ted Hughes, both of which exhibit a range of foregrounded features. Pick out those features that you think are foregrounded, and using the levels model of language, describe how the language use has caused this foregrounding to happen. Make sure that you describe the effect as technically as possible, using linguistic tools of description. Commentaries on these poems can be found at the end of the book.

(41)   *To Autumn*

Season of mists and mellow fruitfulness,
Close bosom-friend of the maturing sun;
Conspiring with him how to load and bless
With fruit the vines that round the thatch-eves run;
To bend with apples the moss'd cottage-trees,
And fill all fruit with ripeness to the core;
To swell the gourd, and plump the hazel shells
With a sweet kernel; to set budding more,
And still more, later flowers for the bees,
Until they think warm days will never cease,
For summer has o'er-brimm'd their clammy cells.

Who hath not seen thee oft amid thy store?
Sometimes whoever seeks abroad may find
Thee sitting careless on a granary floor,
Thy hair soft-lifted by the winnowing wind;
Or on a half-reap'd furrow sound asleep,
Drows'd with the fume of poppies, while thy hook
Spares the next swath and all its twined flowers:
And sometimes like a gleaner thou dost keep
Steady thy laden head across a brook;
Or by a cyder-press, with patient look,
Thou watchest the last oozings hours by hours.

Where are the songs of spring? Ay, where are they?
Think not of them, thou hast thy music too, –
While barred clouds bloom the soft-dying day,
And touch the stubble-plains with rosy hue;
Then in a wailful choir the small gnats mourn

Among the river sallows, borne aloft
Or sinking as the light wind lives or dies;
And full-grown lambs loud bleat from hilly bourn;
Hedge-crickets sing; and now with treble soft
The red-breast whistles from a garden-croft;
And gathering swallows twitter in the skies.

                                        (John Keats)

(42)   Then I crept through the house. You never knew
           How I listened to our absence,
           A ghostly trespasser, or my strange gloating
           In that inlaid corridor, in the snow-blue twilight,
           So precise and tender, a dark sapphire.
           The front room, our crimson chamber,
           With our white-painted bookshelves, our patient books,
           The rickety walnut desk I paid six pounds for,
           The horse-hair Victorian chair I got for five shillings,
           Waited only for us. It was so strange!
           And the crimson cataract of our stair Wilton
           Led up to caverns of twelfth-century silence
           We had hardly disturbed, in our newness.
           Listening there, at the bottom of the stair,
           Under the snow-loaded house
           Was like listening to the sleeping brain-life
           Of an unborn baby.

                                (from Ted Hughes, 'Robbing Myself')

Further reading

Ehrlich (1965) covers the history of Russian formalism, the precursor to modern stylistics. The principles of foregrounding are set out in van Peer (1986), which also contains substantial empirical support for the theory. Early work in stylistics can be found in the collections edited by Fowler (1966, 1975) and Freeman (1970). Leech (1969) is a comprehensive discussion of the application of linguistic techniques to the analysis of poetry, as is Jeffries (1993), while Leech (1966), discusses the language of advertising from what might be defined as a stylistic perspective. Crystal and Davy (1969) is an early work in non-literary stylistics, concerned particularly with the linguistic description of particular styles, and Enkvist (1973), too, is an approach to stylistics very much rooted in the descriptive tradition. Leech (2008) is a collection of essays written over the last forty years, with the concept of foregrounding as a unifying theme, and is highly recommended.

3 Discourse and context I

Function

3.1   Texts as discourse

In Chapter 2 we considered the origins of stylistics in Russian formalism, and the progress made in the analysis of literary texts in response to the developments of descriptive linguistics in the first half of the twentieth century. Many of the insights of the theory of foregrounding, and its various realisations in the analysis of form, are still relevant to stylistic analysis and have been refined and added to as linguistics has increasingly considered context and function as part of its scope. This chapter will introduce some of the main ways in which the consideration of function in language study has affected the way in which stylistics approaches the study of literary and other texts, and will begin by tracing the debates and controversies that accompanied some of these developments.

Stylistics has, on occasion, been the target of attacks from literary critics for what has been seen as an excessive concern with the linguistic form of (literary) texts at the expense of social, historical and other contextual factors that also play a role in a text's meaning. (Similarly, stylisticians have found themselves accused of failing to take adequate account of the important relationship between writer and reader which is mediated by the text. Recent advances in cognitive stylistics have addressed this criticism directly; see Chapters 5 and 6.) While no stylistician would accept that an analysis can incorporate too much linguistic detail, there is perhaps some truth to the point that stylistics has sometimes neglected contextual factors involved in meaning-making. The reason behind this is that stylistics has taken as its guiding light linguistics, which itself began with more formal concerns. Leech and Short (1981: 4) reflect on the changing nature of linguistics in the introduction to the first edition of their influential textbook on the style of prose literature:

> linguistics itself has developed from a discipline with narrowly defined formal concerns to a more comprehensive, if more inchoate discipline, in which the role of language in relation to the conceptualization and communication of meaning has been fruitfully investigated.

The advances in linguistics noted by Leech and Short – incorporating a burgeoning of theories and related methodologies – are also reflected in the developments and scope of contemporary stylistics, as the remainder of this book will illustrate (see also the discussion of stylistics' tendency towards eclecticism in section 1.6.3). Leech and Short (1981: 5) themselves comment upon the range of linguistic traditions which have influenced the development of stylistics and they attempt to characterise what they have in common as

> a tendency to explore for pattern and system below the surface forms of language; to search for the principles of meaning and language use which activate and control the code.

This concern with form, then, does not disappear, just because there has been a rising interest in the functions of the forms described. Leech (2008) sees the link between form and function as vital to the definition of stylistics:

> This interface between linguistic description and interpretation is precisely the sphere of stylistics as I see it: by undertaking a linguistic analysis as part of the interrelation between the two fields of study, we facilitate and anticipate an interpretative synthesis. Within stylistics, that is, linguistic and literary concerns are as inseparably associated as the two sides of a coin, or (in the context of linguistics) the formal and functional aspects of a textual study.

This integration of formal and functional aspects of language is probably not as new as it sounds and of course is not unique to stylistics. Even Saussure, who is often associated with formal analysis, explicitly concerned himself with language as a 'social semiotic' and the whole of systemic-functional grammar, particularly in the work of Halliday (1985), has been concerned to try to describe form and function within the same model. Some of the results of Halliday's work have proved particularly useful for the analysis of the style of literary and other texts, and others have added similar tools of analysis which combine form and function in their model of language. Note that the opposition between form and function is also a 'convenient fiction' both in the sense that Leech (2008) above sees it, since they are 'two sides of a coin' (and thus inseparable), and also in the sense that we could, and some analysts do, divide language up into more than two aspects. Thus, we could say that form is made up of the levels of language discussed in Chapter 2, and that function consists of at least semantics (at each of these levels) and pragmatics (and the grey area between them). In addition, there may be further layers of interpretation that we would want to associate particularly, but not uniquely, with literary texts. These latter are those layers of interpretation which are least closely tied to the text itself, though they may be deduced from the nature of the language.

Before we consider the use in stylistics of some of these functional tools of analysis, let us consider one more of the challenges that stylistics has faced, which is partly concerned with the question of the relationship between form and function. This is the charge of 'interpretative positivism' (see Simpson 1993: 111–16) which was most famously levelled against stylistics by Stanley Fish (1981) and which many stylistics books since then have felt compelled to answer. This charge will be explained below, but it is worth making the connection here with the related controversy about the objectivity of stylistics, which was discussed in section 1.6.2. Here, the attack made by Fish is concerned with the question of whether it is possible, or indeed desirable, to do as he claimed that stylistics did and to 'read off' meaning automatically from text:

> For both critics operate with the same assumptions and nominate the same goal, the establishing of an inventory in which formal items will be linked in a fixed relationship to semantic and psychological values.   (Fish 1981: 75)

Whilst Fish is able to find *some* examples of this kind of apparent rigidity in seeing form and function as having a fixed relationship, in fact stylistics has long embraced the notion that form does not confer a particular meaning in any automatic sense. Thus, though there may be some conclusions one can draw from the form of a text, they are only the *beginning* of literary interpretation, which depends on the conjunction of form with particular content and also with particular contexts of production and reception. Thus, for example, we may wish to comment on the use of long and convoluted sentence structure in a novel to the extent that it draws attention to itself (i.e. is foregrounded). However, the significance of this tendency will depend on its year of production (since longer, more complex sentences have been declining for some centuries in English), on its genre (it would be unusual in a detective fiction novel and less so in a 'literary' one), on its topic (the more philosophical, the less unusual it would be) and on its year of reception (contemporary readers of eighteenth-century fiction would not react adversely to long and complex syntax, though the twenty-first-century reader may do so). In other words, the question of external deviation is not simply a qualitative linguistic calculation. Literary interpretation requires us to recognise which of these, and other, factors are influencing our view of a text, and included in the list of affective factors is the construction of the language itself.

This lack of automation in the move from language to interpretation (form to function) causes Fish (1981: 72–3) to attack stylistics from the opposite direction, for what he calls 'a serious defect in the procedures of stylistics':

> the absence of any constraint on the way in which one moves from description to interpretation with the result that any interpretation one puts forward is arbitrary.

Many stylisticians have found fault with the apparent logic of Fish's attack on their field. Toolan, for example, acknowledges many of Fish's arguments in relation to the more automatic interpretative claims of stylistics, though he also takes up the question of whether stylistic analysis is still worth doing:

> Fish rightly argues that the stylistician's focus on a particular phonological or syntactical pattern in a text is itself an interpretative act. As I hope to have suggested, this in itself does not constitute an overwhelming argument to stop doing stylistics unless (a) that interpretative act is shown to be incoherent or ill grounded, or (b) more coherent interpretative acts are presented, and preferably both.   (Toolan 1996: 131)

Though stylistics as a whole has never been either as rigid or conversely as loose as the worst cases represented by Fish, there is nevertheless some movement to be seen through the history of the subject from a more text-intrinsic approach towards an approach which recognises the reader as an integral part of the construction of textual meaning. Thus, most approaches to stylistics these days see the text (literary and other) as the centre of a communicative event which may take place in a range of places and timescales, and which includes the producer and the recipient. In other words, literary and other texts are considered as discourse events, and not just stable artefacts with stable meanings.

However, it is important to note that there remain some features of the text which *can* be identified and described irrespective of their intended and/or received effect. The interpretation of how such features may affect the writer's meaning and the reader's meaning is one of the more subjective aspects of stylistic analysis, though the link to textual features does at least achieve the scientific standard of explicitness that enables others to see how an interpretation is arrived at (see the discussions of methodology in section 1.6 and Chapter 7). Stylisticians rightly claim that their procedures in analysing literary and other texts are explicit, logically argued and do not assume that language is transparent in its meaning. Together, these aspects of the stylistics methodology make sure that those encountering a particular stylistic description of a text will know how the interpretation is arrived at, and will be able to engage with it on its own terms.

The remainder of this chapter will introduce some of the functional categories that have been applied to stylistic analysis. Where these tools of analysis depend on other linguistic knowledge this will be explained in the relevant section.

3.2   Functional categories and style

Although the analytical tools described in the following sections are often labelled as 'functional categories' in Hallidayan and other systems of description, they are not really categories at all. What we have in most of the cases is a system of related concepts (i.e. meanings) which are realised linguistically in a range of ways, often with a prototypical realisation in one of the systems of the language, but usually including a set of other, less central possibilities for producing the same effect. We will see below how this works for a number of functions, but it is convenient to illustrate the point about how these systems work using negation.

If we take a very strict, grammatical, view of negation, we would probably say that it is realised by a negative particle which is attached to the verbal element of the clause. Thus in 'I didn't know you were coming', the negator, 'not', is attached to the first auxiliary, the operator in the verb phrase, and here occurs in a reduced form ('n't'). A less central, but still clearly negative, form is the use of the adjectival 'no' before nouns in noun phrases as in 'no time' or 'no food'. A still clearly negative meaning is attached to a range of prefixes in English, which have a variety of precise meanings, depending on their root word, but all denote some kind of negation, as in '*in*credible', '*un*successful' and '*a*social'. Whilst their meaning may be clearly negative, these morphemes are not able to be added to all equivalent root forms (note *asincere, *insubtle, *unsecure). This, then, is a less central form than the verbal and nominal negation, which are not similarly restricted. Still less formal is the existence of a range of lexical items in English and other languages where the semantics indicate a negated denotation. These include 'lack', 'loss' and 'absence' as clear members of the group, though the parameters for identifying a lexical item as negative are not clear-cut and result in items being more peripheral to the group, including for example those which have negative evaluation as part of their meaning, such as 'feeble' or 'cruel'. In the case of the clear examples, though it is difficult to establish a straightforward methodology for deciding whether they are performing some kind of negation, we can nevertheless say that their denotation is most easily paraphrased using a negated phrase or clause. So 'lack of x', for example, is clearly denoting the situation where there is 'no x', and 'loss of x' clearly denotes 'no longer having x'. This test is less clear-cut in the latter cases, where we could use a negative definition, or a positive one. Thus, being 'feeble' could be defined as 'having no strength', but it is arguable that most pairs of gradable adjectives have one partner which could be thus defined: cold (absence of heat), calm (absence of strong feelings), short (lack of length).

We will see below that the strength of this arrangement of form–function relationships is in its very lack of one-to-one conformity. Thus, it is the fact that a set of related meanings, such as those we can define under the term *negation*, can be produced by an array of different forms in a language like English that makes all sorts of meanings possible. If there was one, and only one, way to negate concepts in English, the language, and literature as a result, would be thereby impoverished in its potential effects, as we shall see in the sections below. This point, that the lack of one-to-one form–function relationship is at the heart of human language, takes us back to one of the founding principles of stylistics itself, the assumption that style is made up of a series of choices among options provided by the language. We considered this idea in section 1.6.4. Here, we will see how choices made by text producers have the capacity to influence the meaning created by text recipients.

3.2.1   Transitivity

The syntactic system of transitivity is the central component in Halliday's functional grammar, which was conceived in relation to English, and is thus perhaps peculiarly suited to that language, although the development of systemic-functional grammar theory and models is not so restricted.

This system acknowledges that the verbal element is the core of the clause, and that the choice of lexical verb itself is somehow crucial to the rest of the choices in the clause. So, for example, if a clause is being constructed with the verb 'eat' as the lexical verb, the choice of this verb, which is labelled a 'Material

Table 3.1 *Transitivity categories from Simpson (1993)*

Main category	Sub-category	Further sub-category	Participants
Material	Action	Intention	Actor (animate) (Goal)
	Action	Supervention	Actor (animate) (Goal)
	Event		Actor (inanimate) (Goal)
Verbalisation			Sayer (Verbiage) (Target)
Mental	Perception		Senser Phenomenon
	Reaction		Senser Phenomenon
	Cognition		Senser Phenomenon
Relational	Intensive		Carrier Attribute
	Possessive		Carrier Attribute
	Circumstantial		Carrier Attribute

Action – Intention' process, will dictate that the grammatical subject of that verb will be an Actor (an animate being) and there will be a grammatical object following the verb which will be the Goal. Transitivity analysis, then, takes the traditional idea that some verbs require objects (transitive) and some do not require objects (intransitive) one step further, and gives groups of verbs semi-semantic labels, describing them as occurring in the context of a number of participants, also with semantic labels. There are a number of versions of these categories of verb, but here we will draw upon that used by Simpson (1993), as he was using the model specifically for stylistic purposes (see Table 3.1).

Before we consider the problems with this model as well as the uses to which it can be put in stylistics, let us look at some simple examples of the way in which transitivity analysis characterises clause structure:

- The girl on the bicycle saw her brother.   Mental Perception
- The bike hit a rock.   Material Event
- The girl fell off the bike.   Material Action Supervention
- Her brother ignored her.   Material Action Intention
- She was upset.   Relational Intensive
- She shouted at him.   Verbalisation
- He had a grin on his face.   Relational Possessive
- She thought him an idiot.   Mental Cognition

As we will see below, the basic idea that the use of different process types can make a difference to the effect of a text is of use to the stylistician. However, the model is not without its problems. For one thing, there is no single agreed set of transitivity types, as a result of their being based not solely on formal properties. The decision as to how many different kinds of Mental Cognition categories there should be in English, for example, is not a clear-cut one. Similarly, we cannot assign verbs to transitivity categories out of context, because they may have a range of possible transitivity behaviours. Thus, the verb 'drop', for example, may be a Material Action Supervention verb on one occasion (*She dropped the glass in her fright*); a Material Action Intention in some cases (*She dropped the glass to see it shatter*) and a Material Action Event in other cases (*The glass dropped from her hand*). In addition, of course, there may not be enough information in a particular context for us to be sure which transitivity process is intended, though there is often a preferred interpretation, which in the case of 'drop' would be the Supervention one (She dropped the glass).

Of course, very many verbs in English and in other languages are used metaphorically in everyday contexts and much of the time. Whilst this means that we may in some cases distinguish between the core use and the creative use of an item, the normal use of an item may in some cases be the metaphorical one, and this would make the metaphorical meaning more basic. In the case of 'drop', the Goal is the key to its meaning, so that instead of 'She dropped the glass', the utterance 'She dropped the case against him' would bring the metaphorical meaning to the fore. This may still be classified as a Material Action, though it is clearly intentional, whereas the default interpretation in literal cases would be Supervention. The question of how to categorise other metaphorical uses of a verb may be more difficult, so that one could argue about the transitivity of 'She dropped her voice', given that it describes a Verbalisation process as though it were a Material Action.

Despite these problems, which really all stem from the system being on the form–function borderline, transitivity analysis can be helpful in characterising aspects of style that no other tool has yet captured. The key to dealing with the problems of categorisation is not to treat transitivity types as categories at all, but as points of reference on a continuous plane of meaning, which is probably multi-dimensional, but may be likened to the vowel chart of phonetics which represents the mouth in diagrammatic form and in two dimensions. Thus, the different types of transitivity are 'idealised' types of meaning, with concrete actions being the most typical Material Actions, and more abstract 'actions', such as deciding or condemning, having dual identity as material actions and mental cognition or verbalisation respectively.

The question of why and how we would use this tool to address questions of style is answered when we see how well it can explain certain perceived differences in style that were previously difficult to pin down. Simpson (1993: 110) comments on Halliday's own use of transitivity analysis to explain how William Golding manages to convey the mind-style of the Neanderthal people in *The Inheritors*:

> Where the world depicted from the perspective of 'new' people is very much like our own, the world seen by Lok and his tribe is distinctly unfamiliar. Within the limits of Lok's understanding, people appear to move aimlessly, seldom acting directly on objects in their physical environment. This sense of discontinuity, Halliday argues, is created through particular selections from the system of transitivity.

The analysis by Halliday is one of those which Fish (1981) takes exception to, and Simpson (1993) defends. Simpson's description of the problem which Fish identifies is as follows:

> The criticism rests primarily on what might be termed the interpretative positivism shown by stylisticians who simply invoke linguistic descriptions as a way of confirming the decisions they have already taken about a text's meaning.   (Simpson 1993: 111)

The way in which Simpson defends stylistic analysis – in particular transitivity analysis – from Fish's attack is to take another Golding novel, *Pincher Martin*, which is about a drowning man, and subject it to the same kind of analysis that Halliday used on *The Inheritors*. His conclusions are that the two texts, despite their rather different storylines, characters and settings, 'display uncannily similar patterns of language'. Thus, he notes that both texts use an abundance of body parts as Actors (e.g. 'his hand let the knife go') and frequent uses of event processes with inanimate actors where we would normally attribute the actions to human agency (e.g. 'the lumps of hard water jerked in the gullet'). Simpson's point is that stylistic analysis can distinguish between the linguistic choices in a text and their literary (or other) effect, and that in practice 'avoiding interpretative positivism often requires no more than a modicum of caution' (Simpson 1993: 113). The problem, as Simpson points out, is when 'a direct connection is made between the world-view expounded by a text and its linguistic structure'. In comparing his own analysis of *Pincher Martin* with Halliday's analysis of *The Inheritors*, he comes to the conclusion that although the specific interpretation of each novel is different, there is 'an interpretative "lowest common denominator"' which demonstrates that the texts 'despite markedly divergent story-lines, are at one level of analysis stylistically very similar' (Simpson 1993: 113).

Having considered the model of transitivity and the issues arising from its use in stylistics, let us look at some examples of analysis of a prose passage, and consider the contribution of transitivity choices to the style of the text. Here, then, is a passage from the opening pages of *Ever After* by Graham Swift (1992: 3), which is narrated by a university professor who has recently attempted (unsuccessfully) to commit suicide:

(1)   This is the real reason why I say I am prematurely decrepit. My recipe, you see, was at fault. These things (I know from example) can be well executed or hopelessly botched. I was found. They rushed me away, pumped me, thumped me, jump-started me, wired me to the latest gadgets. And the net result of all this was that I opened again these eyes which I thought to have closed for ever and began breathing and thinking for myself (though that phrase begs questions) once more.

This short passage uses transitivity choices which might not be normal for first person narration, where it is to be expected that the narrator will often be the Actor in any material actions that take place. Instead, in this passage at least, the narrator is the Goal of a range of material actions (*rush away, pump, thump, jump-start* and *wire*) because at that point he is unconscious through his efforts to commit suicide. Before this, the passage has another slightly surprising transitivity choice, where he is admitting that he has failed in his (material action) of killing himself, but chooses to use a Relational Intensive process instead: 'My recipe, you see, was at fault.' Here, the cocktail of drugs that he has taken is blamed for the failure, rather than the producer of that cocktail, the narrator himself. This effect is strengthened in the next sentence where the passive constructions ('can be well-executed or hopelessly botched') do not include any agents, and the generic nature of the statements themselves add to the effect of the narrator not taking responsibility for the failed suicide attempt. Once the narrator is conscious again, he becomes the Actor in material processes, though the choice of 'breathing' is interesting as it would probably normally be seen as almost unintentional (supervention?) because we don't have to breathe consciously, but in this circumstance of course, the laboured breathing of one back from the brink of death is almost a conscious choice, as indicated by 'breathing and thinking *for myself*'.

The following passage comes from *A Spot of Bother*, by Mark Haddon (2007: 13), in which another man in his 50s is coping with a breakdown and in this passage is suffering from extreme phobia of flying:

(2)   He stared doggedly at the seat-back in front of him, trying desperately to pretend that he was sitting in the living room at home. But every few minutes he would hear a sinister chime and see a little red light flashing in the bulkhead to his right, secretly informing the cabin crew that the pilot was wrestling with some fatal malfunction in the cockpit.

The enforced immobility of sitting in an aircraft is underlined here by the transitivity choices where the most active that the protagonist can be is to 'imagine' – a mental cognition process, and to 'see' and 'hear' – mental perception processes. This man, it turns out later, is increasingly at the mercy of his mental breakdown, and is swept along by the tide of his emotions. The fear-of-flying episode, then, is a microcosm of his life experience as told in the novel, and prepares the reader for his frequent experiences of this kind, one of which occurs on the following page when his daughter announces that she is planning to marry Ray:

(3)   George had a brief out-of-body experience. He was looking down from fifteen feet above the patio, watching himself as he kissed Katie and shook Ray's hand. It was like falling off the stepladder. The way time slowed down. The way your body knew instinctively how to protect your head with your arms.

The transitivity choices here, then, are varied but on the whole are not intentional material actions, except the two actions he watches himself perform ('kiss' and 'shake'). The others are mental perception ('look' and 'watch'), relational possessive ('had') and material action supervention ('fall'). The final two sentences remove George from the Actor role entirely and in the final sentence we have an example similar to those analysed by Halliday and by Simpson, in which the body seems to take control of the person rather than *vice versa*.

Whereas in the case of Neanderthal people, this transitivity use reflects a lack of understanding of cause and effect on the part of Lok and his relations, and in the case of *Pincher Martin*, it reflects the lack of control of someone who is in physical distress as he drowns, in the case we have here, the lack of control over his body is one of the symptoms of George's mental breakdown. So, it seems that, as Simpson claims, it is entirely possible to see different interpretative points in the use of this particular transitivity pattern, and also to trace the 'lowest common denominator' that he speaks of in terms that can include all of these examples. Thus, the loss of bodily control, or perceived lack of such control, is at the root of all of these examples.

Transitivity analysis is not to be seen as a rigid tool of stylistics, then, but an indicator of the ways in which certain effects can be achieved. Because verbs occur in every clause in English (with only a few exceptions), there is clearly a great deal of transitivity that can be analysed in even a short text. The student of stylistics will need to consider carefully the judicious use of such analysis and the extent to which it can be carried out in any one project. The reader is referred to section 7.1.3 and other sections of Chapter 7 for discussion on these kinds of question.

3.2.2   Modality

Like transitivity, modality is also one of the systems discussed in Hallidayan approaches to linguistic description. This is another system where there is a set of prototypical forms reflecting the meanings of modality, but where there are also more peripheral forms which can produce similar meanings. Let us consider first, then, the general functions of modality, and its various forms, before considering its role in the production of literary meaning.

The general system of modality reflects what Halliday (1994) calls the 'inter-personal' metafunction of language, which is one of three metafunctions he sees as co-existing in linguistic usage. Thus, if transitivity reflects the ideational meta-function, in which language represents the world in certain ways, then modality is intended to reflect the interpersonal function, in which language mediates between people. However, as we will see, modality may be seen as ideational in literary and other texts too. Its main contribution to textual meaning is to reflect the producer's opinion about what s/he is saying or writing. Thus, the modal auxiliary verb *might*, for example, indicates that the speaker is not completely sure that the process following is going to happen. Take the sentence 'Joanne might be home by nightfall', for example. The question of whether Joanne will indeed be home before dark is left uncertain as a result of the use of 'might', and it is the speaker's uncertainty which is communicated.

The auxiliary modal verbs are the prototypical carriers of modal meaning. The set of modal verbs includes at least *will, would, may, might, shall, should, can, could* and *ought* (*to*) and for some speakers, other verbs, which have become lexical for some dialects of English, remain modal too. These include *need* and *dare*, which in their modal form tend to allow the same kind of reduction of form in casual usage that is common for more central modal verbs (*needn't, daren't*). In addition to the modal auxiliaries, there are modal adverbs and adjectives which carry very similar meanings, and can be used to paraphrase clauses with modal verbs:

(4)   She *may* come = It's *possible* she'll come = She'll *possibly* come

(5)   She *ought* to come = It's *advisable/proper/required* for her to come

Notice that these two sets of examples demonstrate two of the main types of meaning that are normally recognised in relation to modality. Thus, the question of whether something is likely/certain or unlikely is covered by the broad concept of **epistemic** modality. It reflects the speaker's level of confidence in the truth of their utterances. Related to epistemic modality, and often thought to be a sub-category of it, is **perception** modality which is usually delivered by verbs of perceiving, such as 'see' and 'hear', though with the meaning of 'understand to be true' as in:

(6)   I see your daughter is off to high school this year.

(7)   I hear that Susan has been short-listed for the job.

The other way that perception modality is delivered is through adjectives and adverbs which relate literally to perception (*apparently, clearly*) but when used modally are used to draw conclusions about the certainty or otherwise of the proposition.

   So, on the one hand we have epistemic modality (including perception modality), which gives information about the speaker's confidence in his/her utterances. On the other hand, however, we have the two related types of **deontic** and **boulomaic** modality, which indicate the necessity and desirability respectively of the proposition in the utterance. The following are examples of these modality types (example 8 indicates deontic modality and example 9 boulomaic):

(8)   You should do more exercise.

(9)   I wish you would help me with the housework.

Note that most of the modal auxiliary verbs have the capacity to deliver more than one of these types of modal meaning, as can be seen in the following groups of examples:

(10)   It *should* come clean with a bit of scrubbing (epistemic)

(11)   You *should* scrub it to get it clean (deontic)

(12)   You *might* have told me that my slip was showing – I'm very embarrassed! (deontic)

(13)   You *might* have told me that my slip was showing – I can't remember! (epistemic)

(14)   You *might* tell me when my slip is showing – Or I'll be embarrassed! (boulomaic)

It is important to note that there is no comprehensive list available of all the modal forms in English, or any other language. This is partly because the work has not been done, but this in turn may be partly because it is possible that such a task can never be complete. Not only adjectives (*definite, certain, unsure*) and adverbs (*possibly, certainly, hopefully*) can be modal, but main verbs also carry modal meaning in some contexts:

(15)   I thought he got there before us (weak epistemic)

(16)   I want you to come home early tonight (boulomaic or deontic)

(17)   I understand you are the owner of the house? (epistemic)

Note that these verbs (*think, want, understand*) are not always unambiguously modal in their meaning. For example, with third person subjects, or with different polysemous senses, they may not reflect the speaker's view of how things are:

(18)   She thought he got there before us.

(19)   He wanted her to get home early tonight.

(20)   I understand the theory of relativity.

Examples 18 and 19 report the thoughts and desires of a third party and are therefore not reflecting the speaker's viewpoint. Example 20 uses a non-modal sense of 'understand' to make a categorical assertion.

In addition to these modal uses of main verbs and the adverbs and adjectives already mentioned, it is possible for modality to be conveyed by more peripheral forms still. For example, the epistemic uncertainty of 'she might get better' can also be conveyed by a shrug of the shoulders or the rising intonation of a question imposed over the less modal form of 'She'll get better?'. Note the use in the last sentence of 'less modal', rather than 'unmodalised' because although this sentence is as certain as English can be about its content, it is nevertheless marginally modal because of the presence of the modal auxiliary *will* (in this case reduced to ''ll'. This is language-specific because some languages do not create future reference in their verbs by use of a modal auxiliary, using instead a future tense form, morphologically created. In English, however, the verb element of clauses does not allow future reference through tense forms, but makes a future form by using the *will* auxiliary to predict the future as accurately as possible. It is quite sensible in some ways for the language to reflect what we know to be true – that the future is not certain – by using a modal auxiliary.

There are a range of possible effects of the different kinds of modality when used in texts, both literary and non-literary. Before we take a look at some examples, there is one more important point to be made in relation to modality, and that is to consider what happens when it is not there. Unmodalised utterances are normally labelled 'categorical' and they assert their propositions with none of the undermining of certainty which would be the case in a modalised utterance. The first of the following examples, which uses weak epistemic modality, then, is very much less certain than the categorical version which follows it:

(21)   The bus might have already left. (weak epistemic)

(22)   The bus has already left. (categorical)

(23)   The bus has definitely already left. (strong epistemic)

What is perhaps surprising, but less so on reflection, is that the third version here, which uses strong epistemic modality, is also less convincing than the categorical version. There is something about modality, even strong epistemic modality, which undermines the certainty of the proposition, even while it asserts it emphatically. It is precisely this emphatic nature of the strong modality which seems to undermine it, probably by drawing attention to the very question of its certainty. The categorical utterance, by contrast, is more confident in its assertions and appears to not even raise the question of reliability.

Let us see how this simple division of clauses into categorical and two main types of modality (epistemic and deontic/boulomaic) may affect a poem's potential for meaning. The following opening of a sonnet by Douglas Dunn recalls the experience of bringing food up to his terminally ill wife:

(24)   To climb these stairs again, bearing a tray,
          Might be to find you pillowed with your books,
          Your inventories listing gowns and frocks
          As if preparing for a holiday.
          Or, turning from the landing, I might find
          My presence watched through your kaleidoscope,
          A symmetry of husbands, each redesigned
          In lovely forms of foresight, prayer and hope.
                    ('The Kaleidoscope', Dunn 1985: 20)

The first eight lines of the poem, rather surprisingly, use epistemic modality to describe what the husband 'might' find when he climbs the stairs, though it is clear that the addressee of the poem is no longer there, and this is confirmed later ('at where you died'). The more obvious modal forms to use in a situation where the bereaved person is wishing his partner was still there would have been the boulomaic forms such as 'wish' or 'want'. Instead, this poem presents the terrible truth of bereavement, which is that the bereaved hope and almost expect to see their loved ones again, which is reflected in the epistemic modals here. This is incongruous for the reality which is boulomaic, since they are desiring or wishing for the return of the person who has died. The use of epistemic modality here is thus foregrounded.

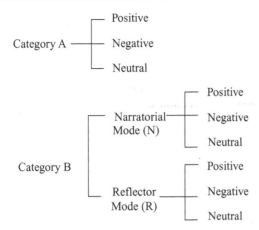

Figure 3.1 *Simpson's modal grammar*

The question of how modality affects literary and other textual meaning has been addressed at some length by Simpson (1993), particularly in relation to narrative fiction. Simpson bases what he terms a 'modal grammar' on the types of modality introduced above, and demonstrates that certain genres of fiction tend to use modality in recognisably different ways, reflecting the viewing position or 'point of view' (POV) of the narrative. His modal grammar of POV is a development from Fowler's (1986) earlier four-way classification of narrative types:

- Internal type A: first person narration, from POV of participating character, foregrounded modality and *verba sentiendi* (words denoting thoughts, feelings and perceptions)
- Internal type B: third person narration; omniscient narrator, privileged access to participants' thoughts and feelings, though no authorial presence, *verba sentiendi*
- External type C: no account of participants' thoughts and feelings, third person narration, no modality or *verba sentiendi*
- External type D: explicit modality, words of estrangement, some first person use, but no privileged access to participants' thoughts and feelings

Simpson introduces the model of modality sketched above into this framework, in order to reflect the more complicated range of narrative types that he observes. Thus, the division of narrative types into first person narration (Category A) and third person narration (Category B) is further sub-divided as shown in figure 3.1.

Simpson's Category B, then, is divided into those narratives which reflect the viewpoint of one (or more) of the characters (Reflector Mode) or no particular viewpoint from within the story (Narratorial Mode). Then each of these categories is further sub-divided into positive, negative and neutral 'shading' which are characterised as follows:

- Positive shading: deontic and boulomaic modality foregrounded; generic sentences and *verba sentiendi* present
- Negative shading: epistemic and perception modality foregrounded; supplemented with 'words of estrangement'
- Neutral shading: dominated by unmodalised categorical assertions; few *verba sentiendi* or evaluative adjectives and adverbs

The resulting classification of narrative types into nine categories allows the analyst to demonstrate similarities and differences of narrative style across a range of genres and text-types. In order to give a flavour of these categories, we will consider a number of passages from narrative fiction here, though there will not be room for nine examples, and as it happens, many narratives are made up of passages from different categories. The following passage comes from McCall Smith (2007: 2–3):

(25)   If people were only more careful, or behaved themselves as they should, then they would not find themselves faced with problems of this sort. But of course people never behaved themselves as they should. 'We are all human beings,' Mma Ramotswe had once observed to Mma Makutsi, 'and human beings can't really help themselves. Have you noticed that, Mma? We really can't help ourselves from doing things that land us in all sorts of trouble.'

Mma Makutsi pondered this for a few moments. In general, she thought Mma Ramotswe was right about matters of this sort, but she felt that this particular proposition needed a little bit more thought. She knew that there were some people who were unable to make of their lives what they wanted them to be, but then there were many others who were quite capable of keeping themselves under control.

The transitivity choices in this passage reflect the different characters of the two protagonists in this detective novel. This is unlike the so-called 'hard-boiled' detective novels of tradition, which Simpson claims use mostly Category A (i.e. first person) narrative style, with neutral shading, so that there is no modality, few *verba sentiendi* and few evaluative adjectives or adverbs. This novel is one of a series about the 'No. 1 Ladies' Detective Agency', set in Botswana, so it is different from the norm of this genre in being about female detectives in an African setting who are not trying to emulate the habits of the male detectives in all details. These novels are written in third person (Category B), but through a combination of modality and free indirect style (see section 3.2.4) give the reader a strong sense of the opinions and views of the two main characters, Mma Ramotswe and Mma Makutsi.

As seen in the passage above, the narrative tends to be in Reflector Mode, though alternating between the viewpoints of the characters. The first section, then, reflects the thoughts of Mma Ramotswe, the senior of the two detectives, and we see the evidence of her opinions in the deontic modality ('behaved themselves as they should') and the use of generic sentences ('human beings can't really help themselves'). This, then, gives a positive shading, where the action is 'located within [the] viewing position of [a] character, offering their opinions and judgements' (Simpson 1993: 75). In the second part of the passage, Mma Makutsi thinks about her employer's views, and though it remains in Reflector Mode, there is a more negative shading with the use of epistemic modality ('she thought Mma Ramotswe was right'; 'she knew that') so that Mma Makutsi's lower self-confidence is reflected in this slightly more 'estranged' style, though the presence of one of the *verba sentiendi* ('she felt that') is more indicative of positive shading.

As the reader will see from this analysis, even in a short extract from a literary work there is no single consistent style that can be categorised according to Simpson's modal grammar of point of view. This demonstrates that just as with the transitivity analysis, what we have are not categories so much as idealised reference points which can be used to characterise the fluctuating style of any narrative. The following is an extract from a rather different kind of novel:

(26)   I was alone again. There was a light this time. A gas jet high up on the wall. It gave a sick, shifting light that made shadows, then killed them. I saw some old blankets in a corner and sat on them. The light made more shapes, snuffed them. I knew where I was. *We'll go home be the water.* I knew exactly where I was. I lay on the floor and covered myself with the blankets. I closed my eyes (...) I woke. There was no water. It was dark. I was hungry. It was years since I'd eaten. A slamming door had woken me – I knew, although I couldn't hear anything now. And I could see nothing. I heard feet, three or four pairs of boots on the damp flags of the passage outside. I heard keys jangling, scraping. It was very dark. I sat up. The door opened and dirty light fell into the room. Followed by a man, who hit the ground hard. The door was closed, the key turned. It was dark again, darker than before. I heard the man breathing through a swollen mouth. I stayed still. The breath rattled. The man groaned.   (Doyle 1999: 302)

This is from *A Star Called Henry*, which relates the experiences of a young Irish man caught up in the Easter uprising in 1916 through his voice and in first person (Category A). In this passage, having been captured and badly beaten by the British soldiers, he shows signs of detachment from his surroundings, with a mixture of categorical assertions ('There was a light this time'), demonstrating neutral shading, and of estrangement through the negative shading of epistemic modality ('I knew') and perception modality ('I heard', 'I saw'). Note that these effects of estrangement and detachment are reinforced by the transitivity choices (see section 3.2.1), which include only the most basic of intentional material actions on the part of the narrator ('I lay on the floor'; 'I sat up') and some which are barely actions ('I stayed still'). Mostly, there are descriptions using intensive relations ('It was dark again') and events ('A slamming door had woken me') as well as one or two of the kind of involuntary movements of body parts – and bodies – that we saw in Halliday's and Simpson's analysis of Golding's novels ('a man who hit the ground hard'; 'the breath rattled'). Though other parts of this novel demonstrate different aspects of Simpson's modality types, so that for example, there are times when the narrator expresses his wishes (deontic modality, positive shading), the life of the young Henry Smart is so traumatic that he clearly learns the skills of staying detached when his body and mind are under attack, and these are experiences that allow him to survive the brutal treatment he gets later.

Modality, as mentioned at the beginning of this section, is often seen by Hallidayan scholars as forming part of the interpersonal metafunction of language, rather than, say, the ideational metafunction. Its use in fiction, however, is not quite as simple as its use in face-to-face interaction. For example, deontic 'should' would be interpersonal if you said to a friend 'You should phone John', because it informs the hearer of the opinion of the speaker. However, in a novel, the use of deontic 'should', though remaining the opinion of the speaker, is no longer directed at the recipient, at least not if that recipient is seen as the reader.

3.2.3   Cohesion

The third functional category we will consider here, as being a useful tool of analysis for style, is cohesion. Halliday was again instrumental in bringing the concept of cohesion to the attention of linguistics, and Halliday and Hasan (1976) describes a model of cohesion that can be used to assess certain distinguishing features of literary and other texts.

The basis of cohesion is the idea that texts are not random sequences of sentences and that there must therefore be some structuring devices that link adjacent sentences in a text, which help the reader to make sense of their relation to each other. Whilst not as strictly rule-governed as the internal structure of sentences, the cohesion between them is nevertheless traceable to certain structural and semantic features which we will investigate in this section as they affect style.

The basic concept of cohesion is the idea of a textual 'tie' between units in different sentences which helps the reader to perceive the referential identity or topical consistency of different parts of a text. The simplest, and most prototypical, tie is that between a pronoun and its antecedent, as in:

(27)   There was *a man* waiting in the shadows by the bus stop. *He* looked around to see if *he* was being watched.

Note that the mysterious man is introduced by an indefinite article ('a man') and in the following sentence the same person is referenced as 'he' twice. This is the normal order of things: a person, animal or thing is introduced in one sentence and is referred to by a pronoun in ensuing sentences until there is a danger of ambiguity, when some further unique referring phrase will be used. This kind of reference is known as 'anaphoric reference', which means that the pronoun refers backwards to a fuller phrase in an earlier sentence. It is possible, though rarer, for the pronoun to precede the phrase explaining its referent, as in 'He was good-looking. The man lit a cigarette and smiled.' The main mechanisms of cohesion are:[1]

- Repetition – of similar or identical words, phrases or clauses.
- Reference – different ways of identifying the same referent.
- Substitution – the use of pro-forms (pronouns and other forms) to replace full phrases.
- Ellipsis – the missing out of highly predictable words and phrases.
- Conjunction – the conjoining of sentences by conjunctions (*and*, *but*, *or*).
- Lexical cohesion – the inclusion of words with semantic relations (e.g. synonymy) between them.

Whilst it is true to say that all texts are cohesive, the variability in the extent of cohesion of a text is quite significant in literary terms. Thus, although some cohesion is necessary for a reader to make sense of the text, some genres and text-types are more likely than others to minimise – or maximise – the concentration of cohesive ties. Children's literature, for example, is highly likely to include a large intensity of cohesive ties, as clues to make sure that the child is following the narrative. The following example is the text of a picture book intended for young children:

(28)   The hour was late. Mr. Bear was tired. Mrs. Bear was tired and Baby Bear was tired, so they all went to bed. Mrs. Bear fell asleep. Mr. Bear didn't. Mrs. Bear began to snore. 'SNORE,' went Mrs. Bear, 'SNORE, SNORE, SNORE.' 'Oh NO!' said Mr. Bear, 'I can't stand THIS.' So he got up and went to sleep in Baby Bear's room. Baby Bear was not asleep either. He was lying in bed pretending to be an aeroplane. 'NYAAOW!' went Baby Bear, 'NYAAOW! NYAAOW!' 'Oh NO!' said Mr. Bear, 'I can't stand THIS.' So he got up and went to sleep in the living-room.   (Murphy 1980)

Here, there is a considerable amount of exact repetition (e.g. 'Oh NO!' said Mr. Bear, 'I can't stand THIS.') as well as some partial repetition of frames with different fillers (e.g. 'So he got up and went to sleep in Baby Bear's room' / 'the living-room'). This short passage also has related lexical items forming a semantic field, and thus giving a semantic cohesion to the passage ('late' – 'tired' – 'bed' – 'asleep' – 'snore'). There is a small amount of substitution of pronouns for names ('he' for 'Mr. Bear'), but less than one might expect in literature for older age groups, perhaps. There is also one example of ellipsis, where 'Mr. Bear didn't' implies 'Mr. Bear didn't fall asleep'. It is one of the features that marks this story out as being suitable for children, rather than babies, because they need to be able to follow the cohesive ties, including the ones where something is actually missed out.

Whilst there are clearly practical and pedagogical reasons for the super-cohesive style of this particular narrative, similar features may be used by other writers wishing to evoke the innocence of children's stories in their own. One writer who does this is McCall Smith, whose series of books about the No. 1 Ladies' Detective Agency are known for their 'simple' style, reflecting a down-to-earth morality from Botswana which the protagonist, Mma Ramotswe, tries to follow. One of the features of this style is the apparent 'overuse' of full names, rather than shorter versions of the names or pronouns, some repetition with variation as we saw in the children's story and a reasonably dense lexical cohesion:

(29)   Mma Ramotswe and Mr J. L. B. Matekoni went home for lunch at Zebra Drive, something they enjoyed doing when work at the garage permitted. Mma Ramotswe liked to lie down for twenty minutes or so after the midday meal. On occasion she would drop off to sleep for a short while, but usually she just read the newspaper or a magazine. Mr J. L. B. Matekoni would not lie down, but liked to walk out in the garden under the shade netting, looking at his vegetables.   (McCall Smith 2007: 30)

The obvious stylistic features to notice in the above extract are:

*   Use of full names: 'Mma Ramotswe' and 'Mr J. L. B. Matekoni' repeatedly used rather than shorter variants.
*   Repetition: 'Mma Ramotswe liked to lie down'; 'Mr Matekoni would not lie down'
*   Semantic cohesion: 'Lunch' – 'midday meal' – 'vegetables'; 'lie down' – 'sleep'

At the other extreme from these highly cohesive texts are those poems which are often seen as 'difficult' to read, partly because they are lacking those cohesive ties that would make the meaning plain and the links between sentences clear. Here is the opening of a poem by McGuckian, to demonstrate (N.B. we began to discuss this poem in Chapter 2; see example 34 in that chapter):

(30)   Once you have seen a crocus in the act
         of giving way to the night, your life
         no longer lives you, from now on

         your later is too late. Rain time
         and sun time, that red and gold sickness
         is like two hands covering your face –
         it hardly matters if a whole summer
         is ruined by a crumpled piece of paper
         or the dry snap of a suitcase closing.
                         (McGuckian 1997)

The subject-matter of this poem is very difficult to work out from the opening lines, though it does become clearer later on. The semantic (lexical) cohesion is almost entirely lacking, if you look at the lexical items in this stanza:

- Crocus, night, life, live, rain, sun, red, gold, sickness, hands, face, summer, ruin, crumpled, paper, dry, snap, suitcase, closing

Each time a semantic link appears (life – live; rain – sun; red – gold) it is followed by another semantic field with no clear link to the ones already established. In addition, though there is a consistent second person pronoun ('you') used throughout, it is not clear who it refers to, nor whether it is intended to be interpreted as second person (i.e. the reader or a particular addressee) or as the equivalent of 'one' (generic third person), which may in turn be interpreted as 'I'.[2] As a text, then, it barely manages the basic cohesion that would make it comprehensible, as there is no clear narrative, the various processes being described as hypothetical, rather than occurring in some kind of time-frame. This will lead the practised reader of contemporary (and particularly of McGuckian's) poetry to search for other links, such as the interpretation of 'rain time' and 'sun time' as seasons, which then link to summer, and possibly also to the red and gold sickness. Crocuses can then be seen as connected to spring, though the connection of all of this with the 'dry snap of a suitcase closing' remains to be inferred retrospectively from other parts of the poem where it becomes clearer that it is a partner that is leaving the narrator.

Cohesion, then, can have an effect on the meaning of a text by making the style either very plain and childlike or difficult to work out, with the effect that the reader has to work extra hard to interpret the text.

3.2.4   Discourse presentation

This chapter has been considering textual analysis beyond the microstructural concerns of the levels model of language, and this has so far led us to consider those systems identified by Halliday and his followers as simultaneously formal and functional. On a similar level of analysis to these Hallidayan systems, there are some other 'local textual functions' (Mahlberg 2007) that are just as useful for stylistic analysis, and which also seem to combine form and function in similar ways. In this section, we will consider one aspect of narratives which has received a great deal of attention from stylisticians in its own right: the presentation by a narrator of others' words (written or spoken) or of their thoughts. This system has frequently been called 'speech and thought presentation' but since writing started to be included, it has become simpler to label it 'discourse presentation' to cover both written and spoken language and also the thoughts that are sometimes presented by narrators as though they were witnessed directly.

The model we will use here is from Leech and Short (2007), which reproduces the model in the first edition of their book (Leech and Short 1981), though there have been changes to the model in other places (e.g. Semino and Short 2004) and this process is continuing in more recent work. The original model, then, includes the following categories of speech presentation:

- Narrative report of speech act (NRSA):   e.g. *He agreed.*
- Indirect speech (IS):   e.g. *He said that he agreed.*
- Free indirect speech (FIS):   e.g. *He was in agreement.*
- Direct speech (DS):   e.g. *He said 'I agree.'*
- Free direct speech (FDS):   e.g. *I agree.*

The formal differences between indirect and direct speech presentation include the following markers, assuming that indirect speech is converted from direct speech:

- The inverted commas are removed
- The speech is marked by a subordinator (e.g. *that*)
- Any first and second person pronouns change to third person
- Any present tense verbs change to past (including auxiliaries)
- Any proximal deixis (see section 6.3) changes to distal (e.g. *this → that*)

(adapted from Leech and Short 2007: 256)

If we look at the following related sentences, all of these changes have taken place:

(31)   I said, 'You have given me this horror of spiders.'

(32)   He said that she had given him that horror of spiders.

The other categories of speech presentation in Leech and Short's model have a range of formal features which distinguish them from the two traditional categories of direct speech and indirect speech presentation. Thus, NRSA does not include any reference to the actual speech itself, though it gives an indication of the speech act that was used. (e.g. 'He agreed'). Note that in later models (e.g. Semino and Short 2004), an even more minimal category has been added which does not even relate which kind of speech act has occurred, and simply states that speech has taken place (e.g. 'He spoke'). This category is labelled 'narrative report of voice' (NV). In many narrative contexts, the use of such minimal reports of speech are useful to progress the narrative, though most writers use them sparingly. Here is an example of NRSA used to avoid reporting a conversation where the detail would not be of great interest to the reader:

(33)   I rushed upstairs, *explained the matter shortly to my wife*, and in five minutes was inside a hansom, driving with my new acquaintance to Baker Street.   (Conan Doyle 2003 [1891]: 328)

Here, the companion of Sherlock Holmes, Doctor Watson, narrates his actions in excusing himself from home and taking the latest 'case' to the great detective.

However 'shortly' he explained where he was going to his wife, the reader would have been frustrated in having to read his words verbatim as it would delay the narrative proper.

The categories of speech presentation vary in their functional aspects in two related ways. At one end of the cline are those categories (NV and NRSA) that indicate the most intrusion by the narrator and, consequently, the most distance from the actual speech referred to. At the other end of the cline, free direct speech (FDS) is speech that is unmediated by a narrator. The examples given above are not unambiguous in their allocation to categories because for some of the categories, context is required in order to be clear which type of speech presentation is involved.

In particular, it is often difficult to identify text extracts as unambiguously FIS, particularly out of context. Thus, the following rhetorical question, out of context, may seem to the reader like the opinion of the narrator (or the text's producer):

(34)   Hadn't people always worn earrings, and got away with it?

There is, in fact, a clue here that this is free indirect speech and this is the use of the past tense form of the auxiliary verb, *have*, which if it were original direct speech or writing, would be in the present ('Haven't people' etc.). The context, as often with FIS, helps the reader to conclude that the 'voice' of this sentence is the character Isabel, as we can see in the following:

(35)   People who had metal piercing in their heads were asking for trouble, Grace
           had once said. Isabel had asked why this should be so. Hadn't people always
           worn earrings, and got away with it? Grace had replied that metal piercings
           attracted lightning, and that she had read of a heavily pierced man who had
           been struck dead in an electric storm while those around him, unpierced, had
           survived.

This short passage from *The Sunday Philosophy Club* (McCall Smith 2005: 73) includes a number of examples of speech presentation as we can see:

*   IS: People who had metal piercing in their heads were asking for
    trouble, Grace had once said.
*   NRSA: Isabel had asked why this should be so.
*   FIS: Hadn't people always worn earrings, and got away with it?
*   IS: Grace had replied that metal piercings attracted lightning, and that
    she had read of a heavily pierced man who had been struck dead in
    an electric storm while those around him, unpierced, had survived.

Note that the FIS here is within a longer passage of reported speech and this sets up the expectation that the FIS sentence is an elaboration of the speech act referred to in the previous sentence ('Isabel asked why this should be so'). The labelling of NRSA assumes that the exact words used are not reflected in 'why this should be so', so it is possible that this is actually IS, if these *were* the words used. This whole passage in turn is part of an internal thought sequence as the character Isabel remembers the conversation being reported. The section begins as follows:

(36)   Isabel felt trapped, and thought: *I'm an unconvincing hypocrite*. There was a silence now at the table of students, and she was aware of the fact that they were listening to the conversation. She stared at them, noticing that one of the boys had a small pin in his ear.

This demonstrates the importance in stylistic analysis of using more than one tool to describe the potential effect of textual features. Here, the use of a verb of perception, 'felt' (see section 3.2.2), with the reported thought make this a Category B(R) narrative with positive shading, in Simpson's modal grammar of point of view. We are seeing the narrative from Isabel's viewpoint, and being presented with her opinions and thoughts. At this point, the section analysed above occurs, as a kind of daydream as Isabel remembers the conversation with Grace which is followed by 'The students exchanged glances, and Isabel turned away.' The narrative then returns to the 'present'.

Though often labelled 'categories', speech presentation types are similar to the so-called categories of Simpson's modal grammar or Halliday's transitivity system in that they are often not clear-cut at all but rather represent points of reference on a continuous, and often multi-dimensional, plane of meaning or function. There is, for instance, no precise formal way of identifying FIS or NRSA, and many analytical decisions rely on context. However, a category-based model of speech and thought presentation remains useful because it allows us to identify prototypical points on a cline. Furthermore, the Leech and Short model of discourse presentation has been developed most recently through large-scale corpus studies, which have necessitated clear decisions about the labelling of items in the corpus. In this respect, a category-based model is essential. We will return to this topic later in this section, but for now we will consider the equivalent types of thought presentation. There exists a similar range of ways of presenting others' thoughts in narratives:

•	Narrative report of thought act (NRTA):	e.g. *He decided.*
•	Indirect thought (IT):	e.g. *He thought that he should do it.*
•	Free indirect thought (FIT):	e.g. *He should do it.*
•	Direct thought (DT):	e.g. *He thought 'I should do it.'*
•	Free direct thought (FDT):	e.g. *I should do it.*

Like the speech presentation system, this range indicates the closest to the 'actual' thoughts at the bottom of the list, and the most narrator intervention at the top. However, the one important difference between the two lists is that speech can be heard by others, and thoughts cannot. The fictional narrator, even if s/he is a non-participating omniscient narrator, can in theory still tell the reader what was said verbatim, so that the reader has some confidence in the faithfulness of the

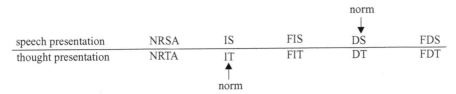

Figure 3.2 *Norms for speech and thought presentation (from Leech and Short 2007: 276)*

words. The reporting of thoughts is always hypothetical, whoever is narrating, and we therefore have a different semantic 'norm' in the two systems, as Leech and Short point out, using figure 3.2 to help them.

The way Leech and Short explain the relevance of the different norms is as follows:

> Thoughts, in general, are not verbally formulated, and so cannot be reported verbatim. Given that the norms for speech and thought presentation are at different points on the continuum, the different values of FIS and FIT can be naturally explained. FIS is a movement leftwards from the norm in figure [3.2] and is therefore interpreted as a movement towards authorial intervention, whereas FIT is seen as a move to the right and hence away from the author's most directly interpretative control and into the active mind of the character. Because the direct perception of someone else's thought is not possible, DT is perceived as more artificial than more indirect forms.

It has, of course, been a standard device of novelists to give the reader insights into the minds of the characters they create. The reporting of thoughts is also tied up with the features that Simpson's modal grammar discusses, so that one of the differences in style between the 'hard-boiled' detective fiction and the romantic novel is that the thoughts of the detective are less readily exposed to the reader, whereas the feelings and thoughts of the romantic heroine are typically on show for all to see. We saw earlier that McCall Smith's lady detective in Botswana does not conform to this stereotype, and neither does his Scottish philosopher-detective, Isabel Dalhousie, whose thoughts regularly bring his style into Simpson's Category B(R) with positive shading as we saw earlier. Here is another passage, where Isabel is thinking about her niece, Cat, and the boyfriend she has spurned:

(37)   What more could Cat want? she thought. Really! What else could a girl possibly require than a Scotsman who looked Mediterranean and could sing? The answer came to her unbidden, like an awkward truth that nudges one at the wrong moment. Jamie was too nice. He had given Cat his whole attention – had fawned on her perhaps – and she had grown tired of that. We do not like those who are completely available, who make themselves over to us entirely. They crowd us out. They make us feel uneasy.

Here, the thoughts are presented as follows:

- DT: What more could Cat want? she thought.
- FDT: Really! What else could a girl possibly require than a Scotsman who looked Mediterranean and could sing?
- NRTA: The answer came to her unbidden, like an awkward truth that nudges one at the wrong moment.
- FIT: Jamie was too nice. He had given Cat his whole attention – had fawned on her perhaps – and she had grown tired of that. We do not like those who are completely available, who make themselves over to us entirely. They crowd us out. They make us feel uneasy.

The whole passage, then, is an internal monologue with only the first sentence needing to indicate that this is thought, leaving the reader in no doubt that the thinking continues in the other sentences. The FDT section is labelled as such because of the exclamation ('Really!') which seems to indicate the 'verbatim' thought, even though, as Leech and Short point out, thoughts are not usually couched in language. The NRTA sentence requires us to consider the transitivity choice that has been made here, as the Actor is inanimate ('the answer') and the result is a material event, with Isabel at the mercy of the inanimate – in this case abstract – world.

The final section, labelled FIT, is Isabel's viewpoint, since it follows the other thought processes with no intervening narrative. The generic sentences ('We do not like' etc.) confirm the Category B status of this passage, and the use of past tense verbs ('was' and 'had') makes this indirect, as they would be present tense if the thoughts were being presented 'verbatim'. McCall Smith presents his characters' viewpoints using all the available speech and thought presentation techniques. As we can see here, the apparently unmediated presentation of thought, by the use of FIT, is one way he may cause readers to feel that they are accessing the characters' thoughts directly.

3.2.5   Other functional categories

In this section, we will introduce two other ways in which functional concepts, realised by a range of forms, may influence the meaning likely to be derived from a text. What these categories share with transitivity, modality and discourse presentation is that they are predominantly conceptual and not formal, though each has a prototypical realisation, like the categories introduced in previous sections.

The first of these local textual functions is the creation of opposites in context. This phenomenon has only recently been fully explored (see Davies 2008 and Jeffries 2010a), though it has been mentioned incidentally in earlier work (Jeffries 1998) and was used as a tool of analysis in Jeffries (2007b):

> This textual creation of what are normally seen as context-free lexical seman-
> tic meanings is just one of the ways in which we can see the symbiotic rela-
> tionship between code and usage or between *langue* and *parole*.
>
> (Jeffries 2007b: 102)

The textually-created opposites, then, draw on what the reader already knows about relationships of opposition, including the fact that there are different types of oppositional relationship. These include as a minimum[3] the mutually exclusive complementaries (*alive/dead*), the mutually dependent converses (*buy/sell*), the gradable antonyms (*dark/light*) and the directional or reversive opposites (*pack/unpack*). The textually created opposites are usually triggered by one of a number of structural features, most prototypically the X-not-Y structure, using negation as a way of setting two concepts in opposition to each other. Other triggers include those which depend on parallel structures to contrast items (e.g. *He wanted X. She wanted Y*) and those that are explicit about the fact that they are being contrasted (*X in contrast to Y*). A very much more comprehensive list of potential triggers of opposition can be found in Davies (2008), though it should be pointed out that, as with modality, it may be impossible to compile a complete list, as this is a fuzzy category with changing boundaries.

Let us consider some of the possibilities for literary effect in the creation of opposites by looking at a poem by Philip Larkin which is built upon created opposition:

(38)   *The Importance of Elsewhere*

> Lonely in Ireland, since it was not home,
> Strangeness made sense. The salt rebuff of speech,
> Insisting so on difference, made me welcome:
> Once that was recognised, we were in touch.
>
> Their draughty streets, end-on to hills, the faint
> Archaic smell of dockland, like a stable,
> The herring-hawker's cry, dwindling, went
> To prove me separate, not unworkable.
>
> Living in England has no such excuse:
> These are my customs and establishments
> It would be much more serious to refuse.
> Here no elsewhere underwrites my existence.

The poem opens with a negated opposite, where 'Ireland' is opposed to 'home', and this is followed by the juxtaposition of 'rebuff' with 'welcome', which are semantically opposed, though not conventional opposites. Here, though, it is the very rebuff which *creates* the welcome, since the whole poem's argument is predicated upon the notion that we only feel that we belong somewhere if other places are strange to us. So, the narrator's feeling of strangeness is important to his awareness of home. In expanding upon this idea, Larkin describes the range of scenes that seemed strange to him in Ireland, adding that they 'went to prove me separate, not unworkable'. Here, then, there is another negated opposition created between 'separate' and 'unworkable', where the feeling of being a foreigner is seen as evidence of difference, but not a chasm that cannot be bridged. Negated opposites are usually complementary, so that there is no conceptual intermediate position between 'separate' and 'unworkable': you have to be one or the other in Larkin's world. Nevertheless, Larkin has played with the conventional idea that strangeness creates unbridgeable distance between people. Here, instead, we see that you can be separate from people without being alien to them. This, in effect, introduces a middle point between unworkable and close, which is separateness, and this intermediate concept in human relations is the one that allows us to feel a sense of belonging at home. In the final line, Larkin's 'deictic centre' (see section 6.3) has returned to England, where he cannot refuse to join in with the customs, as it is his own culture. He ends the poem by reiterating his main theme, using here and elsewhere, rather than the conventional here/there, to emphasise his rootedness in England. The essential link between home and elsewhere is maintained, however, by his existence being dependent on ('underwrites') the other place(s).

The creation of local textual opposites is a phenomenon that, once noticed, is very common in literary, but also in other, texts. Volvo car adverts, for example, have recently been using the line 'less emissions,[4] not less style', which implies that there are some circumstances in which style and low emissions are incompatible, in other words, are complementary opposites, where you can only have one or the other. This 'trick' of advertising is ubiquitous; the argument that you can have value and quality for example is one that many adverts try to make.

The prototypical created opposition is the negated opposition, where a positive and a negative are placed next to each other to create contrast. This means that created opposites are often linked to the final textual function to be discussed in this chapter: negation. Like the other systems introduced here, negation has a prototypical form, which is the negator, *not*, modifying the verb (e.g. *hasn't*, *didn't*), although the premodification of nouns by *no* is also reasonably prototypical (e.g. *no money*, *no food*). However, like the other systems in this chapter, negation also takes a number of other forms, including morphological ones (e.g. *de-humidify*, *unreasonable*), semantic ones (e.g. *lack*, *fail*) and like modality (the shrug) negation can be delivered paralinguistically by shaking the head or waving the hands in certain (probably culturally-specific) ways.

The discoursal significance of negation, and the reason that it is closely tied in to opposition, is that it simultaneously evokes the negated scene, at the same time as denying its existence. So, the opening comment in Larkin's poem above, 'since it was not home', both informs the reader that Ireland is not the narrator's home and also conjures up another place that is indeed his home. Similarly, the following sentence from Kate Atkinson's novel, *Case Histories* (Atkinson

2004: 35), conjures up the very scenes that Rosemary is rejecting in relation to her academic husband:

(39)   Rosemary couldn't imagine Victor anywhere as spirited as a racecourse, nor
              could she see him in the smoky commonality of a betting shop.

This sentence negates two possible scenarios in which Rosemary's own father was habitually to be found, and her comparison of her earthy father with her distant intellectual husband is made more effective by the technique of negation, so that both Rosemary and the reader are invited to envisage the very scenes she is supposed not to be able to imagine, and reject them as unreal. This is taken literally in some advertising where the very thing that is negated is shown happening, or shown not happening. Thus, an advertisement for Drench spring water[5] has the slogan *Dehydrated Brains Don't Perform Well*, which appears after a short video clip of a puppet called Brains (from the popular 1960s marionette series *Thunderbirds*) singing (well) on stage and then falling over, presumably when his brain dehydrates. The negated proposition, then, helps us to envisage both scenarios. The converse is not normally true of positive propositions, such as 'Jackson had arrested a jeweller once' (Atkinson 2004: 74), where the scenario in which Jackson had not arrested a jeweller is not clearly relevant to the narrative. 'Nicola was not a great cook, apparently' (Atkinson 2004: 77), by contrast, does conjure up the kinds of people who are good at cooking, and Nicola is rejected as one of them.

3.3   Summary and conclusions

This chapter introduced a set of stylistic tools of analysis which go beyond the early stylistic analysis in two ways. First, the systems of functional meaning which operate at levels of analysis higher than the sentence have been discussed. These include transitivity analysis and modal grammar, which can be used to comment on individual clauses and also whole texts or text extracts. Similarly, the analysis of cohesion is predicated on the idea that there are structures and functions which work at text level. The final two analytical systems, opposition and negation, work both locally in texts and also more extensively throughout a text.

The second way in which these tools of analysis work differently to those studied in Chapter 2 is that they are all concept-driven. That is, they each address large-scale concepts, such as certainty (modality), representation of events and processes (transitivity) and the more transparent concepts of cohesion, negation and opposition. In each case, there is a prototypical form which delivers the concept most recognisably, and further ways of realising the same kinds of idea, which shade out towards the paralinguistic, the pragmatic and the contextual at the edges of what seem to be 'fuzzy' categories at best, if they are categories at all.

It has been suggested that, perhaps, one way to conceptualise these systems is as a set of reference points to which actual textual examples will approximate, and which help us to understand texts as discourse without constraining us to label (except for the sake of computer analysis) unambiguously in every case.

Exercises

The following extracts, from novels and from a news story, and the poem can be analysed using some or all of the systems featured in this chapter. Each one is introduced to give the reader a little context. Explain how they may jointly help the analyst to describe the style of the texts, and what impact these stylistic choices could potentially have on the reader.

Exercise 3.1

This passage is from Meera Syal's autobiographical novel about growing up in the Midlands of England in a Hindu family.

(40)   Papa was jingling his loose change in his jacket pocket and I knew he wanted to make his way over to the skittle stall. Papa loved gambling; I had watched him playing rummy with my Uncles, everyone sitting cross-legged in a huge circle on our carpet, their coins and tumblers of whisky at their knees, throwing down cards with whoops of triumph or dismay. Or I had followed him into penny arcades during shopping trips, when he would slip away whilst Mama was taking too long over a purchase, and would watch him feed the one-arm bandits carefully, holding his breath as the tumbling oranges and lemons spun to a halt as if expecting a jackpot win every time. Whilst Papa thought of himself as a rakish risk taker, I could see how hard it was for him to gamble without guilt by the way he reluctantly handed over notes for change at the penny arcade booths, or how hesitantly he would place his bets on the carpet whilst my more flamboyant Uncles would be flinging shillings and sometimes notes onto the floor with optimistic battle cries.

(Syal 1997)

Exercise 3.2

This passage is from a book written from the point of view of a nine-year-old boy whose father runs one of the concentration camps (Auschwitz) in Poland, and who makes friends with a boy in the camp through the fence, though he is not aware of why the camp is there, or how the prisoners are being treated.

(41)   'Poland,' said Bruno thoughtfully, weighing up the word on his tongue. 'That's not as good as Germany, is it?'
    Shmuel frowned. 'Why isn't it?' he asked.

'Well, because Germany is the greatest of all countries,' Bruno replied, remembering something that he had overheard Father discussing with Grandfather on any number of occasions. 'We're superior.'

Shmuel stared at him but didn't say anything, and Bruno felt a strong desire to change the subject because even as he had said the words, they didn't sound quite right to him and the last thing he wanted was for Shmuel to think that he was being unkind.

'Where is Poland anyway?' he asked after a few silent moments had passed.

'Well, it's in Europe,' said Shmuel.

Bruno tried to remember the countries he had been taught about in his most recent geography class with Herr Liszt. 'Have you ever heard of Denmark?' he asked.

'No,' said Shmuel.

'I think Poland is in Denmark,' said Bruno, growing more confused even though he was trying to sound clever. 'Because *that's* many miles away,' he repeated for added confirmation.

Shmuel stared at him for a moment and opened his mouth and closed it twice, as if he was considering his words carefully. 'But this is Poland,' he said finally.   (Boyne 2006: 112–13)

Exercise 3.3

This is the beginning of a BBC report from Gaza during the Israeli bombardment of the Palestinian territory in 2009. Such human-interest stories are common ways to bring war zones to the rest of the world.

(42)   Twenty-year-old Yahya Abu Saif lies in his hospital bed looking wide-eyed, gaunt and scared.

He was lucky to survive an Israeli air strike. But, like so many others in Gaza, his life was transformed in an instant.

He lost his right leg in the explosion. The left side of his body is paralysed.

'I had just left the mosque near my home and was going home after prayers,' he says, with a little difficulty.

'They dropped a bomb on the mosque and I was thrown in the air, but I don't remember what happened after that.

'My family told me 15 people were killed and 20 people injured, including me.'

Yahya says he used to go to university and wanted to be a teacher one day.

'Now I will have a life of hospitals. I know I will just need medical care forever.'

As we left the room, we found Yahya's elder brother outside, wiping away tears.

Doctor's dilemma

Al-Wafa Hospital, to which Yahya has been admitted, is the only one in Gaza which specialises in treating amputees.

At a time when hundreds more people need its care, the hospital itself was shelled and damaged in the fighting.

'It was a miserable time for us and the patients,' says Dr Tariq Dardas.

'From midnight on 16 January until 9am, there was constant shelling. We called the Red Cross and civilian defence to help us leave, but nobody would come to this area under those circumstances.

'All the staff members were scared but, of course, we could not leave our patients.'

('Gaza hospital bears heavy strain', Aleem Maqbool, BBC News, Gaza City. <http://news.bbc.co.uk/1/hi/world/middle_east/ 7866159.stm>)

Exercise 3.4

This poem approaches the question of what secular equivalents to prayer exist in the modern world.

(43)   *Prayer*

Some days, although we cannot pray, a prayer
utters itself. So, a woman will lift
her head from the sieve of her hands and stare
at the minims sung by a tree, a sudden gift.

Some nights, although we are faithless, the truth
enters our hearts, that small familiar pain;
then a man will stand stock-still, hearing his youth
in the distant Latin chanting of a train.

Pray for us now. Grade 1 piano scales
console the lodger looking out across
a Midlands town. Then dusk, and someone calls
a child's name as though they named their loss.

Darkness outside. Inside, the radio's prayer –
Rockall. Malin. Dogger. Finisterre.

(Duffy 1993: 52)

Further reading

Readers wishing to pursue the debate about the value and integrity of stylistics may trace the argument through from Fish (1981), who claims that it is ill-founded and illogical, to Simpson (1993: 111–16), whose defence of stylistics from charges of 'interpretative positivism' depends on the notion of 'lowest common denominator' coupled with contextual variation, and to Toolan, who responds from the point of view of 'integrationalism', which attempts to recognise the fluidity of textual meaning throughout stylistic analytical practice and detects at least some literary critical value in the techniques and methods of stylistics.

General discussions of the kind of combined formal/functional tools of analysis described in this chapter can be found in Jeffries (2007b: 12–15) and Jeffries (2010a). Halliday (1994) is the source of the transitivity and modality systems, though readers may find Butt *et al.* (2000) or Halliday and Matthiessen (2004) an easier introduction to Halliday's ideas. Similarly, Simpson's (1993) book on ideology and point of view in literature is accessible and the models of transitivity and modality given there are those used in Jeffries (2007b and 2010a) and the basis of the discussion in this chapter too.

Cohesion is best explained by Halliday and Hasan (1976), though many introductory linguistics books have introductory explanations of the kind also found here. See, for example, Jeffries (2006: 183–7).

Discourse presentation has been developed as a model and analytical tool primarily by Leech and Short (2007: 255–81), Short (1996: 288–324) and Semino and Short (2004), though accessible accounts can also be found in Simpson (1993: Chapter 2) and Toolan 1988: Chapter 4). Applications of the speech and thought model to spoken data can be found in McIntyre *et al.* (2004).

The other tools of analysis presented here, opposition-creation and negation, are less widely covered in stylistic literature at the moment, though opposition is the subject of a monograph (Jeffries 2010a) and a PhD thesis (Davies 2008) and can be seen in practice in Davies (2007) and Jeffries (2007b: 109–19). Negation as a stylistic tool is developed by Hidalgo-Downing (2000), Nørgaard (2007) and Nahajec (2009), and is explained as a tool of critical discourse analysis in Jeffries (2010a).

4 Discourse and context II

Interaction

4.1 Stylistics and pragmatics

Early work in stylistics focused primarily on the analysis of the formal linguistic elements of texts – for example, grammatical forms, phonological features and propositional meanings (see Chapter 2). It is no surprise that such work also focused mainly on the analysis of poems, since such texts are short (making it possible for the stylistician to analyse a complete text) and relatively straightforward in terms of discourse structure. That is, many poems have a single-tier discourse architecture in which the poet addresses the reader directly (Short 1996: 38). This makes a stylistic analysis of such texts relatively straightforward (at least in methodological terms), since it involves identifying stylistic effects at just one discourse level. This is considerably more straightforward than trying to identify the stylistic effects in a text with multiple discourse levels, such as a novel, which involves an address from the author to the reader, embedded in which is an address from a narrator to a narratee, embedded in which are the characters in the fictional world addressing each other. In texts composed of multiple discourse levels, the task for the analyst is considerably more difficult, since the analysis necessitates identifying and isolating stylistic effects at each of the text's constituent discourse levels. Also, such texts tend to be longer, making it unfeasible to produce analyses of complete texts (though corpus stylistics has alleviated this problem to a certain extent; we will discuss this fully in Chapter 7). These methodological issues also explain the comparative neglect of drama by early stylisticians. Dramatic texts, too, have complex discourse architectures, as well as the added complexity that comes if we try to take account of associated performances of the text. (The analysis of the multimodal elements of drama is something stylistics has only just begun to deal with; see, for example, McIntyre 2008.) Stylistics in its infancy was simply not equipped to deal with such text-types, and one reason for this was the lack of appropriate tools for analysing discursive interaction. Only with the advent of pragmatics were stylisticians able to deal with texts – both fiction and non-fiction – which involved (re)presented interaction. The eclectic nature of stylistics meant that it was quick to add pragmatic and sociolinguistic approaches to its analytical toolkit. Our aim in this chapter is to outline some of the key analytical frameworks from pragmatics that stylistics has utilised, and to show how such pragmatic approaches can shed interpretative light on texts that incorporate discursive interaction in the form of (re)presented conversation.

4.2   Interaction in discourse

During the 1970s and 1980s, advances in pragmatics (broadly speaking, the study of how context affects meaning) increased the scope of what stylistics was able to achieve. Previously, while the techniques of grammatical analysis had been available to help stylisticians uncover such aspects of text structure as viewpoint, the tools were not available to reveal the source of interpretative effects deriving from dialogue. For this reason, work on the stylistics of drama to some extent stalled, especially by comparison with work on the stylistics of prose and poetry. But prose, too, often incorporates dialogue (whether presented directly or otherwise), and so, in order to produce stylistic analyses of prose texts that take account of all aspects of discourse structure, the techniques of pragmatics (and other methods of dialogue analysis) are also needed. We will begin by examining the techniques available for the analysis of conversation structure before going on to consider pragmatic aspects of dialogue.

4.2.1   The structure of interactive talk

The notion of stylistics as something of a 'magpie' discipline is amply demonstrated in the extent to which it has borrowed techniques from Conversation Analysis (CA) and applied them in the analysis of dialogue in both fiction and non-fiction texts. The propensity of stylistics for adapting techniques from other disciplines is also demonstrated in the way in which it has taken CA methods and modified them for its own ends, as we shall see.

Conversation Analysis is an ethnomethodological approach to analysing spoken language, pioneered by Harvey Sacks in the 1970s (see Sacks 1995). Conceived as a method of describing and analysing interactive talk, it aims to demonstrate the structures that underlie all conversation. Stylisticians such as Burton (1980) and Mandala (2007) have since demonstrated how such structures are also apparent in fictional dialogue, showing CA to be an analytical method also appropriate for stylistic analysis. Key to CA is the notion of a **turn**. Turns are composed of one or more **turn-constructional units**, which are themselves defined as a complete grammatical unit, such as a sentence or a clause (or, in speech, an utterance; see Biber *et al.* 1999 for a discussion of the units of spoken discourse). In prototypical conversation, a turn-taking system is always in place, wherein participants take it in turns to hold the **floor** (defined as the right to speak and have other participants in the talk listen to you). The turn-taking system is composed of two components: (i) the **turn allocational component** and (ii) the **turn constructional component**.

Table 4.1 *Adjacency pairs (Person 1999: 43)*

First parts	Second parts	
	Preferred	Dispreferred
request	acceptance	refusal
offer	acceptance	refusal
assessment	agreement	disagreement
blame	denial	admission
question	answer	unexpected answer or non-answer

The turn allocational component regulates turn change and assumes that only one speaker may speak at a time. The point in a conversation at which a change of speaker occurs is known as a **transition relevance place (TRP)** and at such places several options become available. The current speaker may select the next speaker (by, for example, asking a question of another participant), the next speaker may self-select (perhaps by rebutting the previous speaker's point) or the turn may lapse. If a lapse occurs, the current speaker may incorporate that lapse as a pause and continue until the next TRP. A turn-overlap at any other point than a TRP constitutes an interruption.

The turn constructional component deals with the length and linguistic complexity of the turn, and turn-length is locally managed. For instance, if you are telling a story and someone begins to talk over you, you might raise your voice as a paralinguistic signal that you need more time to complete your turn. Alternatively, you might signal this metalinguistically by saying, for instance, 'Let me just finish.' (Good examples of the need for management of the turn constructional component can easily be found in political discussion programmes and political interviews.)

But CA doesn't just concentrate on the *production* of talk. It examines how talk is *interactive*, and it does this by looking at how turns relate to each other. Turn-taking in conversation comes about in part because turns often call for another turn in response. Schegloff and Sacks (1974) describe such turns as **adjacency pairs**. An adjacency pair consists of a first part and a second part, and the second part of an adjacency pair may be **preferred** or **dispreferred**. An example will make this clear. A greeting prototypically consists of two parts. The first part involves a salutation from one speaker (for example, 'Good morning'), and the prototypical response to this (the preferred response) would be a salutation in return. A dispreferred response would be to respond with, for example, an invective ('fuck off!') or to ignore the greeting and say nothing at all. Person (1999) summarises some typical adjacency pairs as shown in Table 4.1.

In stylistic terms, a dispreferred response is foregrounded by external deviation and may be regarded as interpretatively loaded. Consider the following example from Dennis Potter's television drama *Pennies from Heaven*:

(1)   [Context: Joan and Arthur, both in their mid-thirties, are married. It is night.
             Arthur has been working away from home and has now returned. He enters
             his and Joan's bedroom, where Joan is sleeping. Joan wakes up.]
             JOAN   Have you been drinking, Arthur?
             ARTHUR (*Mimics*) Have-you-been-drinking-Arthur?
                                                ('Hand in Hand', Potter 1996: 86)

Here, Joan's question constitutes the first part of an adjacency pair, the preferred
second part to which would be an answer. However, by repeating Joan's question
and (as the stage directions explain) mimicking Joan, Arthur gives a dispreferred
second part. The usefulness of CA to stylistics is in the replicability of its method:
by the terms of CA, any analyst would identify Arthur's response as dispreferred
and thus foregrounded.

The next stage in the analytical process is, of course, to interpret the significance of this element of foregrounding, and here is where stylistics differs from
CA. Conversation analysts would claim that we should not speculate on what
a speaker means by a particular utterance, since we can never know for certain
whether our speculation is correct. We must, instead, concentrate our efforts
simply on describing what speakers do within a particular conversation. In so
doing, conversation analysts specifically exclude context in contributing to the
meaning of utterances, and their failure to consider speaker-meaning seems to us
an unremittingly reductive stance to take. Even natural scientists need to interpret
the results obtained from experiments, and it may well be the case that other
scientists might disagree with their interpretation. Nonetheless, the important
thing is that the analytical procedure is such that the experiment can be replicated
and the same results obtained. The same principle applies to text analysis. To
stop short of interpreting the effects – or meanings – of a particular utterance
or element of text structure is to provide an incomplete analysis. With regard to
example 1, we might assume Arthur's utterance to betray his annoyance at Joan's
question. (We will consider the means by which we might legitimately make such
inferences in 4.2.2.)

The necessity of taking into account the implicatures that may be generated
by the second part of an adjacency pair can be seen when we consider those that
seem, on the surface, to be preferred responses but which in practice are not quite
so straightforward. Imagine, for instance, a conversation between two friends:

(2)   A: What about going to the cinema?
             B: Well, er, I've got an essay to write.

In this example we have a question followed by an answer, and in terms of
adjacency pairs we might, at a surface level, say that the answer constitutes a
preferred second part. If we are to suggest that it does not, we have to do so on the
basis that the question by speaker A requires an answer which is either affirmative
or negative. However, to do this means speculating on the meaning of speaker A's
utterance, something that conversation analysts would claim to avoid. It would

seem, then, that it is impossible to analyse conversation accurately without some attempt to interpret speaker-meaning. For this reason, while stylistics utilises the descriptive procedures of CA, it disregards the methodological limitations of CA and prefers instead to incorporate analytical techniques from pragmatics, as we shall see in section 4.2.2.

Despite the problems with CA, then, it still has a part to play in the stylistic analysis of dialogue, especially when used in conjunction with pragmatics. For example, the relative power of speakers in a conversation is often reflected in the turn constructional components of the conversation. Short (1996: 219–20) provides a detailed account of the conversational behaviour of powerful and powerless speakers, explaining, for instance, that powerful speakers tend to dominate conversations and that this is reflected in their relative turn lengths. Of course, there are numerous contextual factors that it is necessary to take account of, as Short points out. First, the notion of power incorporates numerous different types. A speaker may be physically weaker than other conversational participants but may be imbued with substantial power as a result of having a particular institutional role (consider the example of a monarch or president's role as titular head of the armed forces). Second, the context of a conversation may place restrictions on the prototypical linguistic behaviour of participants. Job interviews, for example, usually involve the less powerful participants (the candidates) speaking substantially more than their interviewers. We will consider other structural elements of conversational behaviour in an extended analysis in section 4.3, after we have considered in more detail the pragmatic aspects of dialogue analysis.

4.2.2   From presupposition to implicature

We saw in the previous section the importance of taking into account contextual factors when analysing dialogue. In this section we will examine analytical procedures for uncovering contextual meaning.

Sometimes, meanings are inherent in the structure of what we say. For example, saying 'Lee Harvey Oswald assassinated John F. Kennedy' **entails** that 'John F. Kennedy died'. An **entailment** is what follows from the propositions that are made in an utterance. Entailment, then, is a logical concept, not a pragmatic one. There cannot be any context in the real world where if the first assertion is true the second one is not. Entailment, therefore, relates to the utterance rather than to the speaker. Entailment is different from **presupposition**. The sentence 'Lee Harvey Oswald assassinated John F. Kennedy' presupposes the existence of a person called Lee Harvey Oswald and a person called John F. Kennedy. The difference between entailment and presupposition can be seen if we negate the sentence. If we say 'Lee Harvey Oswald *did not* assassinate John F. Kennedy', the existential presuppositions still hold but the entailment does not. If Oswald did not assassinate Kennedy then Kennedy cannot have died as a result. Presuppositions are also derived from the structural elements of utterances. (Levinson 1983 provides an extensive list of presupposition triggers which includes, for example, change-of-state verbs, comparatives, iteratives, etc.)

Sometimes, however, the full meaning of an utterance cannot be derived from its structural elements alone. For example, saying 'The Vice-Chancellor of the University is a man of profound intellectual foresight' presupposes the existence of a particular Vice-Chancellor but it does not indicate whether the speaker is sincere or sarcastic in what they say. To understand this we need to consider the notion of **implicature**.

Grice (1975) distinguishes between what he calls conventional and conversational implicature. **Conventional implicature** is a type of pragmatic presupposition and is realised through the use of particular lexical items. The conjunction *but* is one such item, as in the following example:

(3)   It's an old house but it has a nice atmosphere.

Here the coordinating conjunction gives rise to the conventional implicature that old houses do not usually have nice atmospheres. In a real-life example (4) taken from a snooker commentary, the conventional implicature arising from the conjunction is unintentionally humorous, suggesting as it does that fine snooker players do not normally come from Wales:

(4)   He's 21, he comes from Wales, but he's turning into a fine snooker player.

The linguistic triggers of conventional implicatures are restricted to a small set of lexemes. **Conversational implicature**, on the other hand, is much more prevalent and arises out of the pragmatic behaviour of speakers. The theory which specifies how this occurs was originally proposed by the 'ordinary language' philosopher, Paul Grice (Grice 1975; see also Chapman 2005, 2006), and postulates a number of commonly held assumptions shared by participants in a conversation. Grice explains his so-called Cooperative Principle (CP) as being:

> [...] a rough general principle which participants will be expected (*ceteris paribus*) to observe, namely: Make your conversational contribution such as is required at the stage at which it occurs, by the accepted purpose or direction of the talk exchange in which you are engaged.   (Grice 1975: 45)

Grice formulates his Cooperative Principle as a series of four sub-maxims, of **quantity**, **quality**, **relation** and **manner**. These may be summarised as follows:

Maxim of Quantity
- Make your contribution as informative as is required (for the current purpose of the exchange).
- Do not make your contribution more informative than is required.

Maxim of Quality
- Do not say what you believe to be false.
- Do not say that for which you lack adequate evidence.

Maxim of Relation
- Be relevant.

Maxim of Manner
- Be perspicuous.
- Avoid obscurity of expression.
- Avoid ambiguity.
- Be brief (avoid unnecessary prolixity).
- Be orderly.

Although formulated as imperatives, Grice's maxims are not instructions to speakers but are best understood as encapsulating the assumptions that we prototypically hold when we engage in conversation. We expect, for instance, that if we ask a question of an interlocutor, we will receive a relevant answer that is truthful, clear and no more or less informative than is required. Nonetheless, in practice it is common for speakers *not* to observe these maxims, and there are a variety of means by which they may be broken. These can give rise to a number of different pragmatic effects, all of which may have stylistic import. We can summarise the means by which speakers can break the maxims as follows.

Flouting
When speakers intentionally fail to observe a maxim, and do so ostentatiously to the extent that it is clear to any interlocutors that the maxim is indeed being broken, then, according to Grice, he or she is **flouting** that maxim. Flouting maxims draws attention to an undercurrent of meaning – and this is what Grice refers to as conversational implicature. The following example from prose fiction demonstrates this:

(5)   [Corky Pirbright and Bertie Wooster are discussing Bertie's young cousin, Thomas. Corky speaks first.]
'A small boy with red hair entertained me. He said he was your cousin.'
'My Aunt Agatha's son and, oddly enough, the apple of her eye.'
'Why oddly enough?'
'He's the King of the Underworld. They call him the shadow.'
(Wodehouse 1991: 191)

Perhaps the most obvious instance of flouting in example 5 is Bertie's statement that his cousin is 'the King of the Underworld'. Although a comic novel, the fictional world is one that is akin to the real world and so Bertie's claim that his cousin is the 'King of the Underworld' is clearly not the case, since this is a supernatural being that has no existence in the real world. Bertie's statement, then, is a flout of the maxim of quality. It is so obviously not true, that Bertie's interlocutor (and we as readers) are forced to look for an alternative meaning in order to make sense of Bertie's remark. This is likely to be that Bertie's cousin shares some of the characteristics of the fabled 'King of the Underworld'; perhaps he is frightening, sly, cunning, unpleasant, etc. This, then, is the conversational implicature arising from Bertie's flout. We might also note that this piece of dialogue also constitutes a flout within the discourse world (see Chapter 6) of the novelist, P. G. Wodehouse. At this discourse level, flouting the maxim gives rise to a humorous effect that would not be present had Wodehouse simply observed the Cooperative Principle by having Bertie state clearly and concisely that his cousin was an unpleasant character.

Violating

'Violating' describes the situation wherein a speaker breaks a maxim on purpose and intends for his or her interlocutor not to notice this. Violations of the maxim of quality are notoriously difficult to spot in real life data, for the simple reason that an effective violation of this maxim is one that is not noticeable. One notable example, however, is the former U.S. President Bill Clinton's claim that he did not have sex with the White House intern, Monica Lewinsky. Following allegations that he did, Clinton said in a statement, 'I did not have sexual relations with that woman.' The status of this remark as a violation of the maxim of quality was revealed by Clinton's later admission that 'I did have sexual relations with Miss Lewinsky, and I am deeply, deeply sorry for the pain I have caused my family and friends.' Politicians can often be observed violating the maxims of manner, relation and quantity as a means of deflecting attention away from the fact that they are not directly answering the question posed to them. Successful violations do not generate conversational implicatures.

Infringing

'Infringing' refers to what happens in those situations where a speaker fails to observe a maxim, though with no intention to deceive or to generate an implicature. For example, infringement may occur if a speaker is tired, drunk or cognitively impaired in some other way. A fictional instance of the infringement of the maxim of quantity can be seen in the following extract from a courtroom scene in the film *A Fish Called Wanda*:

(6)   [George, a diamond thief on trial for robbery, has jumped out of the dock towards the witness box, in response to Wanda – his supposed alibi – having just implicated him in the crime.]

      1. GEORGE   You bitch! You fucking bitch!

      2. JUDGE   Restrain that man! Restrain this man.

      3. GEORGE   Come here, you bastard!

      4. JUDGE   Clear the court! I'm adjourning this matter for an hour. Clear the court! Clear the court! Clear the court! Clear the court! Clear the court! Officers, arrest that man! Clear the court! Clear the court!

                                   (Cleese and Crichton 1988)

Here, the judge's last turn is clearly not intended to create an implicature, and cannot therefore constitute a flout. Nor is it covert and so it cannot be a violation. It would seem that the excitement of the situation causes the judge simply to infringe the maxim of quantity (by repeating the phrase 'Clear the court!') in his eagerness to have George removed from the courtroom.

Opting out

'Opting out' refers to the practice of ostentatiously refusing to be bound by the Cooperative Principle. For example, a politician faced with a potentially incriminating question may prefer to respond with 'No comment'. Of course, one of the problems with such a strategy is that interlocutors will often interpret such an opt-out as a violation and assume that the speaker is deliberately withholding information and/or being unclear. This can lead to instances such as the one below, in which the former British Prime Minister goes to considerable lengths to emphasise that he is neither making implicatures nor withholding information as a result of making no comment:

(7)   JOURNALIST What is your general attitude to surveillance or bugging of friendly countries or United Nations officials? Do you accept to do that would be against the Vienna Convention?

           TONY BLAIR I'm not going to comment on the work that our security services do. No Prime Minister has done that. I'm not going to comment on it. Do not take that as an indication that the allegations that were made by Clare Short this morning are true.

(http://www.number-10.gov.uk/output/Page5432.asp)

A more light-hearted example, highlighting the fact that attempting to opt out of the CP can lead to unintentional implicatures, can be seen in the example below from Richard Curtis's film comedy, *Notting Hill*:

(8)   [William has arrived at his sister's house for dinner and has brought with him Anna Scott, a famous actress he met through a series of coincidences.]
           Int. Max and Bella's kitchen/living room – night. A minute or two later – they are standing, drinking wine before dinner. Bernie with Anna on their own – William helping Max in the kitchen.
           1. MAX   You haven't slept with her, have you?
           2. WILLIAM   That is a cheap question and the answer is, of course, no comment.
           3. MAX   'No comment' means 'yes'.
           4. WILLIAM   No, it doesn't.
           5. MAX   Do you ever masturbate?
           6. WILLIAM   Definitely no comment.
           7. MAX   You see – it means 'yes'.

(Richard Curtis, Notting Hill, 1999)

William's response, 'No comment', in turn 2 constitutes an attempt to opt out of the Cooperative Principle, though Max's statement in turn 3 exemplifies the fact that when speakers attempt to do this, it is difficult for their addressees to avoid making an inference on the basis of it.

In addition to breaking the maxims, there are instances in which the Cooperative Principle may be suspended – i.e. occasions where there is no assumption that speakers will observe the Cooperative Principle at all. In interview situations, for instance, there is usually no assumption that candidates will observe the maxim of quantity, since one of the aims of this particular activity type is to convey as much about oneself as possible (see Culpeper and McIntyre 2010 for a full discussion of the Cooperative Principle in relation to the interview activity type). It is also the case that participants in a conversation will often have different conceptualisations of what it means to be truthful, relevant, concise, etc. Harris (1984) takes this truism as a starting point for her development of the notion of *paradigms of reality*, explaining that interlocutors often begin conversations from radically different perspectives on reality and that these different 'reality paradigms' sometimes clash. Archer (2002) develops Harris's work and suggests that the notion of reality paradigms can explain why an utterance may be interpreted differently by different participants in a conversation – i.e. why one utterance may cause different interlocutors to draw different inferences from it. The different reality paradigms from which characters interpret each other's utterances can give rise to a number of effects in drama, not least humour, as can be seen in the following extract from John Cleese and Connie Booth's celebrated sitcom, *Fawlty Towers*. In this extract, Alan is a guest staying at the hotel with his girlfriend. Basil, the hotel owner, has previously refused to give Alan a double-room because Alan and his partner are not married. Part of Basil's reality paradigm is that sex outside marriage is wrong. Because Basil has this world view, it causes him to draw an inference from what Alan says when, in fact, Alan is not attempting to create an implicature at all:

(9)   1. ALAN   [...] I know it's a bit late but do you know if there's a chemist still open?
          2. BASIL (*drawing the wrong conclusion*) I beg your pardon?
          3. ALAN   Do you know if there's a chemist still open?
          4. BASIL I suppose you think this is funny, do you?
          5. ALAN   Funny?
          6. BASIL Ha ha ha.
          7. ALAN   No, I really want to know.
          8. BASIL Oh do you, well I don't. So far as I know all the chemists are shut. You'll just have to wait till tomorrow. Sorry. Bit of a blow, I imagine.
          9. ALAN   What?
          10. BASIL Nothing, you heard. Is that all?
          11. ALAN Well...
          12. BASIL Yes?
          13. ALAN I don't suppose you've got a couple of...
          14. BASIL Now look!! Just don't push your luck. I have a breaking point, you know.
          15. ALAN I only want some batteries.
                    ('The Wedding Party', Cleese and Booth 1988: 59)

Basil's reality paradigm causes him to interpret Alan's first turn as flouting the maxim of quantity to generate an implicature along the lines of 'Do you know where I can buy some condoms?' In effect, Basil's reality paradigm causes him to see an implicature in Alan's first turn, where there is, in fact, none.

4.2.3   Politeness and impoliteness

As we have seen, there is strong evidence from pragmatics for some kind of Cooperative Principle being at work when we communicate with others. From a stylistic perspective, however, our concern is with the interpretative effects generated by the linguistic choices made by speakers (and writers), and we can gain a better understanding of these if we consider the reasons why participants in a conversation choose to observe or ignore the Cooperative Principle. One reason why participants often flout or violate the conversational maxims is for the sake of politeness (and its opposite, impoliteness), and this is an area that has received considerable attention from linguists.

There are a number of different conceptualisations of linguistic politeness, though of these the most widely adopted has been the model proposed by Brown and Levinson (1987). This is based on the concept of **face** and the notion that everyone has both positive face needs (the desire to be liked and approved of) and negative face needs (the desire to be able to go about one's business unimpeded). Any affront to these face needs is termed a **face threatening act (FTA)**, and in order to mitigate FTAs, speakers may choose to use a variety of politeness strategies designed to appeal to their addressee's positive and/or negative face needs. The extent of the mitigating strategies used by speakers depends on the size of the FTA. A relatively innocuous FTA (asking if someone can spare the time to discuss something, for example) may not require extensive politeness strategies to be used, while a more significant FTA (a manager informing an employee that he or she is to be made redundant) will require substantial mitigation. Examples of these scenarios can be seen in the following extract from the screenplay of Sam Mendes's film *American Beauty*:

(10)   [Lester is an employee of *Media Monthly* magazine. Brad is his boss and is significantly younger than Lester. Brad is faced with the prospect of making Lester redundant.]

1. BRAD   Hey Les. You got a minute?

Lester turns around, smiling perfunctorily.

2. LESTER For you, Brad? I've got five.

Int. Brad's office – moments later. Brad is seated behind his desk in his big corner office.

3. BRAD   I'm sure you can understand our need to cut corners around here.

Lester sits across from him, looking small and isolated.

(Ball 2000)

In turn 1, Brad's request for a minute of Lester's time constitutes a face threatening act, albeit a small one. In acknowledgement of the fact that his desire to speak to Lester is in some sense a threat to Lester's negative face (i.e. his desire to be unimpeded), Brad frames the FTA as an interrogative, a more indirect structure than, say, an imperative ('I want to talk to you'). This is coupled with Brad's friendly greeting (constituting an appeal to Lester's positive face) and the informality suggested by the elision of the verb *have* in his second sentence. Such strategies serve to emphasise the insignificance of the FTA. Of course, given that this is not a substantial FTA, and that Brad has greater institutional power than Lester, Brad could perhaps legitimately have used fewer politeness strategies (e.g. 'Lester, I want to talk to you'). Note, though, that this is a precursor to a much bigger FTA, namely Brad warning Lester that he is likely to be made redundant. Hence, in turn 3, Brad continues to use a number of politeness strategies to mitigate this significantly larger FTA. For instance, he appeals to Lester's intelligence (and hence, his positive face) by acknowledging that Lester is likely to understand the reasons behind the need 'to cut corners'.

Brown and Levinson (1987: 103–227) provide an extensive summary of the variety of strategies open to speakers for mitigating both positive and negative face threats which, for reasons of space, we cannot consider here in much detail. Instead, we will simply note that Brown and Levinson divide these specific tactics among what they term five 'super-strategies': (i) Perform the FTA bald, on record; (ii) Perform the FTA on record using positive politeness; (iii) Perform the FTA on record using negative politeness; (iv) Perform the FTA off record; and (v) Don't perform the FTA. To begin with super-strategy (i), bald on-record politeness simply means that the speaker's utterance is in accordance with Grice's Cooperative Principle; that is, it is maximally efficient in communicative terms. Such an approach may be warranted by the context in which an utterance occurs. As an example, a Private may exclaim 'Look out!' to a superior ranking officer when advancing under fire if he or she notices that the officer in question is in immediate physical danger. The utterance is maximally efficient in terms of observing the maxims of quality, quantity, relation and manner, and the necessity of issuing a warning quickly allows the soldier to disregard the usual need to use the conventionalised polite address form.

In drama, politeness strategies can work as elements of characterisation. In Alan Bennett's *The Lady in the Van*, for example, the character of Miss Shepherd frequently uses the bald on-record strategy, even in circumstances where politeness would be the norm. Inevitably this characterises her as someone who is rude and cares little about social niceties:

(11)   [Miss Shepherd is being visited by a social worker who is concerned about the fact that she is an old woman living alone in a dilapidated van.]
         1. SOCIAL WORKER   Miss Shepherd. I'm Jane, the social worker.
         2. MISS SHEPHERD   I don't want the social worker.
                                        (Bennett 2000: 17)

Miss Shepherd's answer is potentially damaging to the social worker's positive face, though she does nothing to mitigate it, preferring instead to answer in accordance with the Gricean maxims.

In cases where mitigation of the FTA is necessary, super-strategies (ii) to (iv) may be employed.

Super-strategies (ii) and (iii) call for the FTA to be performed on record. This simply means that the FTA should be acknowledged and appropriate tactics used to mitigate it. Performing an FTA on record using positive politeness means using strategies designed to redress the positive face threat to the hearer. Examples might include intensifying one's interest in the addressee, seeking agreement with him or her and avoiding disagreement, using in-group identity markers, joking and making small talk. In the following extract from *The Lady in the Van*, the social worker is responding to an irritable comment from Alan Bennett:

(12)   SOCIAL WORKER Alan, I'm sensing that hostility again.
                                                    (Bennett 2000: 70)

The social worker's choice of words appears to be governed by an awareness that simply telling Alan that he is behaving in a hostile manner would be threatening to his positive face. To mitigate the FTA the social worker uses a number of strategies: (1) She uses Alan's first name to indicate a close relationship to him; (2) she refers not to what Alan is doing but to what she is feeling; (3) she 'distances' the hostility from Alan and herself by referring to it using the distal empathetic deictic term 'that' (see Chapter 6 for an explanation of deixis).

Performing an FTA on record using negative politeness involves using strategies designed to reduce the negative face threat to the addressee. Here, speakers may be indirect, they might hedge, be pessimistic about the outcome of whatever request/statement they are making, apologise, or impersonalise the FTA through the use of passivisation or the use of impersonal pronouns to refer to the speaker and hearer. The next example, again from *The Lady in the Van*, is a rare instance of Miss Shepherd being polite. Here, she is dictating a request to the College of Cardinals in Rome:

(13)   MISS SHEPHERD Might I humbly suggest that at the Papal Coronation
                                            there could be a not so heavy crown, of light plastic
                                            possibly, or cardboard, for instance?
                                                    (Bennett 2000: 70)

Disregarding Miss Shepherd's tenuous grip on reality, her request is one which, if acted upon, would create difficulties for the College of Cardinals. Recognising this, she mitigates the FTA by using indirectness (framing her suggestion as an interrogative), by downplaying her own status (via the adverb 'humbly') and by hedging (using 'possibly' and 'for instance').

Super-strategy (iv), 'Perform the FTA off record', means performing the FTA using an indirect illocutionary act (illocutionary force is discussed in more detail in section 4.2.4). Put simply, this means performing the FTA in such a way that the speaker's utterance might be interpreted in more than one way, allowing the speaker the get-out clause of denying having performed an FTA at all if offence is taken by the hearer. For instance, a speaker wanting a favour from a colleague might say, 'It's really inconvenient that I have to work an evening shift today.' If the colleague replies along the lines of, 'Well I can't help you, I'm busy myself you know!', the indirectness of the first speaker's utterance allows him or her to deny the initial negative face threat by claiming that he or she was simply making a statement as opposed to a request.

Finally, with regard to super-strategy (v), Brown and Levinson note that in some cases an action may be deemed so potentially face-threatening that it is simply not worth performing the FTA. This evaluation of the size of the FTA is what determines the choice between the five super-strategies, along with other contextual factors such as the relative power differential between the speaker and hearer. 'Small' FTAs may be performed bald on record, while weightier ones may require on-record positive or negative politeness, or even an off-record strategy.

It should be apparent from the above explanation of Brown and Levinson's theory of politeness that utilising many of their proposed super-strategies involves breaking the Gricean Cooperative Principle in some way. A clear connection can be seen, then, between these two theories of conversational exchange. What is also the case is that the Cooperative Principle can be broken in the pursuit of less harmonious exchanges: that is, speakers and writers may choose to flout or violate the Gricean maxims in order to be impolite.

It is generally agreed by most scholars working in this area that the Brown and Levinson theory of politeness cannot adequately account for instances of impolite conversation. Nonetheless, a number of these scholars have proposed that impoliteness may be explained using a face-based model similar to that proposed by Brown and Levinson to account for polite verbal behaviour. Culpeper (1996), for example, suggests that if impoliteness is viewed as being the polar opposite of politeness, then strategies for achieving impolite exchanges must be in opposition to the strategies typically used to maintain conversational harmony. In his view (and in that of Lachenicht 1980) impoliteness may be defined as an attack on the positive and/or negative face needs of an addressee. In explaining how this might work, Culpeper identifies five super-strategies for attacking face. These are: (i) Perform the FTA using bald on-record impoliteness; (ii) Perform the FTA using positive impoliteness; (iii) Perform the FTA using negative impoliteness; (iv) Perform the FTA using sarcasm or mock politeness; and (v) Withhold politeness.

With regard to super-strategy (i), Culpeper (1996) points out that while the bald on-record *politeness* super-strategy is usually employed in situations where the context is such that little face damage is likely to result, the bald on-record *impoliteness* super-strategy tends to be used in instances where the converse is true. Super-strategy (ii) governs the use of tactics designed to attack the positive face needs of the addressee (for example, ignoring the addressee, using inappropriate address forms, using taboo language, avoiding agreement and seeking disagreement), as in this example from Quentin Tarantino's screenplay *Reservoir Dogs*:

(14)   [Mr White, a crook who has just robbed a jewellers, is arguing with his
              criminal compatriot, Mr Pink.]
              MR WHITE You little motherfucker!

(Tarantino 1994)

Super-strategy (iii), obviously enough, covers the use of tactics designed to attack
negative face (for instance, hindering, being condescending of the addressee's
position, invading his or her space either literally or metaphorically), as in this
example from later on in the *Reservoir Dogs* screenplay:

(15)   [Mr White is berating another member of the gang for behaving psychotically
              during the robbery.]
              1. MR WHITE   You almost killed me, asshole! If I had any idea what type
                             of guy you were, I never would've agreed to work with
                             you.
              2. MR BLONDE   You gonna bark all day, little doggie, or are you gonna bite?

(Tarantino 1994)

Mr Blonde's reference to Mr White as 'little doggie' is condescending in the
extreme, especially considering the implicature (via a flout of the maxim of
relation) that Mr White is all talk and lacks the courage to attack Mr Blonde
physically.

Super-strategy (iv) refers to the performance of an FTA using insincere politeness forms, as in this response from Mr Pink to Mr White's revelation that he has
told a fellow criminal his real name (despite being expressly instructed not to do
this) because the man in question had been shot and was scared:

(16)   1. MR PINK   Oh, I don't doubt it was quite beautiful –
              2. MR WHITE Don't fucking patronize me.

(Tarantino 1994)

Finally, super-strategy (v) refers to the withholding of politeness when it is
expected, by keeping silent.

There are, of course, issues with Culpeper's approach to impoliteness, as,
indeed, there are issues with any theory, model or analytical framework. Bousfield
(2007a: 63), for instance, questions the necessity of the bald on-record impoliteness strategy, arguing that any bald on-record utterance is threatening to face to
some extent, and that bald on-record tactics might be better thought of as being
subsumed within both the positive and negative impoliteness super-strategies.
Bousfield (2007a: 91) also raises the potential problem of the open-ended nature
of Culpeper's list of the tactics that might be employed in pursuit of any of the
five super-strategies for aggravating face. If there is no theoretical restriction on
the number or type of tactics that might be subsumed within each of the super-
strategies, then the approach itself is in danger of being unfalsifiable. Culpeper
counters this problem to some extent in his more recent work (Culpeper 2005)
by integrating Spencer-Oatey's (2002) notion of rapport-management into his
approach in order to take account of the culturally and contextually managed

aspects of face. Despite the issues, the approach is useful for its capacity for explaining interpretative significance in the analysis of dialogue, and the wealth of research currently being undertaken in this area is likely to result in further refinements and improvements in approaches to analysing impolite exchanges.

4.2.4 From the performative hypothesis to speech act theory

A further pragmatic concept which has been borrowed into stylistics (and particularly the stylistics of drama) is that of the **speech act**. The origins of speech act theory may be traced to the work of J. L. Austin, who first noted that language is not just used to make statements or ask questions, but might also be used to perform actions (see Austin 1962).

Austin distinguished between what he called **constatives** (e.g. 'I like Guinness') and **performatives** (e.g. 'I apologise'), on the basis that performatives can never be said to be true or false while constatives can. There is no sense, for example, in which 'I apologise' can be said to be either true or false. We might discuss the sincerity of the apology but this is a different matter to proclaiming truthfulness or falsity. In further describing the linguistic notion of a performative, Austin points out that as well as being unfalsifiable, all performatives are self-referential; that is, they refer to what the speaker is doing. Austin also distinguished a number of different sub-varieties of performatives. Metalinguistic performatives, for instance, refer to some linguistic act (e.g. 'I say that he is a bounder and a crook!' or 'I propose that capital punishment be reinstated') and by their nature are always successful (**felicitous** in Austin's terms). That is, by uttering a metalinguistic performative no-one can accuse you of not having performed the act specified by the verb. Not all performatives are intrinsically felicitous. Ritual performatives, for example, rely on external factors for their success. Consider, for instance, 'I sentence you to 25 years' hard labour.' While anyone might make such an utterance, only a small minority of people within the criminal law system have the institutional authority to utter this and have it acted upon (i.e. the defendant taken away to prison). The external factors that need to be in place for a performative to be felicitous are referred to by Austin as **felicity conditions** and he outlines these as follows:

A: i)   there must be a conventional procedure having a conventional effect.
    ii)   the circumstances and persons must be appropriate.
B: The procedure must be executed (i) correctly, (ii) completely.
C: Often
    i)   the persons must have the requisite thoughts, feelings and intentions and
    ii)   if consequent conduct is specified, then the relevant parties must do it.

(Austin 1962: 14–15)

Sometimes a speaker may make explicit reference to felicity conditions when uttering a performative, as can be seen in example 17 (the underlining denotes this explicit reference):

(17)   <u>By my authority as Vice-Chancellor</u>, I hereby confer upon you the status of graduates of the University of Huddersfield.

> (Professor Bob Cryan, Vice-Chancellor,
> University of Huddersfield, 2009)

Some performatives are collaborative in nature and require the consent of others to be felicitous. It is impossible, for example, to make a bet unless that bet is taken up by a second party. The effects that can arise from infelicitous performatives can, unsurprisingly, be exploited for dramatic purposes, as in example 18:

(18)   [Citizen Camembert, the Chief of the Secret Police during the French Revolution, is determined to track down the elusive 'Black Fingernail' who has been rescuing aristocrats just before they are taken to the guillotine.]

  1. CAMEMBERT What's this I see! Oh! My own sister ravaged before my very eyes!
  2. SIR RODNEY No, no, it's the other way round!
  3. CAMEMBERT You despicable cur sir! I demand immediate satisfaction!
  4. SIR RODNEY There seems to be a failing in your family.
  5. CAMEMBERT Enough sir! You have insulted the honour of the de la Plumes, to say nothing of ma Tante.
  6. SIR RODNEY Ooh that hurt!
  7. CAMEMBERT As the injured party I have the choice of swords or pistols.
  8. SIR RODNEY Oh well we won't quarrel over that. You have the swords, I'll have the pistols.
  9. CAMEMBERT Do not jest sir! Believe me, I am deadly earnest!
  10. SIR RODNEY And I'm living Rodney and I'm going to stay that way!

> (Talbot Rothwell, *Carry On . . . Don't Lose Your Head*, 1966)

The metalinguistic performative uttered by Camembert in turn 3 ('I demand immediate satisfaction!') is an indirect challenge to Sir Rodney, which fails because it is not taken up by him; indeed, Sir Rodney deliberately avoids responding directly to the performative, thereby giving rise to a number of humorous effects. (Note that although the status of 'demand' as a metalinguistic performative means it is intrinsically felicitous, it is functionally infelicitous when viewed as an indirect challenge.)

Austin's work on what he called his **performative hypothesis** raises interesting issues about the nature of language, but it is inherently flawed. Thomas (1995: 44) summarises the reasons why the performative hypothesis does not work by making three major points. The first is that there is no formal (i.e. grammatical) way of distinguishing performative verbs from other sorts of verbs. Thomas points out that performatives do not necessarily have to be first-person present tense forms (for example, 'Your contract is hereby terminated' and 'The student asserted that he had not plagiarised' are both performatives despite being second- and third-person respectively). Second, the presence of a performative verb does not guarantee that the specified action is carried out (consider if 'I promise to help you paint your kitchen' is indeed a promise if the speaker does not then go through with his or her intended action). Finally, not all performative acts in

English have an associated performative verb. Hinting, boasting, inviting, etc. are all carried out without using a performative, therefore it is clear that performatives are not necessary in order to perform actions in language. Indeed, the fact that there is no direct correlation between the form of an utterance and its force was eventually recognised by Austin, who then proposed a three-way distinction between **locution** (what is said), **illocution** (what is meant) and **perlocution** (the effect on the hearer of what is said). For example, saying 'I'm not bad with a paintbrush' has the form of a statement but may, in the right circumstances, have the illocutionary force of an offer ('Would you like me to help you with your decorating?'). The perlocutionary effect of this utterance may be that the hearer accepts the assistance offered indirectly. Austin's term for an utterance and the situation in which it is used was speech act.

In an effort to systematise Austin's work, one of Austin's pupils, J. R. Searle, attempted to formulate a series of rules to explain how speech acts work. Searle proposed that all speech acts could be broken down into four components: the propositional act, the preparatory condition, the sincerity condition and the essential condition. We can see how this works if we consider the prototypical speech act of 'offering', which we might describe as follows:

Propositional act: The Speaker (S) asks the Hearer (H) if he/she would like either some item (I) or for the speaker to perform some act (A) which the Speaker believes to be in the Hearer's interest.

Preparatory condition: S believes I/A is in H's best interest and is in a position to provide I/A.

Sincerity condition: S wants to provide I/A for H.

Essential condition: S conveys a desire to provide I/A to H.

Following Searle's scheme, the example below constitutes a prototypical offer:

(19)   MAGGIE Would anybody like more tea?
                   (McGuinness 1998: 57)

Conversely, while example 20 may appear on the surface to have the qualities of an offer, it does not fulfil the relevant preparatory condition (i.e. that the speaker believes the offer is in the Hearer's interest) and so, according to Searle, we would look for an alternative explanation of the speaker's meaning. We might, for instance, say that example 20 has the locutionary form of an offer but the illocutionary force of a threat; that is, it is an indirect speech act, which may be defined as one speech act performed by means of another.

(20)   SERGEANT If you want a smack in the ribs, mate, you can have one.
                     (Potter 1996: 230)

In a sense, then, Searle's improvement on Austin's work was a means of explaining how non-literal meaning is conveyed – a similar goal to that of Grice (1975). However, there are problems with speech act theory as a concept that makes Grice's approach to the analysis of non-literal meaning more attractive. For instance, there are certain speech acts that it is difficult to distinguish between.

Orders, commands and requests all have the same felicity conditions, for example (Thomas 1995), so that the only differences between these speech acts are contextual rather than linguistic differences (e.g. that one speaker must be in authority over another in order to command). The other major problem with Searle's approach to meaning is that it is rule-based – and language does not lend itself to being tied down by rules (Jeffries 2007a shows how this is the case in an analysis of the speech act of apology). Thomas (1995) provides a very succinct discussion of the differences between rules and principles in pragmatics, and notes that the advantage of Grice's work over Searle's is that it is principle-based rather than rule-governed. Nonetheless, speech act theory retains some usefulness, especially when applied in the stylistic analysis of dialogue (either fictional or non-fictional), since it provides a means of explaining how foregrounding effects can be achieved in interactive talk. For instance, example 20 has a foregrounding effect that is achieved by deviating from the conventional speech act rules for making an offer, which gives rise to a very different illocutionary force. We should be careful, then, not to throw out the baby with the bathwater when criticising Austin's and Searle's work, not least because of its value for stylistic analysis.

4.3   An extended analysis of an extract from a dramatic text

The analytical approaches described in this chapter will be better understood in the context of a full analysis of a text. We have chosen a light-hearted example to discuss, as it is important to emphasise that stylistic frameworks are appropriate for analysing a wide variety of texts – non-fiction and fiction, literary and non-literary. The extract below is taken from the screenplay of the film *Monty Python and the Holy Grail* (Chapman *et al.* 1974):

(21)   [King Arthur and his servant, Patsy, are looking for knights to join his court at Camelot. As he approaches an impressive-looking castle, he stops a peasant to ask him if he knows who lives there.]

1. ARTHUR   Old woman!
2. DENNIS   Man!
3. ARTHUR   Man. Sorry. What knight lives in that castle over there?
4. DENNIS   I'm thirty-seven.
5. ARTHUR   I – what?
6. DENNIS   I'm thirty-seven. I'm not old.
7. ARTHUR   Well, I can't just call you 'Man'.
8. DENNIS   Well, you could say 'Dennis'.
9. ARTHUR   Well, I didn't know you were called 'Dennis'.
10. DENNIS   Well, you didn't bother to find out, did you?
11. ARTHUR   I did say 'sorry' about the 'old woman', but from the behind you looked –
12. DENNIS   What I object to is that you automatically treat me like an inferior!

13. ARTHUR Well, I am King!

14. DENNIS Oh, King, eh, very nice. And how d'you get that, eh? By exploiting the workers! By hanging on to outdated imperialist dogma which perpetuates the economic and social differences in our society. If there's ever going to be any progress with the –

15. WOMAN Dennis, there's some lovely filth down here. Oh! How d'you do?

16. ARTHUR How do you do, good lady? I am Arthur, King of the Britons. Whose castle is that?

17. WOMAN King of the who?

18. ARTHUR The Britons.

19. WOMAN Who are the Britons?

20. ARTHUR Well, we all are. We are all Britons, and I am your king.

21. WOMAN I didn't know we had a king. I thought we were an autonomous collective.

22. DENNIS You're fooling yourself. We're living in a dictatorship: a self-perpetuating autocracy in which the working classes –

23. WOMAN Oh, there you go bringing class into it again.

24. DENNIS That's what it's all about. If only people would hear of –

25. ARTHUR Please! Please, good people. I am in haste. Who lives in that castle?

26. WOMAN No one lives there.

27. ARTHUR Then who is your lord?

28. WOMAN We don't have a lord.

29. ARTHUR What?

30. DENNIS I told you. We're an anarcho-syndicalist commune. We take it in turns to act as a sort of executive officer for the week . . .

31. ARTHUR Yes.

32. DENNIS . . . but all the decisions of that officer have to be ratified at a special bi-weekly meeting . . .

33. ARTHUR Yes, I see.

34. DENNIS . . . by a simple majority in the case of purely internal affairs . . .

35. ARTHUR Be quiet!

36. DENNIS . . . but by a two-thirds majority in the case of more major –

37. ARTHUR Be quiet! I order you to be quiet!

38. WOMAN Order, eh? Who does he think he is? Heh.

39. ARTHUR I am your king!

40. WOMAN Well, I didn't vote for you.

41. ARTHUR You don't vote for kings.

42. WOMAN Well, how did you become King, then?

43. ARTHUR The Lady of the Lake, (*angels sing*) her arm clad in the purest shimmering samite, held aloft Excalibur from the bosom of the water signifying by Divine Providence that I, Arthur, was to carry Excalibur. (*singing stops*) That is why I am your king!

44. DENNIS Listen, strange women lying in ponds distributing swords is no basis for a system of government. Supreme executive power

derives from a mandate from the masses, not from some farcical aquatic ceremony.

45. ARTHUR Be quiet!

46. DENNIS Well, you can't expect to wield supreme executive power just
'cause some watery tart threw a sword at you!

47. ARTHUR Shut up!

48. DENNIS I mean, if I went round saying I was an emperor just because
some moistened bint had lobbed a scimitar at me, they'd put
me away!

49. ARTHUR Shut up, will you? Shut up!

50. DENNIS Ah, now we see the violence inherent in the system.

51. ARTHUR Shut up!

52. DENNIS Oh! Come and see the violence inherent in the system! Help!
Help! I'm being repressed!

53. ARTHUR Bloody peasant!

54. DENNIS Oooooh! Did you hear that! What a give-away.

55. ARTHUR Come on, Patsy.

56. DENNIS Did you see him repressing me, then? That's what I've been
on about . . .

(Chapman *et al.* 1974: 7–11)

We might start by observing that the situation and dialogue presented in the
extract are absurd, especially when we consider our prototypical expectations for
a conversation between a medieval king and his subjects. We would expect, for
example, a high degree of subservience from those whom the king is addressing.
We might expect them to use respectful forms of address when responding to the
king. In terms of conversational structure, we might guess that the institutional
power of the king would result in his linguistic dominance. None of these prototypical expectations are met in the above extract, resulting in foregrounding
effects which we might point to as the linguistic locus of much of the humour in
the text.

If we start with a simple CA consideration of the text, we can note that, of
the three characters, Arthur takes twenty-six turns, Dennis takes twenty and the
woman ten. On the surface, this would seem to bear out our expectation that the
relative power of the king would lead him to dominate the conversation. We might
also note that the fact that the woman takes fewest turns is perhaps representative
of the subservient social role of women in this period. However, once we start to
examine the mechanics of turn-taking, it becomes apparent that such assumptions
will not hold for this text. For example, despite being the king, Arthur speaks
the smallest number of words – an average of just 6.8 words per turn, which
contrasts significantly with Dennis's 14.4. Even the woman speaks an average
of 7.3 words per turn, which, although not a significant difference from Arthur's
figure, is surprising nonetheless for the fact that it is a higher average per turn
than that of the king.

Arthur's failure to establish his authority is further seen in the mechanics of
turn allocation among the characters. Typically, we expect powerful characters

to allocate turns to less powerful characters. Arthur does attempt this by asking six questions of Dennis and the woman, in turns 3, 16, 25, 27, 29 and 49 (albeit a non-genuine tag question). However, none of these questions is answered, and the peasant characters further defy the stereotype by allocating turns to Arthur through their own questions (see turns 10, 14, 15, 17, 19, 38 and 42). Arthur's relative weakness in the face of their conversational assault is made greater by the fact that he does attempt to answer their questions.

In general, it is not the fact that Arthur is not behaving like a king that gives rise to foregrounding effects, but the fact that Dennis and the woman are subverting our expectations for their characters. We see this if we examine the initiation of new topics in the text. Arthur initiates on four occasions (turns 1, 16, 25 and 27) but so too does Dennis (turns 4, 12, 30 and 50) and so too does the woman (turns 15, 19, 21 and 42). Tellingly, the only character to respond to the initiation of another is Arthur (see turns 5, 7, 9, 11, 13, 20, 39, 41 and 43). Clearly, Dennis and the woman are controlling the conversation. We also see this in the fact that Dennis and the woman have no compunction about interrupting Arthur – Dennis in turn 12 and the woman indirectly, as a result of interrupting Dennis in turns 15 and 23. This relatively straightforward analysis of conversation structure already begins to account for why we perceive the behaviour of the characters to be foregrounded.

We can also note a number of instances of dispreferred responses to Arthur's questions. In turn 4, for instance, Dennis gives a dispreferred response ('I'm thirty-seven') to Arthur's question concerning the inhabitant of the distant castle. The same is true of the woman's response in turn 17. This is arguably even more marked than Dennis's response in turn 4, since at this stage in the conversation, the woman is fully aware that she is addressing the king. These turns are thus foregrounded as a result of being conversationally deviant. Our expectations about the kind of encounter dramatised in the extract are also likely to lead us to interpret as deviant the fact that Dennis fails to give the preferred response to Arthur's orders in turns 35, 37, 45 and 47. Arthur even uses a metalinguistic performative in turn 37 ('I order you to be quiet!') but this still fails to establish his authority. Here again we see the adjacency pairs completed, but with dispreferred second parts.

If we now turn to the pragmatic behaviour of the characters, again we see that Dennis and the woman subvert our expectations for this kind of interaction. This is apparent both in terms of their non-observance of the Cooperative Principle and their lack of regard for politeness when addressing Arthur. Arthur, by contrast, makes substantial efforts to take account of Dennis and the woman's negative face wants by mitigating his FTAs. Despite beginning with a bald on-record request ('What knight lives in that castle over there?'), which may be viewed as appropriate given Arthur's level of institutional power, Arthur does attempt to mitigate the damage to Dennis's positive face caused in his first turn by prefacing his request with a conventional apology. Similarly, in turn 16, Arthur prefaces his direct question to the woman with a conventionalised enquiry as to her health, and also uses a respectful address term ('good lady') to enhance her positive face.

In contrast, Dennis and the woman repeatedly violate the maxim of relation in their failure to answer Arthur's questions. This in itself constitutes a threat to Arthur's positive face and may be construed as impolite behaviour conveyed via positive impoliteness. We can also observe Dennis using sarcasm in turn 14 ('Oh, King, eh, very nice.'), which is clearly insincere politeness given what he goes on to say in the rest of the sketch. Nonetheless, Arthur's behaviour towards them remains fairly reasonable. His orders in turns 35 and 37 for Dennis to be quiet are bald on-record as opposed to positively or negatively impolite, and even when he increases the force of his command by using a metalinguistic performative ('I order you to be quiet!') this is not marked by further impolite strategies. Indeed, Arthur has been remarkably restrained so far, even addressing Dennis's positive face needs in 31 and 33 by communicating acceptance of the political points he is making. Dennis and the woman, meanwhile, fail to acknowledge Arthur's face needs. Their lack of concern for these also escalates as the scene progresses. In turn 44, Dennis flouts the maxim of manner when he says 'Listen, strange women lying in ponds distributing swords is no basis for a system of government. Supreme executive power derives from a mandate from the masses, not from some farcical aquatic ceremony.' The implicature created here is that Arthur's power has no democratic validity, and it seems that Dennis's choice of linguistic strategy here is designed to increase the threat to Arthur's positive face via positive impoliteness. In response, Arthur attempts another bald-on-record strategy by saying 'Be quiet!' (turn 45) and 'Shut up!' (turn 47), though the latter command is even mitigated by the application of a question tag ('will you?'). Only towards the very end of the scene does Arthur break type and use a deliberately impolite strategy when he calls Dennis a 'bloody peasant!', the impolite address form constituting a tactic for aggravating the harm to Dennis's positive face needs.

In addition to the various linguistic elements we have pointed out so far, we might also note that the humour of the scene is accentuated through the characters' use of anachronistic vocabulary and political ideas, giving rise to the incongruity necessary for the creation of humour (see, for example, Nash 1985). Nonetheless, an analysis of the dramatic dialogue enables us to identify the sources of fore-grounding in the text, which arguably constitute the ultimate source of the humour in the scene. A stylistic analysis of the dramatic text, then, provides a means of accounting for our initial reactions to the scene and its effect on audiences.

4.4   Summary and conclusions

In this chapter we have outlined key theories and analytical frame-works for use in the analysis of dialogue. In applying these we are able to account for our initial interpretative responses to texts that contain such dia-logue and (re)presented conversation. We have concentrated particularly on the analysis of dramatic texts, though such techniques are equally applicable to conversation in prose fiction and (re)presented conversation in non-literary texts. (In the exercises below we have used a range of different texts to illustrate this.) The analytical frameworks for the stylistic analysis of dialogue enable us to uncover the pragmatic motives of characters, narrators and writers, but in addition, we might also note that the application of such frameworks uncovers the discoursal equivalent of the foregrounding that arises from deviating from linguistic norms (see Chapter 2). In effect, analysing dialogue using the techniques described in this chapter allows us to identify conversational foregrounding, the upshot of which is to enable the identification of areas of the text which may prove likely to be of particular interpretative consequence.

Exercises

Exercise 4.1

Carry out a Gricean analysis of the following short pieces of dialogue, using the Cooperative Principle to explain any implicatures that the speakers may be conveying, and any humorous effects that you notice.

(22)   [Blackadder and George are soldiers fighting in the First World War. George is upper-class and public-school educated, and Blackadder thinks of himself as considerably more shrewd and worldly-wise than George. In this extract, George enters the trench and greets Blackadder.]
GEORGE   Tally-ho, pip pip and Bernard's Your Uncle.
BLACKADDER In English we say 'Good morning'.
                        ('Captain Cook', Curtis *et al.*, 1998: 349)

(23)   [*All the President's Men* is a film about the Watergate Scandal in Washington DC in 1972. The film focuses on the efforts of two journalists to uncover the source of the scandal.]
The TV set. Sloan is walking along toward a large office building, [sic] *he is flanked by a lawyer. A TV Reporter (it was Daniel Schorr) is walking alongside, mike in hand.*
SCHORR   Mr Sloan, would you care to comment on your testimony before the Grand Jury.
SLOAN   My lawyer says –
SLOAN'S LAWYER The answer is an unequivocal no. Mr Sloan did not implicate Mr. Haldeman in that testimony at all.
                        (William Goldman, *All the President's Men*, 1976)

Exercise 4.2

Analyse the following piece of dramatic dialogue from a CA perspective, paying particular attention to adjacency pairs. What does the characters' linguistic behaviour suggest about their relationship?

(24)   [*Dancing at Lughnasa* is set in 1930s Ireland. Christina and Gerry have a son together, though Gerry is an unreliable partner and father and, until this meeting, has not seen Christina for over eighteen months. He has come to say goodbye, as he has decided to travel to Spain to fight in the Civil War against the fascists.]

1. CHRISTINA Where are you heading for?
2. GERRY   You'd like to know?
3. CHRISTINA I would.
He pats the motorbike.
4. GERRY   Want a spin on this boy?
5. CHRISTINA I might.
6. GERRY   Get on.

(McGuinness 1998: 34)

Exercise 4.3

Analyse the politeness and impoliteness in the following piece of dialogue. What strategies do the characters employ and for what purpose? What does this tell you about the characters and the relationship between them? (It may help you to interpret the effects of the dialogue if you consider the alternative linguistic choices that the writer could have made.)

(25)   [Tam, Richie and their English supervisor (the first-person narrator of the novel) are driving from Scotland to England to erect a high-tensile fence, part of a contract they have from an English farm. Tam has just thrown an empty cigarette packet out of the van window.]

I said, 'You shouldn't drop litter, you know.'
'Why not?' said Tam.
'Well,' I replied, 'You know. It looks bad, doesn't it? Spoils the countryside and everything.'
'That's a load of shite and you know it,' he said.
'No it isn't,' I said. 'You can't just go chucking rubbish all over the place.'
'You can if you want,' said Tam. 'All this stuff about litter is just English pathetic . . . ' He trailed off, and then started again. 'This is Scotland. You're in Scotland and these mountains have been here millions of years. It doesn't make any difference, a few fag packets for fuck sake. That's just English fucking pathetic shite.'
'He's right,' said Richie.
'Yeah . . . I suppose so,' I said.
I couldn't see any mountains.

(Mills 1998: 51)

Exercise 4.4

Choose a dramatic text (a play or a screenplay) and identify a research question pertaining to the linguistic behaviour of one of the characters. How would you go about answering your research question? For example, how would you choose a representative section of the text to analyse? Would this be sufficient for your analysis? What analytical frameworks would you need to use? How objective would your analysis be, and how replicable?

Further reading

For an application of conversation-analytic and sociolinguistic approaches to the stylistic analysis of dialogue see Burton (1980), Short (1981) and Mandala (2007). Jenny Thomas's *Meaning in Interaction* (1995) provides an excellent introduction to key aspects of pragmatics, while such approaches are used in the analysis of drama by Bennison (1993), Cooper (1998), Culpeper (1998) and Bousfield (2007b), and in the analysis of prose fiction by Short (1995). Culpeper and McIntyre (2010) demonstrate a holistic approach to the analysis of drama by integrating a number of different analytical frameworks using activity type theory. Grice (1975) is the classic article on the Cooperative Principle and implicature. Austin (1962) outlines his notion of performatives and speech acts in a very readable collection of lectures, while Searle (1969, 1979) extends and develops speech act theory in considerable detail. Jeffries (2007a) and Short (2007) provide applications of speech act theory in non-literary and literary contexts respectively. Brown and Levinson (1987) is the standard work on politeness, while Culpeper (1996, 2005) demonstrates a face-management model of impoliteness. Bousfield (2007a) tests this model and provides a thorough overview of other work in this area. Levinson's *Pragmatics* (1983) is a higher-level textbook covering many of the pragmatic issues raised in this chapter and is highly recommended.

5 Text and cognition I

Text comprehension

5.1 Cognitive stylistics

In this chapter and in Chapter 6 we focus on an area of stylistics in which interest has grown considerably over the last decade or so. This is an area which has come to be known generally as **cognitive stylistics** ('cognitive poetics' is another term currently in use, though there is arguably no significant difference between what the two terms signify). Cognitive stylistics focuses primarily on hypothesising about what happens during the reading process and how this influences the interpretations that readers generate about the texts they are reading. It proceeds on the assumption that reading is an active process and that readers consequently play an active role in constructing the meaning of texts. Cognitive stylistics has drawn considerable influence from work in areas such as cognitive science generally, psychology, computing and artificial intelligence. Although Stockwell (2002a: 1) claims that cognitive stylistics (he calls it cognitive poetics) 'is all about reading literature', there is in principle no reason why cognitive stylistics should not also deal with non-literary texts (the arguments for why stylistics generally is appropriate for the analysis of both fiction and non-fiction writing can be found in Chapter 1).

In recent years, the theories and analytical frameworks of cognitive stylistics have been outlined in a number of key texts (see Tsur 1992, Semino and Culpeper 2002, Stockwell 2002a and Gavins and Steen 2003), though the roots of such work may be traced back much further. Gavins and Steen (2003: 41) cite Tsur's research in the 1970s as being an important precursor to current work in the area, while West (2007) notes that the work of I. A. Richards in the 1930s may be seen as protocognitive in orientation. In fact, any evaluative stylistic analysis (cf. purely descriptive stylistics; see Leech 2008 on this distinction) will always necessitate some consideration of the reading process, and most stylisticians would claim that they have always tried to take account of this. We might, then, see cognitive stylistics as an effort to systematise the way in which this aspect of stylistic analysis should be taken into account.

We will focus in this chapter on the cognitive processes by which readers respond to particular aspects of texts, and the real-life schematic knowledge that they bring to bear in interpreting them. In so doing we will begin with a discussion of **schema theory**, a theoretical consideration of how we package world knowledge and use this in the interpretation of texts. We will then consider the cognitive concept of **figure and ground** and how prior knowledge drives our recognition of spatial foregrounding, before going on to discuss **cognitive metaphor theory**, a theoretical exposition of how we use schematic knowledge to structure our view of key concepts in our lives. With this groundwork in place, we will go on in Chapter 6 to focus on cognitive theories designed to explain how readers monitor their progression through a text as they read.

5.2   Schema theory

Cognitive stylistics is predicated on the notion that readers are actively involved in the process of meaning-making. Meaning is not located solely in the formal structures of the text but is, in a sense, negotiated as a result of readers utilising aspects of their pre-existing background knowledge of the real world as they read. In a discussion of how readers make sense of the fictional worlds of poems, Semino (1997: 125) makes a useful distinction between what she terms **projection** and **construction**. Although her discussion is centred primarily around explaining how readers generate images of fictional worlds, Semino's terms are useful more generally for explaining the way in which readers make sense of what they read. Texts *project* meaning while readers *construct* it. That is, texts contain triggers which activate aspects of readers' background knowledge. This then allows readers to construct mental representations of the world of the text.

A useful and related notion is the psychological distinction between **bottom-up processing** and **top-down processing**. Used in relation to text comprehension, the former refers to the practice of inferring meaning from textual cues while the latter term describes the practice of utilising background knowledge to aid understanding. Bottom-up processing maps onto the notion of projection, since both refer to the means by which meaning is drawn from a text by the reader. Top-down processing maps onto the notion of construction, since both of these terms refer to readers utilising pre-existing world knowledge to make sense of what they read. In practice, reading a text involves engaging in both bottom-up and top-down processing simultaneously. What we will concentrate on in this section is what it means to invoke pre-existing knowledge in the interpretation of texts. In this respect, we will explain some of the theoretical notions concerning how readers are able to store prior knowledge and access it as they read. The various suggestions for how this might work may be taken together as constituting what is often referred to as **schema theory**.

5.2.1   Schemas, scripts and frames

The term **schema** refers to an element of background knowledge about a particular aspect of the world. We have schemas for people, objects, situations and events. As an example, most people will have a JOB INTERVIEW schema which they will use to help them navigate their way through such a situation. This schema may include such information as how the interview room is likely to be set out, how many people are likely to be on the interview panel, what is expected of the candidate, etc. Schemas (or *schemata* to use the Latinate plural) also encompass linguistic behaviour. For instance, anyone with a well-developed JOB INTERVIEW schema will be aware that it is common practice in such a situation for interviewees to violate the Gricean maxim of quantity (Grice 1975; see section 4.2.2) as they attempt to provide as much information about themselves as is possible (Culpeper and McIntyre 2010 provide a full discussion of what the linguistic contents of a JOB INTERVIEW schema might be, and how particular stylistic effects might be generated by deviating from this).

At this point we should make it clear that while *schema* is a general term for an element of background knowledge, some writers prefer alternative terms in order to flag up the varied nature of schemas. Minsky (1975), for example, uses the term **frame** to describe knowledge related to visual perception (e.g. background knowledge about different kinds of buildings). Schank and Abelson (1977) introduce the term **script**, explaining that scripts are composed of schematic information about complex sequences of events. These have various **slots** which will be filled by different elements according to the particular script. So, there may be slots for props (desks, chairs, etc), roles (interviewer, interviewee), scenes (entering, greeting the interviewer), entry conditions (having applied for the job) and results (being offered the job, being turned down for the job). Scripts can also have different **tracks**, each of which may have different slots. For example, a person's JOB INTERVIEW schema may include a 'Saturday job' track, an 'academic job' track and a 'corporate management job' track, and each of these will vary in respect of their constituent slots. For instance, in the props slot for a 'corporate management job' track, we are likely to expect the clothing of the interviewee to be very formal (a suit, perhaps). The equivalent slot for the 'academic job' track may be filled with a different expectation – perhaps that the interviewee may be dressed much more informally. With regard to the scenes slot, we might expect a restricted number for a 'Saturday job' track, while the 'corporate management job' track may well include many more – for example, an assessment centre scene, a team-building scene, a social event scene, etc. It is worth being aware of this varied terminology; we will use *schema* as an overarching term and *frame* and *script* where appropriate.

It should be clear from our discussion so far that schemas are distilled from past experiences. Nevertheless, we do not have to have experienced something directly in order to build a schematic conception of it. For example, it is likely that most people have a script for a murder investigation, though only a few people will have constructed this schema from direct experience. For the majority of people, such a script will have been composed from watching television police dramas and reading crime novels. It follows too that schemas are not static. Rather they are dynamic, in the sense that they develop as a result of experience. For example, a football supporter's FOOTBALL TEAM schema may be developed if the team in question acquires a new player. This kind of schema development is referred to by Rumelhart (1980) as **accretion**; that is, the new information extends the schema but requires no fundamental change to it. **Tuning**, on the other hand, refers to the modification of an existing schema to take account of new experiences. For example, floppy disks have now been supplanted by hard drives as the primary means of storing electronic data, and this development will have involved a modification to the WORD-PROCESSING schema of anyone familiar with the old way of saving documents. Finally, **restructuring** refers to the generation of new schemas. New schemas may be based on pre-existing ones (a person new to flying might generate an AIRPORT schema out of a BUS STATION schema) or may, theoretically, be induced solely through experience, though this latter type of schema creation is arguably much rarer.

5.2.2   Triggering schemas

Knowing that we bring our schematic knowledge to bear when we read texts, the next issue to consider is how schemas are triggered. Schank and Abelson (1977: 49–50) propose that scripts are triggered by **headers** – that is, textual cues that relate to elements of the script in question – and that at least two headers are required to instantiate a schema. Headers come in the following four types:

1. **Precondition headers** refer to a necessary precondition for the application of the script in question. For example, 'Dan was feeling ill' may work as the precondition for the triggering of a DOCTOR/PATIENT INTERVIEW script.
2. **Instrumental headers** refer to actions that may lead to the invocation of a particular script. 'Dan entered the doctor's surgery' may be instrumental in triggering the DOCTOR/PATIENT INTERVIEW script.
3. **Locale headers** are references to locations where the script in question is likely to be activated. 'The doctor's surgery was a cold and forbidding place' provides a locale wherein we might expect the DOCTOR/PATIENT INTERVIEW script to be instantiated.
4. **Internal conceptualisation headers** are references to actions or roles from the script. 'The doctor asked Dan how he was feeling' includes reference to both a role ('the doctor') and an action (asking how the patient feels), both of which are likely to instantiate the script in question.

One issue with schema theory as we have outlined it so far concerns our capacity for confusing elements of our various schemas. For instance, a child who accidentally calls her school teacher 'mummy' is clearly mixing up her TEACHER and PARENT schemas. If schemas are discrete, as we have so far suggested, why should such slip-ups occur? Schank (1982) proposes an explanation for such occurrences by postulating the existence of what he calls **memory organisation packets** or **MOPs**. He begins with the suggestion that specific schemas have a subordinate relationship to more general schemas. So, for instance, a DOCTOR/PATIENT INTERVIEW script will be embedded within a higher-level INTERVIEW schema. Schank refers to this superordinate schema as a **scene**. He then proposes that MOPs act as organising structures for particular groups of scenes, all of which are oriented towards the achievement of some particular goal. For example, experiential knowledge concerning going to an academic conference is encapsulated in a CONFERENCE MOP (M-CONFERENCE). Such a MOP might incorporate the following scenes: PLAN + SUBMIT ABSTRACT + BOOK ACCOMMODATION + PAY REGISTRATION FEE + TRAVEL TO CONFERENCE + CHECK IN + REGISTER + PRESENT PAPER, etc. What is significant about MOPs is that some of their constituent scenes may be shared by other MOPs. So, the REGISTER scene that is a part of M-CONFERENCE may also be found in M-MARATHON RACE, M-DANCE COMPETITION, M-CONVENTION, and others. Returning now to the example of the school pupil mistaking her teacher for her mother, one potential reason for this might be that the activity in which the child is engaged when she makes the mistake is a scene that is a constituent part both of a MOP that is appropriate to school and one that is appropriate to home – say, READING A BOOK. In school, this scene may be part of M-LESSON, while at home it may be part of M-GOING TO BED. If, within M-GOING TO BED, the child's schematic knowledge postulates a mother in the role slot for the READING A BOOK scene, it is perfectly likely that this role slot may be activated within the READING A BOOK scene in M-LESSON, thereby causing confusion (and probably embarrassment) for the child.

In addition to MOPs, Schank also proposes the notion of **TOPs**, or **thematic organisation points**. TOPs can begin to explain why it is that we see similarities between different events or experiences. For instance, some viewers may discern a similarity between the Francis Ford Coppola film *Apocalypse Now* and the Joseph Conrad novel *Heart of Darkness*. The concept of MOPs cannot explain this, whereas the notion of a TOP can. A TOP, according to Schank, is an impermanent memory structure that arises during processing. The reason for seeing similarities between *Apocalypse Now* and *Heart of Darkness* is that both share goals (exploration), conditions (brutality, imperial adventure) and features (exploitation of another culture, madness) that taken together constitute a TOP.

5.2.3   Applying schema theory in stylistic analysis

So far we have considered schema theory as a means of explaining the ways in which readers' background knowledge is triggered for use in the interpretation of texts. Schema theory has considerable explanatory power beyond this, however. Consider, for instance, the following extract from Umberto Eco's novel *The Name of the Rose*:

(1)   [*The Name of the Rose* is set in Italy in the Middle Ages. Adso, the narrator, is a novice monk and scribe to Brother William of Baskerville.]

William slipped his hands inside his habit, at the point where it billowed over his chest to make a kind of sack, and he drew from it an object that I had already seen in his hands, and on his face in the course of our journey. It was a forked pin, so constructed that it could stay on a man's nose (or at least on his, so prominent and aquiline) as a rider remains astride his horse or as a bird clings to its perch. And, one on either side of the fork, before the eyes, there were two ovals of metal, which held two almonds of glass, thick as the bottom of a tumbler. William preferred to read with these before his eyes, and he said they made his vision better than what nature had endowed him with or than his advanced age, especially as the daylight failed, would permit. They did not serve him to see from a distance, for then his eyes were, on the contrary, quite sharp, but to see close up. With these lenses he could read manuscripts penned in very faint letters, which even I had some trouble deciphering. He explained to me that, when a man had passed the middle point of his life, even if his sight had always been excellent, the eye hardened and the pupil became recalcitrant, so that many learned men had virtually died, as far as reading and writing were concerned, after their fiftieth summer.   (Eco 1980: 74)

What becomes apparent as we read extract 1 is that Adso has limited frame knowledge about what we would call 'glasses' or 'spectacles'. He does not know a word to describe them and is therefore forced to describe their appearance and purpose. In effect, Adso is what Fowler (1986) describes as 'underlexicalised'. This leads to a fairly long-winded description, in which the precondition header 'William preferred to read with these before his eyes' might be said to fully invoke our frame knowledge of the object Adso describes. What this also suggests is that Adso's implied addressee is not a reader such as ourselves. Adso's supposition is clearly that his addressee will not have frame knowledge of what he describes, hence the necessity of his extended description. One of the effects of this is to distance the reader of the novel from the character of Adso, since there is a substantial difference in the amount and type of schematic knowledge that Adso has.

Schemas may also be manipulated to create foregrounding effects, which in turn can lead to incongruity and absurdity, as in the following example:

(2)   *Cut to Mr Glans who is sitting next to a fully practical old 8mm home projector. There is a knock at the door. He switches the projector off and hides it furtively. He is sitting in an office, with a placard saying 'Exchange and Mart, Editor' on his desk. He points to it rather obviously.*

      1. GLANS   Hello, come in. *(enter Bee, a young aspirant job hunter)* Ah, hello, hello, how much do you want for that briefcase?

      2. BEE   Well, I . . .

3. GLANS   All right then, the briefcase and the umbrella. A fiver down, must be my final offer.

4. BEE   Well, I don't want to sell them. I've come for a job.

5. GLANS   Oh, take a seat, take a seat.

6. BEE   Thank you.

7. GLANS   I see you chose the canvas chair with the aluminium frame. I'll throw that in and a fiver, for the briefcase and the umbrella . . . no, make it fair, the briefcase and the umbrella and the two pens in your breast pocket and the chair's yours and a fiver and a pair of ex-German U-boat commando's binoculars.

8. BEE   Really, they are not for sale.

9. GLANS   Not for sale, what does that mean?

10. BEE   I came about the advertisement for the job of assistant editor.

11. GLANS   Oh yeah, right. Ah, OK, ah. How much experience in journalism?

12. BEE   Five years.

13. GLANS   Right, typing speed?

14. BEE   Fifty.

15. GLANS   O-levels?

16. BEE   Eight.

17. GLANS   A-levels?

18. BEE   Two.

19. GLANS   Right . . . Well, I'll give you the job, and the chair, and an all-wool ex-army sleeping bag . . . for the briefcase, umbrella, the pens in your breast pocket and your string vest.

20. BEE   When do I start?

21. GLANS   Monday.

22. BEE   That's marvellous.

23. GLANS   If you throw in the shoes as well.

(Chapman *et al.* 1990: 2)

The initial stage directions in this extract contain both a locale header ('He is sitting in an office, with a placard saying "Exchange and Mart, Editor" on his desk. He points to it rather obviously.') and an instrumental header ('enter Bee, a young aspirant job hunter') which are likely to trigger for the reader a JOB INTERVIEW script. What follows, though, deviates from this schema considerably. The content of Glans's turns is more appropriate for a SELLING schema, until turns 11 to 19, where Glans appears to be behaving as we would expect according to our JOB INTERVIEW script. However, Glans then deviates again, generating further absurdity. The incongruity that arises in this extract comes about because we cannot reconcile the linguistic behaviour of Glans with the JOB INTERVIEW script that is triggered at various points throughout the sketch.

Examples 1 and 2 show how schema theory might be used to account for particular stylistic effects in texts, though schema theory has also been used more generally to discuss the notion of literariness. Cook (1994), for example, has argued that literary texts are distinguished from non-literary texts by their capacity to induce **schema refreshment**. Cook's argument is that literary texts are 'representative of a type of text which may perform the important function of breaking down existing schemas, recognizing them, and building new ones' (Cook 1994: 10). In this sense, we may view certain texts as literary because they cause restructuring or tuning of existing schemas, such that we see the world differently as a result. This, clearly, is a cognitive variant of the theories of defamiliarisation which were discussed in Chapter 2 and demonstrate that a strong tradition of believing in the separateness of literature as a text-type has outlasted the move from formal stylistic to more contextualised and in this case cognitively-informed practice.

Semino (1997) draws on Cook's work to produce an 'approach to text analysis that combines linguistic description with schema theory in order to account for how readers imagine (different types of) text worlds in reading texts' (Semino 2001: 345). Whilst Semino explicitly distances herself from Cook's use of schema refreshment as the defining feature of literary texts, she accepts the usefulness of the distinction Cook makes between schema refreshment and reinforcement.[1] Jeffries (2001) takes issue with Cook's proposal that literary texts are primarily distinguished from other texts by their schema-refreshing function, and argues that they may also cause **schema affirmation**; that is, we find literary texts satisfying because they reinforce our world view by reflecting our schematic knowledge. This 'thrill of recognition' (Jeffries 2001: 340) is significant in many cases, she argues, because individual readers may have a set of schemas resulting from their particular identity (as a woman, as a black person, as a lesbian, as a victim of crime and so on) and some of these schemas may be limited to the particular groups that s/he is a member of. Such 'suppressed meanings' (Jeffries 2001: 340) may be made explicit in literary or other texts and produce a strong reaction in a reader. Like schema refreshment, these may be quite significant for the reader, but they will not necessarily result in cognitive changes as a result. This concept of schema affirmation, Jeffries argues, applies also to non-literary texts such as propaganda and advertising; hence, the notion is unsuitable as a defining characteristic of literature.

Schema theory, then, provides a useful theoretical base both for understanding text-types and for identifying the local effects that are generated in particular texts. A broad appreciation of the notion of schemas is also useful for understanding a number of other cognitive stylistic approaches, as we shall explain in sections 5.3 and 5.4.

5.3   Figure and ground

In Chapter 2 we explained the importance of foregrounding theory for stylistics, outlining how foregrounding effects are achieved through deviation and/or parallelism at one or more linguistic levels. The psychological reality of foregrounding has been demonstrated in empirical tests (see van Peer 1980, 1986, 2007), the results of which suggest that readers do indeed attach more

Figure 5.1 *Rubin's face/vase illusion*

interpretative significance to foregrounded elements of texts. The concept of **figure and ground** adds a further cognitive dimension to the notion of foregrounding by providing an explanation of why we are attracted to deviant and parallel structures.

Notions of figure and ground have their origins in the work of the Gestalt psychologists of the early 1900s, and particularly in the work of Rubin (1915). Rubin proposed that our visual field is organised in such a way that we make a distinction between figures and backgrounds, and that we are able to distinguish the contours of separate objects when there is a strong contrast between their respective colours and degrees of brightness. For example, a particularly bright object will stand out against a dull background and will consequently be perceived as figural and therefore prominent. Rubin's famous illustration of figure and ground is the face/vase illusion, reproduced in figure 5.1.

When we look at the picture, we either see two black faces in profile or a white vase-like object. The point here is that we can only see *one* of these images at any one time; we cannot see both the vase *and* the faces simultaneously. The explanation for this is that the object we choose to concentrate on (the **figure**) seems to us to have special properties. For example, if we choose to concentrate on the faces then they appear to the viewer to have form and structure, whereas the white **ground** seems formless and unstructured. Alternatively, if we concentrate on the white space then that appears to have contours that allow us to discern the figure as a vase. The figure appears to be in front of the ground and we therefore perceive it as being more prominent. Research also suggests that we attach more importance to figures, that they are memorable and that they are likely 'to be associated with meaning, feeling and aesthetic values' (Ungerer and Schmid 1996: 157).

5.3.1   Image schemas

It is relatively easy to see how the concept of figure and ground as employed in the visual arts may be extended by analogy to language, and how, in so doing, the notion of a figure equates to the linguistically foregrounded elements of texts. It is also the case that textual figures may be dynamic; that is, they may be imbued with a sense of movement. This is explained by the cognitive notion of an **image schema**.

Stockwell (2002a: 15) makes the point that in prose fiction, characters are figures against the ground of the story's setting. He explains that we can view them as being figures 'because they move across the ground, either spatially or temporally as the novel progresses, or qualitatively as they evolve and collect traits from their apparent psychological development' (Stockwell 2002b: 16). Within a fictional world, of course, it is not just characters who constitute figures, but other objects too. Stockwell goes on to explain how movement is prototypically represented in the verb phrase, through verbs of motion, and/or by locative expressions of space and time, realised through prepositional phrases – for example, 'over there', under the table', etc. Key to our understanding of movement in texts are image schemas, defined by Ungerer and Schmid as 'simple and basic cognitive structures which are derived from our everyday interaction with the world' (1996: 160). Essentially what this means is that as a result of repeated experiences of certain concepts, we form a schema for these in the same way that we have schemas for people, places, objects and situations (see section 5.2). So, with regard to movement, one of the image schemas we have is of the locative expression OVER/UNDER. This arises out of our repeated encounters with objects moving over other objects. (There are other image schemas of movement, of course. Stockwell 2002b: 16 lists some of these as JOURNEY, CONDUIT, UP/DOWN, FRONT/BACK and INTO/OUT OF.) In this image schema the *figure* is referred to as a **trajector**, and the *ground* that it is moving over is called the **landmark**. And as a trajector moves over a landmark, it follows a **path**. Consider the following extract from Milner Place's poem 'Favela':

(3)   The sun hammers the corrugated iron,
         cracks the thin boards; but over the sea
         the clouds push their black hearts closer
                       (Place 1995)

Here, the clouds are the trajector following a path above the sea, which constitutes the landmark. All OVER/UNDER image schemas make use of this basic conceptual structure.

5.3.2   Figure and ground in stylistic analysis

Having established an understanding of the concepts of figure and ground and image schemas, we might now examine how these concepts can be employed to help us understand and interpret longer texts. To do this, we will consider how the concept of figure and ground is useful in explaining the mechanism by which a reader might make sense of the following poem by Edward Thomas:

(4)   *Tall Nettles*

         Tall nettles cover up, as they have done
         These many springs, the rusty harrow, the plough

> Long worn out, and the roller made of stone:
> Only the elm butt tops the nettles now.
>
> This corner of the farmyard I like most:
> As well as any bloom upon a flower
> I like the dust on the nettles, never lost
> Except to prove the sweetness of a shower.
>
> (Edward Thomas)

In this poem the speaker describes his[2] favourite spot in a farmyard, evoking a nostalgic image of a place neglected and overgrown with nettles. As we read, we are likely to picture the scene being described and we are likely to see it in a particular way. For example, it is probable that we will picture the nettles as being in the foreground of the scene. We might picture the harrow, the plough and the roller to be behind the nettles, only barely visible. Why is it that we are likely to 'see' the scene in this way? Obviously, this is in part to do with the propositional content of the phrasal verb 'cover up', but the concept of figure and ground can also help us to explain why it is that we imagine the scene in the way that we do.

In terms of figure and ground, the nettles can be seen as the figure in the poem for a variety of reasons. The noun phrase 'tall nettles' is foregrounded as it is the title of the poem. It is also the grammatical subject of the first sentence. We therefore read this noun phrase twice as we begin reading the poem, and because it is unusual to have the same noun phrase repeated in immediate succession, it is likely to attract our attention, causing the object to which it refers to be perceived as figural. The items that the nettles cover up, the rusty harrow, the worn out plough and the stone roller, are in the object position in the sentence, and are preceded by an adverbial that further distances them from the subject of the sentence. This grammatical structure corresponds with the propositional content of the phrasal verb 'cover up' and helps to evoke an image of the nettles being in front of the farm implements. As a result, we are likely to picture the nettles as being in the foreground of the scene. In effect, the 'tall nettles' constitute a trajector moving over several landmarks – the rusty harrow, the worn out plough and the stone roller. The way that we 'see' the scene is governed by the OVER image schema that we have.

Figures and grounds, though, are not necessarily fixed across the course of a whole text. Instead, as we read, other elements of a text are likely to catch our interest and shift our attention. In the case of this poem, other trajectors appear and follow paths across other landmarks. In the fourth line of the first stanza, we are likely to shift our attention on to the image of the elm butt. This is a new grammatical subject, and likely to attract our attention because it is a new element of the scene. 'Newness' plays a major part in making something figural in a text. Additionally, phonological parallelism help to foreground the image of the elm butt. The adverb 'only' and the noun 'elm' both contain lateral and nasal sounds. Parallel structures like this set up a relationship of either opposition or equivalence. In this case it would appear to be a relationship of equivalence, and this foregrounds the relationship between the two words and emphasises the fact that the elm butt is the only object not entirely covered by the nettles. This is contrasted with the alliterative relationship between the object noun 'nettles' and the adverb 'now', both of which begin with the nasal consonant /n/. Again we can see a relationship of equivalence between 'nettles' and 'now'. However, there is a wider parallel structure at work within this clause, at both the level of phonology *and* grammar. Both the subject and the object of the clause are phonologically parallel with their related adverbials. Also, we can note that before the predicator there is an adverbial ('only') followed by a noun phrase ('elm butt'), and after the predicate this structure is reversed as we encounter a noun phrase ('the nettles') followed by an adverbial ('now'). This parallelism sets up a relationship of opposition between the subject and the object of the clause, which we might see as a figure/ground relationship. This throws into relief the image of the elm butt and focuses our attention away from the nettles and on to this object, thus changing the figure in the poem.

In the second stanza, the syntactic deviation that arises as a result of the grammatical object being placed first in the clause works to foreground the image of 'this corner of the farmyard'. One way of imagining the scene that is conjured up by the poem is to think of it in filmic terms. Up until this point it seems that we have had a shot of the tall nettles, followed by a shot of the elm butt. We now pull out from a close-up of the elm butt to a wider view of the corner of the farmyard as a whole, almost as if a camera were pulling back on the scene being shot. 'This corner of the farmyard' thus replaces the 'elm butt' as the figure, and the image of the elm butt is backgrounded, along with the image of the tall nettles.

As we continue to read, the figure changes again. This time our attention is focused on 'the dust on the nettles'. The fronting of the adverbial 'As well as any bloom upon a flower' causes us to pay particular attention to the clause 'I like the dust on the nettles' (notice that this is because we would expect this clause, prototypically, to come *before* the adverbial). Within this clause, we can also notice that a figure/ground relationship emerges between the image of the dust and the image of the nettle. This can be explained by the locative prepositional phrase which suggests that the nettle forms the ground on which the dust settles. Consequently we see the dust as the figure. The dust, then, is the trajector here and the nettle becomes the landmark onto which the trajector moves. If we return to the film camera metaphor, it would appear that what we experience at this point in the poem is another close-up shot, this time of the nettle leaves.

The figure/ground distinction is a useful addition to basic foregrounding theory as it allows us to explain more clearly how we as readers shift our attention between various parts of a text as we read. It also helps to address the common criticism that stylistics is too concerned with formal features of language and does not take into account what real readers do when they interpret texts. We will continue in this vein in the next section, where we shall examine cognitive approaches to the analysis of metaphor. This move from examining figure and ground to looking at metaphor is especially pertinent, given Stockwell's (2002a: 105) point that much of the language we use when discussing figure and ground is itself metaphorical. The underlying patterns of thought behind such terminology should become clearer once we have discussed the way in which we as readers process figurative language.

5.4   Cognitive metaphor theory

One of the most influential aspects of cognitive stylistics has been **cognitive metaphor theory**, developed initially by Lakoff, Johnson and Turner (see Lakoff and Johnson 1980, Turner 1987, and Lakoff and Turner 1989) and subsequently developed by, amongst others, Semino *et al.* (2004), Crisp (2002), Steen (2007) and Semino (2008). Cognitive metaphor theory proceeds on the basis that metaphor is not limited to literary texts but is a pervasive phenomenon in all text-types. Furthermore, it asserts that metaphor is not merely a feature of language but a matter of thought which is central to our conceptual system and the way in which we make sense of ourselves and the world we live in.

A basic definition of metaphor is that it is the practice of talking about one thing as if it were another, on the grounds that there are some notional similarities between the two entities. The following simple example from a Tony Harrison poem illustrates clearly a prototypical metaphor:

(5)   Death's a debt that everybody owes
                    (Harrison 1975)

Using the terms of traditional rhetoric, 'death' is the **tenor** of the metaphor (i.e. that which is being discussed), whereas 'a debt' is the **vehicle** (what Leech (1969: 151) calls the 'purported definition'). Clearly the meaning that is being conveyed here is that death has some of the qualities we associate with debts – perhaps in the sense of being unwished for, being something inescapable or something to be feared. These are what traditional rhetoric would refer to as the **grounds** for comparison. Leech (1969: 156) describes metaphor as 'covert comparison', contrasting this with the overt comparison of simile, where the comparison between the two entities is made explicit, as in the example below:

(6)   As mute as monks, tidy as bachelors,
            They manicure their little plots of earth
                        ('Men on Allotments',
                            Fanthorpe 1978)

However, the traditional distinction between metaphor and simile is one that only exists in formal grammatical terms. Both figures of speech (to use the generic term from rhetoric) involve the comparison of two separate entities; fundamentally, they achieve their effects via the same conceptual process. From this it becomes clear that a traditional rhetorical approach to metaphor is limited to providing descriptive categories for different types of metaphor. Such an approach offers no insight into the cognitive basis of metaphors, nor the means by which we process and make sense of them. For this we must turn to cognitive metaphor theory.

The pervasiveness of metaphor in all discourse types has been one of the major findings of cognitive metaphor theory. In addition, we have noted that cognitive metaphor theory makes the point that metaphor is not just a matter of language but a matter of thought. To see more clearly what is meant by this, consider the following conventional metaphors:

(7)   I feel as if I'm going nowhere.

(8)   You'll get there, I promise you!

(9)   He overcame a lot of hurdles to gain his degree.

Cognitive metaphor theorists would note that all these sentences are different linguistic instantiations of the same underlying metaphor. Each sentence describes life as if it were a journey that we make. In cognitive metaphor theory this underlying metaphor is called a **conceptual metaphor**. Conventionally, conceptual metaphors are written in small capitals, as in LIFE IS A JOURNEY. All conceptual metaphors consist of a **target domain** (that which is being discussed; equivalent to the tenor in traditional approaches) and a **source domain** (the 'source' of the metaphor; similar to the vehicle). In the above example, LIFE is the target domain and JOURNEY is the source domain. When we interpret conceptual metaphors we map concepts from the source domain onto the target domain. For example, when we use the conceptual metaphor LIFE IS A JOURNEY, one of the mappings that we make between the source domain and the target domain is to think of the person living the life as a traveller. For instance, we might say 'I feel as if I'm going nowhere!', or 'He's getting ahead of himself.' Other mappings (along with corresponding examples) are:

(10)   Purposes are destinations (e.g. 'You'll get there, I promise you.')

(11)   Difficulties are obstacles on the journey (e.g. 'She overcame a lot of hurdles to gain her degree.')

What should be apparent from these examples is that conceptual metaphors are cognitive structures that underpin our metaphorical use of language. Since cognitive metaphor theory makes clear the connection between language and thought, it has the capacity to be a useful analytical tool for cognitive stylisticians, not least because of its explanatory as well as descriptive capability. For example, applying cognitive metaphor theory can show up ideologies that underlie the surface form of the text. This will be apparent in the following example:

(12)   Mr Blair was attacked by the Liberal Democrats for 'hypocrisy'
                                (BBC News 5 July 2002)

Clearly, the notion of Mr Blair being attacked is not meant to be interpreted literally. Instead, 'attacking' is a conventional metaphorical way of describing the action of criticising someone. Consider a couple of similar examples:

(13)   Commons leader Robin Cook has come under fire from John Prescott for attempting to use politicians' families to score political points.
                                                                    (BBC News 5 July 2002)

(14)   Leaping to Mr Blair's defence, Mr Prescott said he 'deplored' members of the media or other politicians who brought family members into politics in this way.   (BBC News 5 July 2002)

There is a similarity to examples 12 to 14 because they all share the same underlying (and common) conceptual metaphor: ARGUMENT IS WAR. In this conceptual metaphor, concepts from the source domain of WAR are being mapped on to the target domain of ARGUMENT. Being criticised is likened to being shot at ('coming under fire') and supporting someone's argument is likened to physically defending them ('leaping to Mr Blair's defence'). When we talk about arguments and arguing we use the same kind of language as when we talk about war and fighting. The conceptual metaphor ARGUMENT IS WAR is deeply entrenched in (at least) Western society and the implications of using this metaphor are significant. Cognitive metaphor theorists have begun to see these patterns as evidence that, far from being inactive, these conventional metaphorical ways of talking about particular activities and practices suggest that we conventionally think about these things in particular ways. With regard to ARGUMENT IS WAR, Lakoff and Johnson (1980: 4) explain that 'Many of the things we do in arguing are partially structured by the concept of war.' We can therefore begin to see how the way we use language reveals a lot about how we conceptualise the world around us. When we use the metaphor of war to refer to arguments what we're really doing is showing how much we think about arguing as being like war. Fairclough (1992: 195) makes the same point when he claims that 'the militarization of discourse is also a militarization of thought and practice'. This is a disturbing concept, and perhaps the very fact that we have these underlying conceptual ideas about how the world works begins to explain why concepts like diplomacy and international relations are so very difficult to manage (see Goatly 2007 for an extended discussion of the capacity of metaphor to shape ideology).

5.4.1   Novel conceptual metaphors

Cognitive metaphor theory, then, provides a means of describing and explaining the prevalence of conventional linguistic metaphors in all discourse types. However, it does not ignore the more obvious kinds of metaphor typically found in literary language. The new and unusual metaphors that we often find in poetry may be explained using the same principle as cognitive metaphor theory uses to explain conventional linguistic metaphors. Underlying all unusual linguistic metaphors will be a **novel conceptual metaphor**. Again, though, novel metaphors are not restricted to literary language, and as with the examples of conventional metaphors that we have examined, using a novel conceptual metaphor reveals something of the way in which the user conceptualises the world. Consider the following example from a newspaper article reporting Air Marshal Brian Burridge's experience of fighting in the Gulf War of 2003/4:

(15)   During the cold war, he knew where he would be fighting, the weather, the name of his enemy. He compared his job then to 'the second violin of the London Symphony Orchestra. You had a sheet of music with clear notation'. Now, he said, 'it's jazz, improvising.'   (*The Guardian* 11 March 2003)

In example 15 concepts are mapped from a novel source domain onto the target domain of war. The novel conceptual metaphor that underlies the linguistic metaphors that Burridge uses is WARFARE IS MUSIC. Modern warfare is described as jazz, meaning perhaps that it is improvisational and that there are no hard and fast rules. This, for many people, would be quite a disturbing metaphor, since music is more commonly perceived as an art form and participation in music as a pleasure. Here, though, the domain of music is being used to talk about war and arguably the underlying conceptual metaphor gives warfare a frivolity and a licence that it shouldn't have. This could easily be seen to detract from the gravity of war and consequently Air Marshal Burridge lays himself open to criticisms of being gung-ho and inconsiderate of the suffering that war causes.

5.4.2   Types of conceptual metaphor

So far we have shown in general terms how conceptual metaphors underlie particular linguistic metaphors. Lakoff and Johnson (1980) distinguish a number of different types of conceptual metaphor. While we do not have the space to discuss all of these, below is a summary of some of the most prominent.

The CONDUIT metaphor

Much of our metalinguistic capability uses what has been referred to as the CONDUIT metaphor. As Lakoff and Johnson put it, 'The speaker puts ideas (objects) into words (containers) and sends them (along a conduit) to a hearer who takes the idea/objects out of the word/containers' (Lakoff and Johnson 1980: 10). The CONDUIT metaphor is thus an overarching metaphor for the following conceptual metaphors:

IDEAS AND MEANINGS ARE OBJECTS
LINGUISTIC EXPRESSIONS ARE CONTAINERS
COMMUNICATION IS SENDING

Some linguistic instantiations of the CONDUIT metaphor are:

(16)   I'm finding it hard to put my ideas into words.

(17)   You've given me an idea!

(18)   What the teacher said carried little meaning.

(19)   You need to get your ideas across if you're to succeed.

Orientational metaphors

The metaphors that we have examined so far are, Lakoff and Johnson note, 'structural metaphors' (1980: 14). That is, they structure one concept in terms of another. Orientational metaphors are somewhat different in that rather than structuring a concept in terms of another, they provide a concept with a spatial orientation. The category of orientational metaphors begins to explain many otherwise odd expressions that we commonly use in language. Why, for example, do we talk about being in *high* spirits when we're happy but feeling *down* when we're depressed? And why do we talk about *climbing* a career ladder or being at the *bottom* of the class? The answers to these questions can perhaps be found in the following conceptual metaphors:

*   HAPPY IS UP
*   SAD IS DOWN
*   CONSCIOUS IS UP
*   UNCONSCIOUS IS DOWN
*   GOOD IS UP
*   BAD IS DOWN
*   HEALTH AND LIFE ARE UP
*   SICKNESS AND DEATH ARE DOWN
*   MORE IS UP
*   LESS IS DOWN
*   HIGH STATUS IS UP
*   LOW STATUS IS DOWN
*   THE FUTURE IS AHEAD
*   THE PAST IS BEHIND

The above conceptual metaphors certainly help to explain why we use phrases such as 'he's at the top of his profession', but we might well ask just why it is that such conceptual metaphors are ingrained in our consciousness. The answer to this seems to be that many of these orientational metaphors have their origins in a physical basis. For example, we talk about waking *up* and *falling* asleep because humans sleep lying down and stand up when they are awake.

Ontological metaphors

Lakoff and Johnson (1980) point out that, typically, we tend to conceive of events, activities and emotions as entities and substances. Such ontological metaphors are used for a variety of purposes, among which are quantifying ('America has *a lot of political capital* invested in Iraq'), setting goals ('Dick Whittington went to London to *seek his fortune*') and referring ('her *fear of flying* is a huge problem'). In each of these cases, the italicised part of the sentence is being treated metaphorically as a substance. A further ontological metaphor noted by Lakoff and Johnson is the CONTAINER metaphor. Noting that humans are territorial by nature, Lakoff and Johnson suggest that the notions of bounded objects and bounded physical spaces are prime candidates for metaphor. A boundary between one space and another may be denoted by what a person's visual field can encompass, leading to the conceptual metaphor VISUAL FIELDS ARE CONTAINERS. Typical linguistic instantiations of this metaphor include the following:

(20)   The attacker was *outside* his victim's field of vision.

(21)   The sailors had been *out of* sight of land for weeks.

(22)   The hang-glider hove *into* view.

One of the points that become clear when we examine conceptual metaphors is that many of the source domains in these metaphors derive from bodily experience. In this respect we can make a connection between cognitive metaphor theory and the notion of image schemas, namely that image schemas often work as source domains in conceptual metaphors. For example, a CONTAINER image schema is working as the source domain in examples 20 to 22. However, although image schemas are important to conceptual metaphors, there appears to be some principle at work that restricts which image schemas (indeed, which schemas in general) can work as source domains for which target domains. Lakoff (1993) has described this as the **invariance principle**. The invariance principle hypothesises that the mappings between domains of a conceptual metaphor preserve the schematic structure of the source domain in a way that is consistent with the structure of the target domain.

To illustrate this, Lakoff and Turner (1989: 82) use the example of the conceptual metaphor DEATH IS A DESTROYER, realised in such linguistic instantiations as 'Death cut him down' and in the classic image of the Grim Reaper. Lakoff and Turner argue that while DEATH IS A DESTROYER is a commonly understood metaphor, a metaphor such as DEATH IS A MUSICIAN would be less easily understood. This is because DEATH IS A DESTROYER is a specific instantiation of a **generic-level metaphor** EVENTS ARE ACTIONS. According to the invariance principle, the generic-level schemas of the generic-level metaphor must be preserved in the specific instantiation of it. So, in DEATH IS A DESTROYER, DEATH is a specific instantiation of the generic EVENT. Our schematic conception of death is that it brings about a sudden physical change in an entity. Hence, this schematic concept has to be preserved in the source domain of the metaphor. The action of destroying preserves the schematic concept of bringing about a sudden change, so DESTROYER is an appropriate source domain. The action of playing music, however, does not bring about a sudden physical change, meaning that using MUSICIAN as a source domain seems inappropriate. Of course, while the invariance principle appears to be at work in everyday discourse, literary discourse often disregards the invariance principle in the pursuit of novel metaphor. Stockwell (2002b), for example, examines the breakdown of the invariance principle in surrealist literature.

5.4.3   Blending theory

We will end this discussion of cognitive metaphor theory with a brief consideration of a related area that emerged as a result of efforts to remedy some of the theoretical issues with the notion of conceptual metaphors. The oft-quoted exemplar of a basic problem with cognitive metaphor theory is the metaphor THE SURGEON IS A BUTCHER. Evans and Green (2006) note that this example is not easily explained by cognitive metaphor theory, since the metaphor suggests incompetence on the part of the surgeon, despite the fact that butchery is a highly-skilled profession.[3] Cognitive metaphor theory cannot explain where the negative assessment of the surgeon originates from. A potential answer to the conundrum lies in the **blending theory** developed by Fauconnier and Turner (see, for example, Fauconnier and Turner 2002). Blending theory draws on Fauconnier's mental spaces theory (Fauconnier 1985) by proposing a model for emergent meaning that is based on the idea that meaning is generated as a result of blending elements from different input spaces. While cognitive metaphor theory proposes the notion of mapping concepts from one domain of knowledge onto another, blending theory suggests that meaning construction is dependent not necessarily on such *pre-existing* knowledge domains, but on *temporary* knowledge structures created during online processing (the **mental spaces** of Fauconnier's 1985 work). An **integration network** is a model of how these temporary structures give rise to emergent meaning. The example, THE SURGEON IS A BUTCHER is explained by the integration network in figure 5.2.

In the diagram in figure 5.2 there are two input spaces in which we can identify elements associated with SURGEON and elements associated with BUTCHER. The unbroken lines between input spaces 1 and 2 represent mappings between these two domains. The two input spaces are linked by means of a generic space, in which we find higher-order elements that are shared by the input spaces. The blended space includes some information from the two input spaces, and some that is to be found in neither input space. In the case of the SURGEON IS A BUTCHER example, the blended space contains a concept of the SURGEON and the BUTCHER as being one and the same. Only in the blended space can this be the case. The blended space also blends together the goal of healing with the means of butchery. Again, only in the blended space can this be the case. These blends generate an emergent meaning of a surgeon attempting to heal a patient using the techniques of butchery, a clearly inappropriate endeavour which leads to our conception of the surgeon as incompetent.

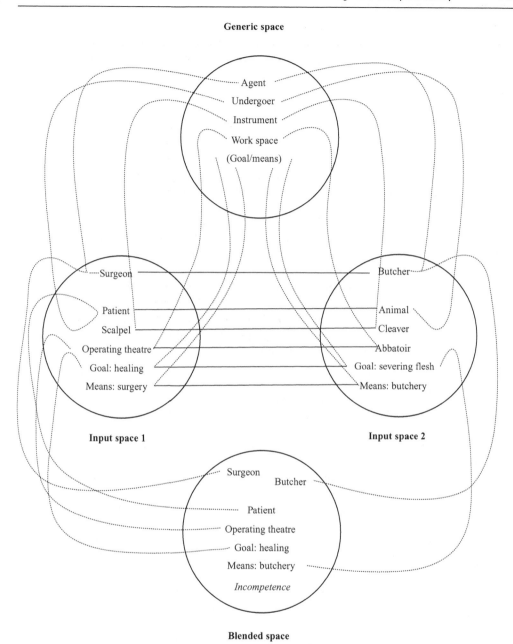

Figure 5.2 *Conceptual integration network for* SURGEON IS A BUTCHER *(based on Evans and Green 2006: 406)*

The value of conceptual blending for stylistics is that it can begin to account for particular stylistic effects. An example of this can be seen in the following extract from James Meek's novel, *The People's Act of Love* (for reasons of space we have abridged the extract):

(23)   [Samarin, the Mohican, Matchstick and the Gypsy are prisoners in a Siberian labour camp in 1919. The Mohican has been protecting Samarin from the harshness of camp life, and has been providing him with extra rations in order to build up his strength for the escape attempt that the Mohican has assured him they will make together. In this extract, Samarin is reporting a conversation he overheard between the Mohican, Matchstick and the Gypsy.]

'I heard raised voices in the other part of our barracks. The other authorities, Matchstick and the Gypsy, Gypsy who'd spread into the niche left when Machinegun was murdered, were after something from the Mohican. Matchstick said: "You've got to share. He's too much for one." The Gypsy said: "It's the end, finished. Time to do the town, brother. Just a little piece, a tiny little piece. I'll have the heart, me. Raw heart, still hot, that's what I like."

'The Mohican says: "It's the end. What I have I keep. What I keep goes with me. You go do the Prince and his people. They've got enough champagne and caviar to keep you all high till spring."

[. . .]

'And Matchstick says: "You've got to share. Where are you going with him? Run in midwinter? You won't get five miles, you and your pig."

'And the Mohican says: "I told you not to use that word in here."

[. . .]

'"I'm going to have this one," says Matchstick. "I'll cut him like an artist and then I'll kill him."

'"You'll not be an artist," says the Mohican. "You haven't got the imagination."

'Listening by the stove, I heard the Gypsy shout. I never heard the sound of the Mohican killing Matchstick. Knives are quiet things, in themselves. I heard the Mohican telling the Gypsy to take the body, and the Gypsy running away, and the Mohican coming to me. He pushed through the screen of blankets, still holding the bloody knife. He said it was time to leave, that they had stopped handing out rations that morning. I asked him what Gypsy and Matchstick had wanted, and he said: "They wanted something I couldn't give them."

'For a moment, I thought I knew why animals don't speak – not because they can't, but because the terror stops them at the moment they need to beg for their life, the fear and hopelessness hits them when a two-legged creature comes at them with a sharp shiny blade in its coiled white fingers, and they understand how much they've been fed and how slow and weak they are, and how greedy and stupid they've been, and how their hooves and paws can't do what fingers can do, and they're outclassed, already dead, already meat. For a moment I was an animal. I was a pig, ready to squirm under the butcher's hands, and squeal, only not to speak. Then I started grabbing words. I said: "Was that something me?" I said: "Am I the pig?"'   (Meek 2005: 207–8)

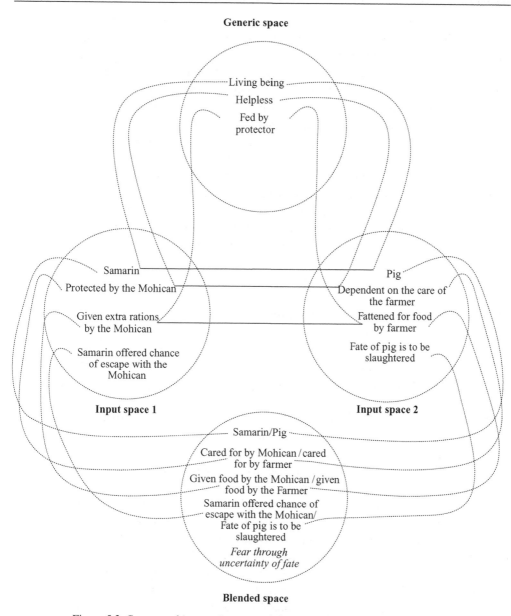

Figure 5.3 *Conceptual integration network for example 23*

This deeply unsettling scene culminates in Samarin's horrified realisation of what his fate is likely to be. This reaction is likely to be shared by the reader since it is at this point in the novel that we are for the first time able to recognise that the actions of the Mohican constitute metaphorical mappings. Conceptual blending theory helps to explain in explicit terms how Samarin's realisation of his fate comes about, whilst also spelling out the dilemma that Samarin faces. This is detailed in figure 5.3.

Input spaces 1 and 2 are akin to the target and source domains of a conceptual metaphor. The mappings between these two domains are indicated by the unbroken lines between them. In the generic space are the shared concepts from the two input spaces. The blended space is where we find the emergent meaning being generated. In this space, the entities of Samarin and the pig are blended together. However, input space 1 contains one structure that has no equivalent in input space 2. This is the offer of escape from the Mohican to Samarin. Since this has no direct equivalent in input space 2 (indeed, the source domain predicates the slaughter of the pig), this causes a mismatch in the blend which gives rise to deep uncertainty for Samarin. The Mohican is offering him a way out of the labour camp but on the (so far unmentioned) proviso that if their supplies run out during their escape march, the Mohican will kill Samarin and eat him. The blended space is where Samarin's horrific dilemma – whether to stay in the camp and die or take his chances with the Mohican – is generated.

5.5   Summary and conclusions

In this chapter we have outlined a selection of key cognitive theories that may be used to explain the active role that readers take in interpreting texts. The concept that links the three theories we have discussed is background knowledge. Schema theory suggests that readers make extensive use of pre-existing world knowledge to make the processes of communication and interpretation efficient. The notion of figure and ground in language works on the basis of our applying schematic knowledge about spatial relations in our analysis of texts. And cognitive metaphor theory takes the notion of image schemas and other types of schematic knowledge and demonstrates how such knowledge structures can function as source domains in conceptual metaphors. In the case of each theory, substantial interpretative benefits can be gained from its application in stylistic analysis. What will be apparent from our discussion, of course, is that some of these theories are more fully developed than others. While there is empirical support for some of these approaches (evidence for the existence of schemas, for instance, can be found in the work of Steffensen and Joag-Dev 1984, while Gibbs 1994 has found empirical evidence for conceptual metaphors), there is still considerable work to be done in this area. Evans and Green (2006: 781), for instance, note the problems of the apparent unfalsifiability of blending theory, postulating as it does the existence of 'the conceptual structures that it attempts to demonstrate evidence for'. Similarly, though some evidence is produced for the importance of schema theory in reading, Semino (2001: 349) claims that 'schema theory is rather unprincipled in what can count as a schema, so that it is hard to *disprove* empirically'. Nonetheless, these cognitive theories are promising new approaches for stylistics and will gain in currency as they develop through empirical and analytical testing.

Exercises

Exercise 5.1

How might schema theory account for why some readers react to the same text differently? Consider this question in relation to texts with which you are familiar.

Exercise 5.2

Read the following extract from Louis de Bernières's novel *Captain Corelli's Mandolin*, set on the Greek island of Cephalonia during the Second World War. Using schema theory, try to explain why Corelli is so concerned, how you know this and why Lemoni seems unconcerned. In your account, include reference to the notions of frames, scripts and headers. (N.B. Lemoni is a child and Corelli is an Italian army officer.)

(24)   'I saw a great big spiky rustball,' Lemoni informed the captain, 'and I climbed all over it.'
            'She says that she saw a great big spiky rustball and she climbed all over it,' translated Pelagia.
            'Ask her if it was on the beach,' said Corelli, appealing to Pelagia.
            'Was it on the beach?' she asked.
            'Yes, yes, yes,' said Lemoni gleefully, adding, 'and I climbed on it.'
            Corelli knew enough Greek to recognise the word for 'yes', and he stood up suddenly, and then just as suddenly sat down. 'Puttana,' he exclaimed, taking the little girl into his arms and hugging her tightly, 'she could have been killed.'
            Carlo put it more realistically; 'She should have been killed. It's a miracle.' He rolled his eyes and added, 'Porco dio.'
                                                    (de Bernières 1994: 260)

Exercise 5.3

Read example 25, an editorial from the British tabloid newspaper, *The Sun*, and answer the following questions:

1.   What conceptual metaphor does the writer use to describe the Labour government?
2.   What are the mappings between domains?
3.   What is the reader's place within the conceptual metaphor? What role does the conceptual metaphor impose on him/her?
4.   What effect does the conceptual metaphor have on how you perceive the topic of politics?

(25)   WALK TALL, YOU TORY DWARFS
              Twelve months ago, Iain Duncan Smith dubbed himself The Quiet Man. Invisible Man, more like it.

The Government has never been in more trouble.

In the country, voters' trust is ebbing away.

Last week The Sun reflected the concern of the nation by showing Mr Blair a yellow card – and warned him the red could follow.

At the moment the PM is still on the pitch – but is struggling to find his goal-scoring touch.

Labour's fumbling has left IDS facing a series of open goals – health, transport, asylum, taxes.

So far he has missed the lot.

The Leader of Her Majesty's Opposition should be giving Tony Blair the savaging he deserves.

But The Invisible Man has had less effect than a mosquito biting an elephant's backside.

The performance of today's Tories shames a once-great political party and is a danger to the nation . . .

This week in Blackpool, IDS and the Tory party must raise the roof if they are to avoid disappearing off the political map.

Democracy depends on a fierce unending debate. Without it, power tips one way and society suffers.

That is what is happening in Britain today.

Last week Tony Blair admitted that improving public services would be a test of his mettle. Now IDS faces a test of HIS mettle.

Can he ever exploit Labour's failings? The omens are not good.

At the Brent East by-election, the Tories surrendered before campaigning began.

And in Blackpool, the Tories will hold just 13 hours of debate, half of what Labour had in Bournemouth.

Hardly the actions of a party bursting with energy and hungry for power.

With the Lib Dems breathing down their necks, the Tories must be bold.

Gordon Brown has flung down the gauntlet over public spending and tax cuts. IDS should pick it up and slap Brown in the face with it.

His weekend pledge to cut taxes was a good start.

The Tories must not let Brown get away with the idea that only the State can provide public services.

Many say IDS is uninspiring, a vote loser not a winner. But even an uninspiring leader can make an impact – if he is brave enough.

IDS must attack the Lib Dems without mercy, making clear how far to the Left that ragbag party is.

But most important of all, he must stamp the Tories in the public mind as the main Opposition.

Not the third-raters they look right now.

                                              ('The Sun Says', 6 October 2003)

Exercise 5.4

A cartoon by Austin appeared in *The Guardian* newspaper on the same day that the poet laureate, Andrew Motion, published a poem critical of America's and Britain's justification for the war in Iraq. The cartoon shows the President of the U.S. in the background, seated at a desk, and a secret serviceman in the foreground with his hand inside his jacket, presumably to draw his gun. He is shouting, 'Incoming poem, Mr President!'

Answer the following questions:

1. What is the main underlying conceptual metaphor in the cartoon?
2. Is the conceptual metaphor novel or conventional?
3. What are the mappings between the two domains of the conceptual metaphor?
4. Can you think of any other linguistic instantiations of this conceptual metaphor, either novel or conventional?
5. What political comment do you think the cartoonist is making?

Further reading

Semino and Culpeper (2002) is an excellent collection of chapters dealing with recent applications of cognitive theories in stylistic analysis, as is Gavins and Steen (2003). Stockwell (2002a) provides an introductory summary of a number of cognitive stylistic approaches, including those discussed in this chapter, while Evans and Green (2006) is a comprehensive (and challenging) introduction to cognitive linguistics in general. Semino (1997) provides a detailed summary of schema theory, taking into account a number of different conceptions of it. A particular strength of Semino's summary is her concentration on the linguistic mechanisms by which schemas are triggered, as well as demonstrations of its application in stylistic analysis. Figure and ground is covered by Ungerer and Schmid (1996) and Stockwell (2002a, 2003). The classic works on cognitive metaphor theory are Lakoff and Johnson (1980), Turner (1987), and Lakoff and Turner (1989). For recent additions to this area, Steen (2007), Goatly (2007) and Semino (2008) are particularly recommended.

6 Text and cognition II

Text processing

6.1 The reading process

In the previous chapter we considered the active role that readers play in the construction of meaning. We focused on the prior knowledge that readers bring to texts and which they use in the process of interpretation, and from this it becomes clear that the process of meaning creation is a result of the interconnection between textual triggers and readers' world knowledge. Or, to restate this in Semino's (1997) terms, texts *project* meaning while readers *construct* it. The means by which readers go about constructing meaning is, as we explained in Chapter 5, the central concern of cognitive stylistics. In this chapter we will continue our consideration of this branch of stylistics by focusing on how readers navigate their way though texts. While Chapter 5 considered the stylistic effects that can arise as a result of, say, deviant schemas or novel conceptual metaphors, in this chapter we will focus primarily on a descriptive account of how readers process textual meaning. In so doing we will outline some of the most influential theories of text processing to have been adopted by stylistics. One caveat to the whole cognitive stylistics enterprise, of course, is that it is important that it does not reject the more linguistically and textually orientated approaches described in the earlier chapters of this book. Rather it should seek to enrich these by adding a cognitive layer to the explanation of how readers react to texts.

6.2 Text world theory

Text world theory is a theory of discourse processing developed initially by Paul Werth in a series of papers (see, for example, Werth 1994, 1995, 1997) and outlined in full in his posthumously published book, *Text Worlds: Representing Conceptual Space in Discourse* (Werth 1999). Werth's aim in the development of text world theory was to account for how we as readers and hearers 'make sense of complex utterances when we receive them' (Werth 1999: 7). His suggested answer was that we do this by constructing 'mental constructs called text worlds' (1999: 7). Werth defined text worlds as 'conceptual scenarios containing just enough information to make sense of the particular utterance they correspond to' (1999: 7). The cognitive nature of the theory is made clear by Werth in his clarification of the necessity of three elements – author, text and reader[1] – in the creation of a text world:

> the author creates only a text; he/she will have a particular text world in mind, but there is no guarantee at all that the reader will manage to produce the same text world on reading that text. We cannot say that the author's text world is the definitive one, since, in fact, there is no such thing. We may say, therefore, that a text world does not come into being until each of the three elements – author, text and reader – are present.   (Werth 2007: 155)

Werth's work has been particularly influential within stylistics and has been taken up enthusiastically by a number of researchers (see, for instance, Gavins's 2007 subsequent development of text world theory). At its heart is the conceptual metaphor THE TEXT IS A WORLD, and text world theory is an exposition of how readers (and hearers) mentally construct such worlds as a means of interpreting discourse in context.

Text world theory makes an initial distinction between the **discourse world** and the **text world**. The discourse world is the immediate real-world situation in which a writer communicates with a reader. The text world is what is constructed by the reader to make sense of the communicative event. Included within the discourse world is the schematic knowledge of all participants in the discourse, as well as all surrounding physical objects and entities, and together these form a **context**. Werth defines context as 'the relevant situational background(s) for and in a particular discourse' (1999: 117). The key word here is 'relevant', since the potential context for any given discourse world is vast. Discourse participants restrict this by only considering **common ground** information: i.e. only that information which is necessary for the interpretation of the discourse in question.

Participants in the discourse world use the textual and common ground information present within it to construct a text world – a mental representation of the text. Text worlds are composed of **world-building elements** and **function-advancing propositions**, both of which are recovered from the text. World-building elements consist of time (realised through the tense and aspect of verb phrases), location (realised through adverbials and noun phrases specifying place), characters (realised through proper nouns and pronouns) and objects (realised through nouns and pronouns). Function-advancing propositions work to develop and advance events within the text world, and are realised in verb phrases. Here it is useful to return to the functional grammatical categories introduced in our discussion of transitivity in Chapter 3, since function-advancing propositions can be seen as mapping onto these Hallidayan processes. Function-advancing propositions may take the form of material processes (that is, intentional, super-ventional or event processes), relational processes (intensive, possessive and circumstantial) and mental processes. In text world theory, material processes are indicated diagrammatically by vertical arrows, while relational and mental

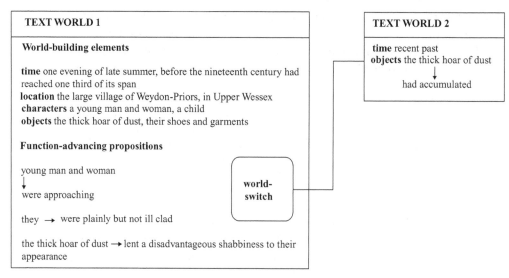

Figure 6.1 *Text world (including temporal world-switch) generated through reading the opening paragraph of* The Mayor of Casterbridge

processes are indicated by horizontal arrows. An example of a text world can be seen in figure 6.1, which represents diagrammatically the opening paragraph of Thomas Hardy's *The Mayor of Casterbridge*:

(1)   One evening of late summer, before the nineteenth century had reached one third of its span, a young man and woman, the latter carrying a child, were approaching the large village of Weydon-Priors, in Upper Wessex, on foot. They were plainly but not ill clad, though the thick hoar of dust which had accumulated on their shoes and garments from an obviously long journey lent a disadvantageous shabbiness to their appearance just now.

(Hardy 1987[1886]: 1)

What is apparent in figure 6.1 is that processing this opening paragraph involves the setting up of two text worlds. The first (text world 1) is generated by the third-person past-simple narration and includes the characters of the young man and woman and the child, as well as the specification of location and time, the characters' shoes and garments and the 'thick hoar of dust'. However, the past perfect verb phrase 'had accumulated' requires the reader to generate a second text world (text world 2), wherein the dust accumulates on the shoes of the young man and woman. Gavins (2007) notes that a change in tense such as that in example 1 invokes a temporal **world-switch** that results in the instantiation of a further text world. The world-switch is indicated in the diagram by a rounded rectangle. Gavins introduces the term *world-switch* to replace Werth's preferred **sub-world** on the basis that subsequently developed text worlds are not necessarily subordinate to the primary text world. Following this logic, we use Gavins's term here. As Gavins (2007: 52) explains, *world-switch* also maps onto Emmott's (1997: 147) notion of a *frame-switch* in contextual frame theory (see section 6.4), thereby providing a useful link between these two approaches to text processing.

Example 1 constitutes a relatively simple text in processing terms, though text world theory is also able to account for much more complex discourse through its concept of **modal worlds**. Drawing on Simpson's (1993) modal grammar and adapting Werth's (1999) notion of sub-worlds, Gavins (2007) postulates the concepts of **boulomaic, deontic** and **epistemic** modal worlds. Respectively, these modal worlds represent the desires, obligations and beliefs of participants in the discourse world or characters in the text world (see Chapter 3 for full definitions of boulomaic, deontic and epistemic modality). These modal worlds are generated as we read example 2, an extract from Larry McMurtry's novel *Lonesome Dove*:

(2)   [*Lonesome Dove* is set in the American West of the mid-1800s. Newt is a young cowboy with the Hat Creek Cattle Company outside the town of Lonesome Dove. Lorena is a prostitute with whom he is infatuated.]

On an average day, Lorena occupied Newt's thoughts about eight hours, no matter what tasks occupied his hands. Though normally an open young man, quick to talk about his problems – to Pea Eye and Deets, at least – he had never so much as uttered Lorena's name aloud. He knew that if he did utter it a terrible amount of ribbing would ensue, and while he didn't mind being ribbed about most things, his feeling for Lorena was too serious to admit frivolity. The men who made up the Hat Creek outfit were not great respecters of feeling, particularly not tender feeling.

There was also the danger that someone might slight her honor. It wouldn't be the Captain, who was not prone to jesting about women, or even to mentioning them. But the thought of the complications that might arise from an insult to Lorena had left Newt closely acquainted with the mental perils of love long before he had had an opportunity to sample any of its pleasures except the infinite pleasure of contemplation.

Of course, Newt knew that Lorena was a whore. It was an awkward fact, but it didn't lessen his feeling for her one whit.   (McMurtry 1985: 24)

There are a number of world-building elements in this passage. Time and location are recoverable from what we have read previously and so we know that the story as a whole takes place in a town called Lonesome Dove somewhere in the American West in the mid-nineteenth century. Time is specified more specifically through the adverbial 'on an average day'. What this also suggests is that we are not dealing with what we might term a concrete text world. The text world presented in this paragraph is a compression of a number of other text worlds in which the action of Newt daydreaming about Lorena has happened. With regard to characters, the primary ones in this text world are clearly Newt and Lorena, though others are mentioned (Pea Eye and Deets, the Captain and 'The men who made up the Hat Creek outfit'). The mention of these other characters also helps to specify place, since these characters are anchored to a specific location. Newt is a cowboy with the Hat Creek Cattle Company, as are Pea Eye, Deets and the

Captain, therefore mention of Pea Eye, Deets, the Captain and the Hat Creek outfit provides a specification of location as a result of our pragmatic knowledge of these characters.

In addition to the world-building elements that help us to populate this text world, the modal verbs in the passage trigger the generation of a number of modal worlds, all of which are as rich as the primary text world of which they are offshoots, in the sense that they too contain world-building elements and function-advancing propositions. For example, the sentence 'There was also the danger that someone might slight her honor' triggers a boulomaic modal in which another member of the Hat Creek outfit insults Lorena and Newt is forced to acknowledge his love of her by defending her honour. 'It wouldn't be the Captain' triggers a negative epistemic modal world in which the Captain *does* insult Lorena (Chapter 3, section 3.2, considers more fully the local textual functions of negation; see also Nørgaard 2007 and Nahajec 2009). In causing us to generate such a modal world, the text foregrounds the unlikelihood of this event ever happening, thereby giving us an indication of the Captain's character. A further epistemic modal world is triggered by the sentence 'Of course, Newt knew that Lorena was a whore.' This reference to what Newt believes to be the case about the world that he inhabits generates an element of conflict in the story. Newt would like nothing more than to marry Lorena, though the content of this epistemic modal world conflicts with the content of the boulomaic modal world in which he and Lorena live happily ever after.

What is also apparent in this passage is that the modal worlds generated are not **participant accessible**. That is, the reader has no way of verifying the truth of these modal worlds, since the content of these is inaccessible to participants in the discourse world. Rather, these are **character accessible** only, hence Newt's beliefs about what would result from a declaration of his love for Lorena are necessarily true only in his modal worlds. We have no means of determining whether this would be the case in the framing text world, were it to happen.

The generation of a number of modal worlds in this passage has several effects. It indicates, for example, that Newt is a character who is thoughtful and not prone to impulsive behaviour. It also generates some of the conflict that is necessary for the advancement of the narrative. Of course, as Stockwell (2002a: 145) notes, a text world theory analysis is not necessarily required to uncover this kind of analytical detail. Nonetheless, text world theory does offer a principled explanation of the way in which we might keep track of narrative information as we read. One of the key aspects of text world theory is the concept of the reader **toggling** between different text worlds, modalised or not, in order to process the events that constitute the narrative. This will result in several shifts of position within the text world in order to take account of the viewpoints of a variety of characters (note, too, that this is also the case for non-fiction texts). For this reason, we will focus in the next section on a theory of text processing that aims to account more specifically for the means by which readers shift mental positions as they read.

6.3   Deictic shift theory

Deictic shift theory was originally developed by an interdisciplinary research group consisting of linguists, psychologists, computer scientists and literary critics, among a number of others. The theory as a whole is outlined in a collection of papers edited by Duchan *et al.* (1995), though for reasons of space we concentrate here specifically on those aspects of the theory that have had applications with stylistics. What we will also attempt to do is demonstrate how deictic shift theory might be used to add a cognitive layer of explanation to how readers process point of view when they read.

Deictic shift theory was developed to account for the way in which readers can come to feel deeply involved in what they are reading, to the extent that they forget about their position within the real world (the discourse world, in text world theory terms) and begin to interpret events in the narrative as if from a position within the text world. If text world theory provides an explanation of the means by which readers make sense of a narrative, then deictic shift theory provides a means of explaining the sense of involvement that readers often have as they navigate their way *through* that narrative. Segal, one of the original proponents of deictic shift theory, suggests that the reader 'takes a cognitive stance within the world of a narrative and interprets the text from that perspective' (Segal 1995: 15). At the heart of deictic shift theory is, as the name suggests, the concept of **deixis**.

Prototypically, deixis refers to the linguistic encoding of spatial and temporal relations between objects and entities. **Deictic terms** are the specific linguistic expressions that encode this information. Following Levinson (1983), we can distinguish five different types of deixis: (i) place deixis, (ii) temporal deixis, (iii) person deixis, (iv) social deixis and (v) empathetic deixis. The first of these encodes the relative position in space of specific objects or entities. Pure place deictics include adverbs such as *here* and *there* which can only be interpreted by reference to the position of the speaker or writer of these words. *This* and *that* are further examples of pure place deictics, since they rely for their interpretation on a knowledge of the location of the speaker or writer. Pure deictics tend to come in pairs, one of which will indicate proximity to the speaker or writer in question, while the second indicates distance from that speaker or writer. Locational deictic expressions are slightly different in nature in that they are interpreted in relation not to the speaker or writer but to the position of other referents within the situational context. Consider, for example, the adverbials in example 3:

(3)   She had a sign painted in bright colours, which was then set up just off the Lobatse Road, on the edge of town, pointing to the small building she had purchased: THE NO. 1 LADIES' DETECTIVE AGENCY.

                                                              (McCall Smith 1998: 4)

The prepositional phrases 'off the Lobatse Road' and 'on the edge of town' can only be interpreted if we know where both the Lobatse Road and the town are situated within the text world. Since this is information included in the world-building elements of the text world, these expressions are not difficult to interpret. The point is that they are not reliant on our knowing the position in space of the narrator, as expressions such as *here* and *there* are. For this reason, they are not considered to be pure deictics.

While place deictics encode physical position within the situational context, temporal deictics encode distance in time from the moment of speaking or writing. Pure temporal deictics include *now* and *then*, and *yesterday*, *today* and *tomorrow*. Temporal deixis can also be expressed through such time expressions as, for example, *a week ago*, *some years previously*, etc. In the same way that temporal deixis encodes metaphorical distance from the moment of speaking, person and social deixis encode the speakers and hearers within a situational context and their relative distance from the speaker or writer. Person deixis is realised through personal pronouns (e.g. *I*, *you*, *he*, *she*, etc.). Social deixis is related to person deixis and encodes perceived social distance between particular characters.[2] This may be realised through, for example, the use of titles and honorifics to encode social distance (e.g. Professor Jeffries, Dr McIntyre) and the use of first names and short forms to indicate social proximity (cf. Lesley and Dan). Finally, empathetic deixis encodes psychological attitude. Compare, for example, the difference between 'So, tell me about *this* new colleague of yours' and 'So, tell me about *that* new colleague of yours'. The second may generate a sense that the speaker harbours less positive feelings towards the colleague in question than the first (though context too may play a part in the choice of demonstrative here).

Pure deictics, as we have explained, are interpreted in relation to the position in space and time of the speaker or writer. This position is known as the **deictic centre** and is a central concept in deictic shift theory. It is our knowledge of the deictic centre to which deictic expressions refer that allows us to interpret them. In everyday conversation we have a tendency to regard ourselves as the deictic centre for all deictic terms. However, we also have the capacity to suspend our egocentric conception of deixis and **project** a deictic centre that is not our own; that is, we are able to interpret deictic terms as having a reference point other than that which we might prototypically expect. As an example of this, imagine receiving instructions over the phone from an IT technician about how to solve a problem with your computer. Such instructions might include phrases like 'Remove the flash drive from the USB port on your left and try the USB port on your right'. In such an instance, the person giving the instructions would be using locative deictic expressions relevant to *your* deictic centre as opposed to their own. In effect, they would be engaging in **deictic projection**. This capacity for deictic projection is at the heart of deictic shift theory, since the theory suggests that readers are able to feel involved in a narrative by experiencing vicariously events from a viewpoint other than their own. Clearly, this involves deictic projection.

Deictic shift theory attempts to spell out precisely how readers understand projected deictic centres. In her explanation of how this happens, Galbraith (1995) suggests that narratives have numerous **deictic fields**, which Stockwell (2002a: 47) defines as a set of deictic expressions all relating to the same deictic centre. The term *deictic field* comes originally from the work of Bühler (1982 and 1990 [1934]). In fiction deictic fields are related either to characters, narrators or narratees, and in non-fiction to what text world theory would term *enactors* – essentially, non-fictional characters within the text world in question. In Galbraith's (1995) summary of Bühler's work she notes that there are three aspects to a speaker's deictic field. The first is the immediate physical space and the immediate time in which a speaker is located. This aspect of the deictic field is realised linguistically through the use of pure deictic terms such as *here* and *now*. The second aspect is the pragmatic context in which a speaker is communicating. Galbraith notes that an awareness of this pragmatic context enables a speaker's addressees to understand the speaker's deictic references. Finally, the third aspect of any given deictic field is its capacity to extend beyond a speaker's immediate physical and temporal location, and to refer to that speaker's memory or imagination. This is a much simplified summary of Bühler's definition of a deictic field, though it will suffice for our purposes (for a full discussion and critique of the notion of a deictic field see McIntyre 2006: 99–107).

Deictic shift theory suggests that readers assume the spatial, temporal and social coordinates of deictic fields not to be egocentric and related to the discourse world, but to be anchored within the text world itself. Suspending our normal assumptions about deictic reference involves making a **deictic shift** into the text world, in order to take up the cognitive stance that Segal (1995) explains results in a feeling of involvement in the narrative. McIntyre (2006: 107) notes that while it is not possible in real life to inhabit exactly the same deictic field as another person, in fiction this limitation does not apply and it is entirely possible to take up a position within a character or enactor's deictic field as we read. It follows that deictic shifts must be triggered somehow and that such triggers may be linguistic or non-linguistic in type. The first deictic shift we make when reading, for example, is triggered simply by picking up a book and starting to read. Once centred within the text world, we move around it by shifting into and out of the deictic fields of which the narrative is composed. And if whatever deictic field we happen to be in is not regularly reinstantiated by further deictic reference, it will eventual **decay**. This process can result in interesting stylistic effects and is particularly prominent as a technique in many contemporary films. For example, Roberto Benigni's *Life is Beautiful* begins with voiceover narration. We therefore understand that the fictional world we see on screen is embedded in the framing narration of the voiceover. However, once the action begins, the voiceover is not continued. The deictic field of the framing narrator thus decays, and we forget that we are watching an embedded narrative. Only at the end of the film is the voiceover narration reinstantiated, causing us to shift deictic fields again, from the embedded narrative level to the framing narrative level.

The means by which we shift around the deictic fields of a text are described by the terms PUSH and POP. A PUSH is defined by Galbraith as a movement 'from a basic level to a less available deictic plane, such as episodic memory (known as "flashback" in fiction), fictional story world (this may be a fiction within the fiction), or fantasy' (Galbraith 1995: 47). Conversely, the term POP refers to movement out of a particular deictic field. According to deictic shift theory, we PUSH into deictic fields and POP out of them. We can see how this works if we consider an example:

(4)   During the night of the fifth of December, the train ran in a south-easterly direction for about fifty miles; then, going up a like distance to the north-east, it drew near to Great Salt Lake.

About nine o'clock in the morning, Passepartout went out on the platform to take the air. The weather was cold, the sky grey, but it was snowing no longer. The sun's disc, magnified by the mist, looked like an enormous gold coin, and Passepartout was busy calculating its value in pounds sterling, when his attention was diverted from this useful occupation by the appearance of a somewhat strange personage.

This man, who had taken the train for Elko station, was tall, very dark, with black moustache, black stockings, a black silk hat, a black waistcoat, black trousers, a white tie and dog-skin gloves.   (Verne 1994 [1873]: 110–11)

This extract from the beginning of Chapter 27 of *Around the World in Eighty Days* is a third-person narrative in which Passepartout's point of view of the events in the text world is prominent. As a reader, we are likely to feel fairly involved in the text world because of our capacity for interpreting the deictic expressions within it as referring to the character of Passepartout's deictic centre. The adverbials 'During the night of the fifth of December' and 'About nine o'clock in the morning' specify the temporal coordinates of Passepartout's deictic field, and our knowledge of the story so far allows us to interpret these more fully as occurring in the year 1872. The other deictic terms in the passage also relate to Passepartout's deictic centre, meaning that to interpret these we have to take up a cognitive stance in the text world that is the equivalent of Passepartout's. For example, the narrator tells us that 'Passepartout went out on the platform'. The place-deictic verb *went* indicates movement away from a deictic centre and generates the sense that we the reader are in the same deictic position as Passepartout. As a means of further verifying this, consider the difference in effect had the sentence been 'Passepartout came out on the platform'. This sentence gives the impression that we are already positioned on the platform and Passepartout is moving towards us.

The more deictic information we are provided with by a text, the richer our conception of the deictic field will be, thereby increasing the degree to which we feel involved in the text world. For instance, the proximal place deictic *this* is used to refer to the man that Passepartout notices, suggesting his physical proximity to Passepartout. Again, to compare an alternative rendering of this, consider the effect generated had the sentence been '*The* man, who had taken the train for Elko station [. . .]'. The deictic references in the text, then, assist the reader in constructing a relatively rich deictic field, at the deictic centre of which is Passepartout. To use the terms of deictic shift theory, we PUSH into Passepartout's deictic field. The cognitive stance that we take up within the text world is reinforced by the other point-of-view indicators in the passage that reflect Passepartout's viewpoint. For example, Passepartout's first sight of the man in black is described using indefinite reference ('a somewhat strange personage'). Indefinite reference is typically used to introduce new information, and because the sight of the man constitutes new information for Passepartout, it is presented to the reader as new information too in order to reflect Passepartout's point of view.

At this point we are in a position to draw some parallels between deictic shift theory and text world theory. Text world theory provides a principled account of how we conceive of the meanings projected by texts. Conceiving of a text world involves taking up a cognitive position within it. Deictic shift theory specifies how we do this through its concept of deictic fields and the notion of pushing and popping between these. There is, though, a problem with the notion of POPs and PUSHes. McIntyre (2006) discusses this in detail and we summarise the issues here.

The first problem is that there are different types of PUSHes and POPs. So, for example, a flashback in a narrative constitutes a PUSH back along the temporal continuum of a story. However, a move out of the fantasy world of a character and back into the basis-level text world constitutes a POP up a level of discourse. At the very least, then, deictic shift theory needs to specify the kinds of PUSH and POP that readers engage in.

A more serious problem concerns the nature of these cognitive movements as a whole. One unfortunate consequence of the terms PUSH and POP (both of which were borrowed from computer science) is that while PUSH suggests an active movement on the part of the reader, POP suggests a movement that is involuntary. Cognitive stylistics puts substantial emphasis on the active role of the reader in text processing and so the notion that a cognitive movement may be involuntary seems counter-intuitive. Furthermore, it must be the case that such movements occur as a result of triggers, be these linguistic or non-linguistic. It would seem, then, that there is little difference in theoretical terms between a move into a deictic field and a move out of one. Both are cued by a trigger and both are active movements on the part of the reader. For example, a POP out of one deictic field must involve a PUSH into another. We suggest, then, that it may be more useful to disregard the terms PUSH and POP and refer instead simply to **deictic shifts**, specifying the type and direction of these (see McIntyre 2006: 108–12 for more detail on this issue).

6.4   Contextual frame theory

The final theory of text processing that we will consider in this chapter is Emmott's contextual frame theory (outlined in full in Emmott 1997). We should point out, of course, that none of the theories discussed in this chapter exist in isolation from each other. Text world theory, for example, is designed to explain how we construct rich mental models as we read, while deictic shift theory complements this by providing an explanation for why we can come to feel deeply involved in the text worlds of a narrative. By the same token, contextual frame theory provides a further connection between these theories by providing an explanation of how we keep track of the elements of a narrative as we read. Of course, the complexities of such an activity are vast and it would be reasonable to ask what contribution stylistics might make to our understanding of this process, especially when the insights provided by psychology into the nature of reading remain at a relatively basic level. Emmott herself suggests an answer when she explains that '[w]hilst textual analysis cannot prove what goes on in a reader's mind, it can reveal the complexity of texts and can thereby indicate the nature of the task to be undertaken' (Emmott 1997: 99). In this respect, the insights of cognitive stylistics might be used to form hypotheses about the nature of reading that would then be available for testing by empirical psychologists and linguists.

Contextual frame theory suggests that readers make sense of narrative events by relating them to the contexts in which they occur in the text world. To do this, readers construct **contextual frames**. Emmott (1997: 121) describes a contextual frame as 'a mental store of information about the current context, built up from the text itself and from inferences made from the text'. Contextual frames contain information which may be **episodic** or **non-episodic** in nature. Episodic information is that which is true at a particular point in the narrative in question, but which is not necessarily relevant beyond this point. Non-episodic information, conversely, is that which *is* true 'beyond the immediate context' (Emmott 1997: 122). As an example, in Jonathan Coe's novel *The Rotters' Club*, the fact that the main protagonist, Benjamin Trotter, is a schoolboy growing up in the 1970s constitutes non-episodic information: i.e. it is information which remains true across the course of the narrative as a whole. We may compare this with an instance of episodic information. In Chapter 7 of the novel, Benjamin arrives for a school swimming lesson only to find that he has forgotten his swimming trunks. Since the punishment for this is to swim naked, Benjamin is mortified and prays to God for an answer to his dilemma. As he does so, a locker door swings open and Benjamin sees that inside the locker is a pair of swimming trunks. This, then, is episodic information: i.e. a one-off occurrence in the narrative. While Emmott notes that episodic information does not have to have relevance beyond its immediate context, in this particular case it does, since the discovery of the swimming trunks leads Benjamin to believe that his prayer has been answered. As a result of this, Benjamin becomes convinced of the existence of God and embraces Christianity, an action that is to have a significant impact on his behaviour throughout the remainder of the novel.

In addition to the episodic and non-episodic information stored within contextual frames, Emmott explains that such frames also hold information relating to the situation in question as well as details of descriptions and events recently referred to. Such information is necessary for a reader to interpret anaphoric references, as may be seen in the following example:

(5)   By everyday standards, it was an exceptionally disastrous swimming period. Benjamin was chosen to be part of a relay team captained by Culpepper, and was clearly the weakest link in the chain. By the time he had completed his two purple-faced, asphyxiated, floundering lengths of butterfly stroke, their lead had been all but erased[.]   (Coe 2004: 72)

In just this short extract we can see that the pronoun *he* in the third sentence relies for its interpretation on the reader having retained from the preceding sentence the frame knowledge of Benjamin being part of a relay team (there is a clear link between this cognitive concept and the linguistic notion of cohesion; see section 3.2.3). This enables us to link *he* with both the proper noun *Benjamin* and the noun phrase *the weakest link in the chain*. Note too that the description in the preceding sentence of Benjamin as a weak swimmer allows us to infer that *he* refers to Benjamin as opposed to Culpepper, since this description is consistent with the negatively-charged adjectives *purple-faced, asphyxiated* and *floundering* used to describe Benjamin's swim in the latter sentence.

Emmott explains that this kind of contextual monitoring allows readers to create an overall context for the narrative. However, while it is possible for readers to hold information about more than one context at any given time, we tend to focus our attention on one particular context. The terms **binding** and **priming** explain the means by which we do this. Binding refers to the process of linking particular entities to particular contexts, while priming refers to the process by which particular contextual frames are brought to the forefront of the reader's mind. For example, Ian Fleming's James Bond novel, *Dr No*, begins with a scene in a Jamaican street in which three blind beggars make their way slowly along the road. These three characters are *bound* into this particular situational context. The scene then switches to a gentlemen's club where Brigadier Bill Templar, John Strangways, a professor from Kingston University and a criminal lawyer are playing cards. These four characters are bound into this second situational context. At this point in the reading process, the scene in the cardroom of the gentlemen's club constitutes the primed context, since this is the context on which the reader's attention is currently focused. The characters of Strangways, Templar and the two others are therefore primed as well as bound. Nonetheless, the three beggars of the first scene remain bound into their own particular context, despite the fact that it is now unprimed.

Binding and priming are thus processes of monitoring that readers engage in. Characters that are primed will remain in a reader's mind even if they are not referred to directly in the text. A primed character that is referred to in a sentence is said to be **overt**. One that is present in the scene but not referred to is said to be **covert**. If we return to our *Dr No* example, in the following paragraph Templar is the overt primed character, since he is referred to directly in the proper noun and its appositive noun phrase, and by the pronoun *he*:

(6)   Bill Templar, the Brigadier, laughed shortly. He pinged the bell by his side and raked the cards towards him. He said, 'Hurry up, blast you. You always let the cards go cold just as your partner's in the money.'

(Fleming 1985 [1958]: 7)

The other characters (Strangways, the professor and the lawyer) are, at this point in the narrative, covert, since they are not mentioned in the text but remain primed; that is, we remain aware of their presence within the scene, despite the fact that the text does not refer to them. Only primed characters may be overt or covert. Unprimed characters – that is, characters not present in the primed frame but bound into some other context – are neither overt nor covert, but simply bound into the reader's main context.

Contexts such as those described above are, of course, continually modified across the course of a whole narrative. The reader's attention will shift to new contexts, and these new contexts will involve new entities and characters. The means by which readers track such context changes is also covered by contextual frame theory. Emmott suggests, for instance, that **frame modification** occurs when characters enter or leave a particular location. For example, the sentence that follows the one in example 6 describes Strangways leaving the club: 'Strangways was already out of the door.' As a result of this, the reader modifies the contextual frame in which Strangways was previously bound. The other elements of the frame remain in place – we assume, for instance, that Templar, the professor and the lawyer remain in the cardroom – and so the frame is not radically altered but simply modified by Strangways becoming unbound from the frame.

This example is an instance of the modification of a primed frame, though unprimed frames may also be modified. However, this cannot be done via overt reference or it would prime the frame in question. The way in which unprimed frames can be modified without consequently priming them is via covert reference. For example, in Chapter 2 of *Dr No* the character of James Bond enters the narrative. Bond, at this point, is in London, hence he is bound into this contextual frame. At the beginning of Chapter 4, however, Bond is on board a plane to Jamaica. We assume, therefore, that he has become unbound from the previous contextual frame (the London scene), despite the fact that there was no overt reference to this happening. (Note that frame modification is similar to the notion of tuning a schema. Some variants of schema theory even make use of the term *frame* to describe schematic knowledge; see section 5.2.1 for details.)

Frame modification, then, refers to the adding or removing of a character from a particular frame. The notion of a **frame-switch** refers to the process by which a reader stops monitoring one frame and starts monitoring another. Frame-switches generate new frames, usually leaving the previously established frames intact (albeit potentially modified). Frame-switches may be instantiated pragmatically or via adverbials of time or place. They may also be **instantaneous** or **progressive**. Instantaneous frame-switches involve a sudden mental leap in space or time, such as that triggered by the mention of Bond being on a plane to Jamaica rather than in an office in London. A progressive frame-switch is one which does not involve such a mental leap, but where the temporal or locative change is tracked explicitly, as in the following example:

(7)   Strangways [. . .] walked quickly across the mahogany panelled hallway of
             Queen's Club and pushed through the light mosquito-wired doors and ran
             down the three steps to the path.   (Fleming 1985 [1958]: 8)

Frame-switches do not discount the possibility that a previously primed frame may be re-primed. If characters remain bound into an unprimed frame, then the potential exists for **frame recall**. The potential for frame recall diminishes over time. For instance, if a year passes within the text world we might assume that one set of characters are no longer bound into the same contextual frame in which we left them. Similarly, if we happen to be reading a particularly long text, the sheer length of time between one mention of a set of characters and another may reduce our capacity to re-prime the frame into which those characters were initially bound. The author is likely instead to be forced into re-establishing the triggers for the construction of a renewed frame.

   Contextual frame theory, then, provides a number of hypotheses about the nature of reading and how readers monitor the progression of a narrative. The concepts described so far, of course, refer to the activities of a reader who experiences no difficulties in processing a narrative. Occasionally, though, a reader may make a mistake, or be intentionally misled by an author/narrator. When this happens, the reader makes a **frame repair** in order to recover the sense of the narrative in question. Writers often exploit both a reader's capacity for making such misjudgements and their capacity for repairing them in order to generate particular stylistic effects. Emmott (2003a), for example, shows how contextual frame theory can account for the way in which readers react to short stories that incorporate a 'twist in the tale', prime examples of which are the short stories of Roald Dahl. Further examples of this kind of technique can be seen in science fiction narratives, ghost stories and fantasy novels. A typical instance of this occurs in John Masefield's classic novel for children, *The Box of Delights*. In *The Box of Delights*, the schoolboy Kay Harker is given a magical box by an old Punch and Judy man, Cole Hawlings. The box enables Kay to travel in time, to fly and to reduce himself in size. Its magic is considerable and, as such, it is much sought after by the wicked Abner Brown and his associates, foxy-faced Charles, Joe, and Sylvia Daisy Pouncer. After undergoing a number of adventures in which he manages to keep the box out of the hands of Abner Brown, Kay is finally able to make it to the Christmas Eve midnight service at Tatchester Cathedral. The following example comprises the final paragraphs of the book:

(8)   Organ and brass band struck up, full strength, the Vestry door curtains fell
        back to each side and out came the great Cathedral crosses and blessed
        banners with all the Cathedral choir and clergy, voices lifted aloft in 'O
        Come all ye Faithful'. By this time the triforium and clerestories, as well as
        every space in the Cathedral, were packed with faces: all there sang as they
        had never sung, the singing shook the whole building.
             Somehow it seemed to Kay that it was shaking the Cathedral to pieces –
        Kay himself was being shaken to pieces, his own head was surely coming
        off, still singing, through the Cathedral roof.
             In fact, the Cathedral was not there, nor any of all that glorious company.
        No, he was in a railway carriage on a bitterly cold day, the train was stopped,
        he was at Condicote Station with his pocket full of money, just home for the
        holidays and Caroline Louisa was waking him.
             'Why, Kay,' she was saying, 'wake up, wake up. You have been sound
        asleep. Welcome home for the holidays! Have you had a nice dream?'
             'Yes,' he said, 'I have.'   (Masefield 1984 [1935]: 167–8)

At this point in the narrative, the reader will have primed a contextual frame
into which Kay and the other members of the Cathedral congregation are bound.
Kay is consequently a primed character, as well as the focus of attention as a
result of the overt reference to him via the proper noun *Kay* and subsequent
masculine pronouns. The beginning of the third paragraph, however, invokes a
frame modification as a result of the narratorial claim that 'In fact, the Cathedral
was not there'. This is contrary information to that which we have so far assumed,
and it is difficult to make the necessary modification to the current primed frame.
Further confusion is caused by the statement that 'No, he was in a railway carriage
on a bitterly cold day'. This suggests both a temporal and locative frame-switch
that is difficult to reconcile, since we have not been provided with an explanation
for why the Cathedral was suddenly no longer there in the previous contextual
frame. The necessary clarification comes with the revelation that Kay has, in fact,
dreamt the whole adventure. As a result of this, the reader is forced to make a
frame repair in order to make sense of the earlier statement, 'In fact, the Cathedral
was not there'. This also means that it is necessary for the reader to reappraise all
previous contextual frames, and view them as subordinate to the current primed
contextual frame in which Kay is woken from his dream.

6.5   Summary and conclusions

In this chapter we have outlined three cognitive theories that deal
with various aspects of the reading process. Each of these have pros and cons
associated with them, perhaps the most significant of which is the relative lack
of empirical testing that each theory has received. Nonetheless, each generates a
number of hypotheses which may be subjected to empirical tests, and herein lies
their potential value for stylistics. Indeed, some empirical research into these areas
is already underway. Emmott, for example, has conducted several experiments

into the psychology of reading that have demonstrated support for some of the claims that contextual frame theory makes (see, for example, Emmott 2003b and Emmott *et al*. 2007). Both text world theory and deictic shift theory are open to empirical testing too, and some of the results with regard to the latter can be found in the volume edited by Duchan *et al*. (1995).

What should also be apparent from our discussion of these theoretical approaches is that there are considerable interconnections between the three. While text world theory provides a means of accounting for the way in which we construct vivid mental models of a narrative as we read, deictic shift theory accounts for the degree of involvement we might feel in such texts, and contextual frame theory provides an explanation of how we keep track of the complex information that it is necessary to manage in order to achieve these rich representations of a narrative world. It is also possible to map certain elements of these theories onto each other. For example, the notion of a frame-switch from contextual frame theory is roughly equivalent to the notion of a world-switch in text world theory (indeed, Gavins 2007 explains that Emmott's term motivated her choice of the term *world-switch* as a replacement for Werth's 1999 *sub-world*). Readers should also be able to note a number of connections between the theories discussed in this chapter and those outlined in Chapter 5. Contextual frame theory, for instance, makes use of several aspects of schema theory in accounting for the frame assumptions that readers have as they monitor contextual frames.

At this point we should also make clear that in our attempts to explicate some of the key ideas in cognitive stylistics, we have made something of an artificial distinction in this chapter and the last between the notions of text comprehension and text processing. Our focus in Chapter 5 was on the means by which readers bring their prior knowledge of the world to bear in the interpretation of texts. In Chapter 6 we have focused primarily on how readers manage the multitude of complex information in a narrative in order to navigate their way through it and make sense of its propositions. However, text comprehension necessarily involves text processing, and *vice versa*. Contextual frame theory, for instance, involves the management of schematic information as well as more obviously textual information. It is, then, important to realise that the various strands of cognitive activity involved in the reading process cannot in practice be separated out as easily as we might have suggested over the course of this and the previous chapter. Nonetheless, we hope that our presentation of these ideas here has helped to clarify some of the main distinctions between them.

Exercises

Exercise 6.1

Compare the following two openings of novels and consider the differences between them in terms of text world theory. Identify the world-building elements and function-advancing propositions and try to explain the differences in stylistic effect between the two texts. Consider also how deictic shift theory and contextual frame theory might elucidate your analysis.

(9)   *Text 1*

The summer day was drawing to a close and dusk had fallen on Blandings Castle, shrouding from view the ancient battlements, dulling the silver surface of the lake and causing Lord Emsworth's supreme Berkshire sow Empress of Blandings to leave the open air portion of her sty and withdraw into the covered shed where she did her sleeping. A dedicated believer in the maxim of early to bed and early to rise, she always turned in at about this time. Only by getting its regular eight hours can a pig keep up to the mark and preserve that schoolgirl complexion.

Deprived of her society, which he had been enjoying since shortly after lunch, Clarence, ninth Earl of Emsworth, the seigneur of this favoured realm, pottered dreamily back to the house, pottered dreamily to the great library which was one of its features, and had just pottered dreamily to his favourite chair, when Beach, his butler, entered bearing a laden tray. He gave it the vague stare which had so often incurred the censure – 'Oh, for goodness sake, Clarence, don't stand there looking like a goldfish' – of his sisters Constance, Dora, Charlotte, Julia and Hermione.

(Wodehouse 1980 [1969]: 1)

(10)   *Text 2*

Peter saw her first.

She was sitting on a stone, quite still, with her hands resting on her lap. She was staring vacantly ahead, seeing nothing, and all around, up and down the little street, people were running backward and forward with buckets of water, emptying them through the windows of the burning houses.

Across the street on the cobblestones, there was a dead boy. Someone had moved his body close in to the side so that it would not be in the way.

A little farther down an old man was working on a pile of stones and rubble. One by one he was carrying the stones away and dumping them to the side. Sometimes he would bend down and peer into the ruins, repeating a name over and over again.

All around there was shouting and running and fires and buckets of water and dust. And the girl sat quietly on the stone, staring ahead, not moving. There was blood running down the left side of her face. It ran down from her forehead and dripped from her chin on to the dirty print dress she was wearing.

(Roald Dahl, 'Katina' in Dahl 1973 [1945]: 83)

Exercise 6.2

Read the following poem and identify the deictic terms and the deictic centres to which they refer. On the basis of having identified these, use the principles of deictic shift theory to describe how a reader is likely to navigate their way through the text world of the poem. What stylistic effects does such an analysis help you to uncover?

(11)   *The Rhodora: On Being Asked Whence Is The Flower*

> In May, when sea-winds pierced our solitudes,
> I found the fresh Rhodora in the woods,
> Spreading its leafless blooms in a damp nook,
> To please the desert and the sluggish brook.
> The purple petals, fallen in the pool,
> Made the black eater with their beauty gay;
> Here might the redbird come his plumes to cool,
> And court the flower that cheapens his array.
> Rhodora! if the sages ask thee why
> This charm is wasted on the earth and sky,
> Tell them, dear, that if eyes were made for seeing
> Then beauty is its own excuse for being:
> Why thou went there, O rival of the rose!
> I never thought to ask, I never knew:
> But, in my simple ignorance, supposed
> The self-same Power that brought me there brought you.
>
> (Ralph W. Emerson, 1834, pub. 1847)

Further reading

Paul Werth's original conception of text world theory can be found in Werth (1999), while Gavins (2007) is an accessible introduction to the theory that also incorporates several modifications. Applications of text world theory in stylistic analysis can be found in Hidalgo Downing (2000), Gavins (2003) and Lahey (2003). Since the roots of text world theory are located in the possible worlds theories of logic, philosophy and semantics, Ryan (1991), Ronen (1994) and Semino (1997) are all recommended as comprehensive introductions to this area. Deictic shift theory is outlined in Duchan *et al.* (1995) and discussed with particular reference to stylistics (and drama in particular) in McIntyre (2006). Stockwell (2002b), McIntyre (2007) and Jeffries (2008) demonstrate how deictic shift theory might be applied to uncover the source of particular stylistic effects. Contextual frame theory is described in Emmott (1997) and applied in Emmott (2002, 2003a) and in Stockwell (2000). More general discussions of the value and limitations of cognitive stylistics can be found in Leech and Short (2007) and Leech (2008).

7   Methods and issues in stylistic analysis

7.1   Methodological considerations

Teaching people to 'do' stylistics is a very difficult task. This is partly because stylistics draws on a wide range of theories and methods from linguistics, and as a result does not have a single set of parameters which define the discipline.[1] This eclecticism is not a weakness, but a theoretically-legitimate strength. The purpose of theories is to shed light on the subject under consideration and as a result they tend to produce models which are simpler in some respects than the data they relate to. This is in order to generate fuller understanding of particular aspects of the data separately. Trying to capture the whole 'truth' about the data in one single unified theory of textual meaning would be unilluminating in its complexity.

As a result of this theoretical eclecticism, the question of how to go about a stylistic study is a complicated one, and requires the researcher to answer a number of questions, which will be introduced and discussed in the sections below. Note that any piece of stylistic research should aim to make clear the basis on which the analysis and interpretation is made, so that others are in a position to judge the results with an understanding of where they originated. This requirement – that stylistics should be as objective as possible in being rigorous and transparent – has at times been questioned by those who saw in this desire for clarity a claim to be 'scientific'.

We have already seen (Chapter 3) Stanley Fish's argument against the claim of stylistics to be scientific, and the responses from Simpson (1993) and Toolan (1996) defending the aims of stylistic analysis from his attacks. Here, we quote Short *et al.*'s (1998) explanation of the stance of stylistics towards this subject at some length as a summary of the approach we also subscribe to:

> For a stylistician, then, being objective means to be detailed, systematic and explicit in analysis, to lay one's interpretative cards, as it were, clearly on the table. If you believe that the number of interpretations that a text can hold is not indefinitely large (see Alderson and Short 1989 and Short and van Peer 1989 for empirical evidence to support such a view), then interpretative argumentation and testing will have to depend not upon something as unreliable as rhetorical persuasion, but on analysis of the linguistic structure of texts

in relation to what we know about the psychological and social processes involved in textual understanding. This is what stylistics has traditionally involved. Of course, . . . we cannot expunge our personal response from our analyses, and would never want to. Like the natural and social scientists, we are human analysts, not machines. But, like them (. . .), we do think that it is incumbent upon us (a) to produce proper evidence and argumentation for our views, and to take counter-evidence into account when making our interpretative claims, (b) to make claims which are falsifiable and (c) to be explicit and open about our claims and the evidence for them. This does not constitute a claim to be natural scientists, but merely to be systematic, open, honest and rational.

The following sections aim to guide the student/researcher through the kinds of decisions that will need to be taken at the outset of a project in stylistics in order to make sure that the research fulfils these expectations.

7.1.1   Research questions – what are they and how do you develop them?

One of the best ways of approaching a new project is to develop a set of research questions that you intend to answer through your analyses. This might be a small set (about 3) of equally important questions, or it might be a single main question which is quite broad, and some subordinate questions specifying the detailed issues that are involved. Here are some hypothetical examples, reflecting these different possibilities:

(1)   Three related questions of equal status for the study of pronoun use in contemporary poetry:

 • How does pronoun use situate the reader in the text world of (specified) poems?
 • Does pronoun use correlate with other deictic features in these poems?
 • How clear are the antecedents in these poems and do they differ in this regard?

(2)   One main question:

 • How does the style of novelist A differ from that of novelist B?

   Subordinate questions which each indicate one possible way of addressing the main question:

 • What are the keywords of (one example of) each writer's work, as compared with a reference corpus?
 • Which of Simpson's modal categories does (one example of) each writer's work fall into?
 • What kinds of discourse presentation are used in (one example of) each writer's work?

Note that example 1 is a quite limited study of a small number of poems, perhaps suitable for a single assessed piece of work for a student, or a journal article for a senior researcher. Example 2 on the other hand has the potential to be a very large study of two or more novels. Example 2 also demonstrates that the list of supplementary questions can be expanded or varied, depending on the tools of analysis that the researcher thinks it appropriate to use. A main research question about something as general as 'the style of X' is almost bound to need quite a lot of focusing in the supplementary questions, which will determine the kinds of tool that will be used. Thus, a general question about style may be followed by particular questions about formal features (phonology, morphology etc.) or by questions about the kinds of conceptual metaphor, blending or other cognitive aspects of the texts concerned. These decisions will reflect the preferences of the researcher, who may find some tools of analysis more enlightening than others, but it may also reflect hypotheses that the researcher has developed about the data from a more informal survey of its linguistic features.

Note that the discipline of formulating research questions is a very useful one to acquire as it requires the researcher to think clearly about what the study is attempting to discover. Although one might first of all develop a hypothesis, such as 'Alan Bennett's prose works use the same stylistic features as his plays', this is only a beginning, and needs to be broken down into specific research questions before you can start planning the actual research itself.

7.1.2   Quantitative and qualitative approaches

Once the research questions are written, they act as an anchor for the rest of the project planning that is needed before the research proper can begin. Though many research projects in stylistics combine some aspects of both quantitative and qualitative research, it is certainly worthwhile being clear from the start about the extent to which, and where, each of these approaches will be used.

It is possible to use quantitative methods on any type or amount of data, but it is important to be clear from the start that once a study begins to count things, it must take seriously the need to test the significance of any statistical findings it intends to use. Thus, the counting of, say, pre-modifying adjectives in a short lyric poem would probably not produce enough statistical information to be reliable, whereas comparing the occurrence of certain grammatical features (e.g. intensive verbs) across two novels would certainly be a statistic worthy of testing.

Note that it remains important to recognise that stylistics, whatever its detractors say, does not 'read off' meanings from linguistic features, so the discovery of a significant (statistical) difference between two texts, though interesting, does not in itself constitute an interpretative finding. The question of why this difference is there often requires more detailed analysis both of the co-text and the context, and this is time-consuming work. The result is that one common way for research projects to progress is to start with a quantitative study of a large corpus of data to discover large patterns, and then to extract samples of the data in order to carry out in-depth qualitative analyses.

Let us say, for example, that the project aims to find out what kind of discourse presentation is used in the detective novel genre, and whether this differs from other novel genres. One way to approach such research questions would be to assemble a corpus of detective fiction, annotate it for types of discourse (speech, thought and writing) presentation, and then compare this statistically with existing corpora of other fiction. This process would reveal any large-scale differences in types of discourse presentation between this genre and fiction in general. The next stage would probably be to consider whether the detail was also different. For example, even where the amounts of FIS or NRSA were similar in the two corpora, there may be differences in the type of context in which they are used. This kind of analysis, which takes context as part of the process, is bound to be qualitative, as there is unlikely to be a pre-ordained set of categories into which each example would fit, even if there was time to look at enough examples to warrant statistical analysis. Though there may be some conclusions which demonstrate patterning, there may also be none, with each example appearing to differ from the others. This kind of research is basically inductive (i.e. bottom-up) as it does not adopt any pre-conceived ideas as to the likely outcome – in other words, it has no specific hypotheses about what will be found.

Before we consider the nature of qualitative analysis, it is worth reiterating the importance of statistical testing in quantitative studies. Whilst percentages and pie charts etc. often look impressive, the differences they purport to show may in fact be insignificant and may be exaggerated by the manner in which they are presented. The tools of quantitative studies are increasingly automated as large corpora become ever more accessible and software is produced to analyse them. This software (see section 7.2.2) usually includes significance testing in producing its results, so the researcher does not usually need to carry out complex calculations her/himself. Nevertheless, it is useful to understand basic concepts, such as normal distribution, how significance testing works and the relevance of levels of significance to a project's findings in order to truly understand the results of your research.[2]

Note also that corpus stylistics is not the only quantitative research that can be said to belong under the umbrella of stylistic research. There has been a distinguished tradition of empirical study (see for example van Peer *et al.* 2007) within stylistics since its inception, much of which involves the measuring and comparison of reader-responses using statistical methodologies.

As for qualitative research, this has been the basis of most of the stylistics of the last hundred years or so, until recently, when computer technology started to make corpus stylistics more attractive. Qualitative work allows the analyst to describe features that are not category-driven, and as we saw in Chapter 3, many of the functional systems of language have prototypical, rather than absolute, categories. Thus, a corpus study which uses these systems (such as transitivity or modality) would need to make sometimes arbitrary decisions about the categorisation of a particular example in order to complete the annotation of the corpus. This is not necessarily a problem if all the data is treated in the same way, though it precludes discussion of the subtleties that are often raised by the difficulties of categorisation.

Another reason why a researcher may choose qualitative research over quantitative is the nature of the data and/or the scope of the research questions. For example, the project may aim to describe in some detail the foregrounded features of a single poem or a small number of poems simply in order to demonstrate the linguistic basis of the foregrounding and perhaps to illuminate the process(es) by which the poem(s) contribute to the reader's meaning. Such a study would be unlikely to require any quantifying of features, and the more appropriate technique would be to provide a commentary on the poem(s) either line by line or under linguistic headings (phonology, morphology, syntax, semantics etc.). Similarly, a student could wish to explain linguistically why a particular passage from fiction seemed to have a particular literary effect, and this would also be a task best suited to qualitative analysis.

In the next section, we will consider the nature of 'data' in stylistics, and how it relates to the questions of qualitative and quantitative methods that we have been considering here.

7.1.3   Data

We saw in Chapter 1 that the data of stylistics, though typically literary, can in fact be potentially any text which uses language.[3] The question of how much data and what kind of data should be analysed is difficult to answer in general terms as it is dependent on the research questions, the methodology and the tools of analysis to be used. In qualitative studies, the more data to be collected, the more sparse the analysis will be to cover it all. Conversely, a study looking only at one linguistic feature (such as speech presentation) will be able to cover a larger collection of texts than one where a number of tools of analysis are to be used.

The question of how much and which data will be analysed is also related to the question of how many tools of analysis will be applied. It is not straightforward to apply many of the stylistic tools to data as there are decisions to be made about how intensively the data will be analysed. For example, if the study is to look at transitivity choices, does that mean the main clauses only, or does it include subordinate transitivity choices too? If the latter, will this include single participles which are barely even separate clauses, and catenative verbs whose status as subordinate clauses is also debatable? If the study is about speech presentation, is it concerned with only certain character-interactions, or all interactions?

All such decisions about the scope of the data and how it is to be treated will follow from the research questions, and should be made clearly and explicitly at the outset, so that they can be described to others. Sometimes, these decisions need to be changed when problems arise from earlier decisions, but in such cases the analysis will begin again.

7.1.4 Stylistic models and tools of analysis

The kind of stylistic analysis which is carried out in any study will depend partly on the underlying assumptions that the researcher makes about the nature of textual meaning. Thus, there are some researchers who are keen to emphasise the reader's role in the creation of textual meaning, and who therefore take a cognitive model of textual meaning as their starting point. There are others who, whilst acknowledging the importance of the experience and understanding that readers bring to textual meaning, nevertheless wish to focus on the properties of the text itself. Some researchers may favour each of these approaches for different projects.

The student/researcher embarking on a project should take a view of the kinds of theoretical position s/he wishes to take as a starting-point, though in many cases the careful elaboration of research questions will make a particular theoretical standpoint inevitable. Thus, a project wishing to address the question of what interpretative common ground there is for readers of a poem will place emphasis on readers' meaning, though there remains the question of whether the empirical collecting of reader responses or the application of cognitive models of understanding is to be chosen. In either case, this being stylistics, there will be close and continual reference to the text at the centre of the process.

If an initial hypothesis is more definitive than this, and suggests that readers *will* overlap in their interpretation of the surface meaning of a poem but differ in their broader interpretative strategies, then there is a latent assumption that one can distinguish theoretically between what might be called semantic and pragmatic meanings of such texts. Note that this distinction, between semantics and pragmatics, is a contentious area of debate, and one that is normally negotiated in relation to spoken face-to-face interaction. Stylistics, then, can appropriate techniques and debates where relevant, but also contribute to them by introducing new kinds of data, in this case written literary texts.

7.2 Stylistic studies

Having described in section 7.1 some of the key elements of stylistic analysis, our aim in this section is to give a flavour of the kind of studies carried out within stylistics, and of the range of methodologies employed by stylisticians. We hope that this will serve as a useful indicator of the range of approaches taken to the stylistic analysis of texts. Of course, in the space available we can do no more than provide a brief summary of typical studies and approaches. Nonetheless, we believe it is useful for the beginning student to have at least some measure of the analytical and methodological possibilities available. We have chosen to focus on three main areas – the qualitative analysis of literature, corpus stylistics, and responses to texts – though there remain, of course, a number of other approaches to stylistic analysis. For these, the reader is referred to the further reading section at the end of this chapter.

7.2.1   The qualitative analysis of literature

The qualitative analysis of literary texts has traditionally been the mainstay of stylistic analysis and will no doubt continue to be so. The importance of qualitative analysis can be seen in the fact that even the corpus-based and protocol analyses described in the subsequent two sections do not ignore this aspect of the analytical process. As West (2008: 137) notes in an article assessing the current state of English Studies, 'the object of study of English is literature written in the English language'. While stylistic analysis may be carried out on languages other than English, West's point is clear: for stylistics, the text is key.

If we take a look at the range of qualitative stylistic studies that have been reported in recent years in *Language and Literature*, the main international stylistics journal,[4] we find that, unsurprisingly, there are some that investigate the style of a single poem. These include Freeman (2005), which takes a conceptual metaphor approach to Sylvia Plath's poem 'The Applicant', and Melrose (2006), which looks at the stylistic ambiguities in Robert Browning's 'My Last Duchess'. What is noticeable about these studies is that they each take a specific stylistic approach to the poem, and that in each case they are comparing their approaches with others'. Thus, Freeman is comparing her analysis with that of Semino (1997), who applies schema theory to the same poem, and Melrose is using stylistic analysis to explain the range of existing literary interpretations of the Browning poem.

Other studies of poetry include those which appear to try to encompass rather large bodies of material, such as Duffell (2002), who surveys the use of Italian metrical lines in English poetry after Chaucer. This work is inevitably reliant on his encyclopaedic knowledge of English poetry of a very long historical range, but can also, of course, draw upon metrical studies by others, since there is a long tradition of such work in English literature. Much more central to stylistics are those studies which focus on a particular poet, such as Somacarrera (2000), who investigates the effects of parallelism in a collection of poems by Margaret Atwood, or Goodblatt (2000), who compares three poems by three poets (Whitman, Williams and Hughes) to demonstrate stylistically the phenomenon noted by critics that after Whitman the unitary poetic (monologic) voice seems to have been displaced by multiple voices (Bakhtin's 1981 concept of 'heteroglossia'). Perhaps the most focused article on poetry is Cauldwell (1999), which looks at just a few lines of Larkin's 'Mr Bleaney', and in particular attempts to relate Larkin's own varied renderings of these lines in recordings to the range of interpretations that have been attached to the poem by others.

Qualitative studies of larger bodies of data, such as prose fiction, are also frequently found in *Language and Literature*. Short fiction is one way to keep the amount of data manageable, and this is illustrated by Ryder (2003), who considers two short stories about time travel, and Malmkjær (2004), who takes a stylistic approach to questions of translation, in particular translations of Hans Christian Andersen's stories. There are also those which attempt to characterise aspects of the style of a whole novel, such as Chapman and Routledge (1999), who take a pragmatic approach to the detective novelist Paul Auster's *City of Glass*, Hidalgo-Downing (2000), who applies text world theory to Joseph Heller's *Catch-22*, and Wallhead (2003), who considers metaphors for the self in A. S. Byatt's *The Biographer's Tale*. Notice that each of these studies has a different way of making the large amount of data manageable, by taking a particular strand of the whole to investigate, usually from a particular theoretical angle. Another way to do this is to specify an extract or extracts to study, as in Cecconi's (2008) study of the trial scene in Dickens's *Pickwick Papers*. As we saw in relation to poetry, some researchers wish to compare versions of texts, either because they have been performed a number of times (see Cauldwell 1999) or because the author drafted and re-drafted the work. Sopčák (2007) considers foregrounding in the drafts of Joyce's *Ulysses*, and this, by its nature, limits the sections of the work that needed investigation, as Joyce will not have changed all of it entirely.

Other comparative studies may involve two (or more) novels. Fraser Gupta (2000), for example, compares two Singaporean novels, whilst Heywood *et al.* (2002) compare extracts from a popular and a serious novel, to identify the different challenges they raise for metaphor identification. Studies which range even wider across prose fiction are Harvey (2000), which investigates the representation of 'camp talk' in post-war English and French fiction, and Rash (2000), which considers the question of language use in Swiss (German-language) literature. Each of these studies makes a manageable project by taking a single theme which thereby reduces the amount of data that needs to be considered. There remain, however, significant challenges in ensuring that such wide-ranging studies are rigorous, replicable and explicit.

Recent developments in qualitative stylistics have included consideration of how stylistic methods may help us to interpret and analyse plays and films. These often take the textual aspects of the script or screenplay as their starting point. So, for example, Culpeper (2000) considers the cognitive stylistic features which give us insights into Shakespeare's characterisation of Katherina in *The Taming of the Shrew*, Ivanchenko (2007) takes a conversation analysis approach to overlap in Caryl Churchill's *Top Girls* and McIntyre (2004) considers how point of view is indicated linguistically in the text of Dennis Potter's *Brimstone and Treacle*. Others compare novels and their realisation in film versions. Thus, Clark (1999) compares Trevor Griffiths's *Fatherland* with Ken Loach's film and Forceville (2002a) compares styles of narration in the novel and film of *The Comfort of Strangers*. These latter exemplify the increasing move in stylistics towards multimodal analysis, though progress is relatively slow in this field, there being a lack of clear analytical procedures for non-linguistic aspects of texts, which makes comparisons difficult.

The final type of qualitative stylistic study that occurs in *Language and Literature* is the investigation of non-literary texts. In the same way that a researcher may investigate everything from an individual poem (or a few lines of a poem) to a whole poetic movement or era, these studies vary in their scope. As with all stylistic study, the broader the scope, the less detail it is possible to include and the less comprehensive it is possible to be. An example of a broad study is by Beal (2000), who takes the representation of the Geordie dialect as her theme, and investigates it across a wide historical range of data including poems, prose and cartoons. A similarly broad study is Seargeant's (2007) study of the representation of epidemic disease in the texts (sermons, pamphlets and so on) of Early Modern England. The focus in this case, on the representation of disease, is what makes the project (relatively) manageable.

More focused studies often depend on corpora of data, though not all of them use quantitative methods to examine this data. Lambrou (2003), for example, draws on a set of recordings of oral narratives to consider the way in which speakers may move from one speech genre to another and Fitzmaurice (2000) investigates politeness phenomena in the letters of Margaret Cavendish. More focused still are those studies which concentrate on a single text or small number of texts, such as Pearce (2001), who examines a single party election broadcast by the British Labour Party, and Montgomery (1999), who analyses the reactions of Tony Blair, the Queen and Earl Spencer to the death of Princess Diana, and the public reception of these reactions. Another way to limit the data that one is investigating is to concentrate on a single word, and this is the strategy of Montgomery (2005), who studies the context and meanings of the word 'war' immediately after the attack on the World Trade Center on 11 September 2001.

In addition to the journal articles explored above, and those of other relevant journals, such as *Style*, *Journal of Literary Semantics* and *English Text Construction*, there are book-length studies which include stylistic analysis of work by genre, author, period and so on. The 'Language of Literature' series (Palgrave), for example, includes Blake (1989), Todd (1989), Jeffries (1993), Fowler (1995) and Lester (1996). These books of course have little chance of being comprehensive, and each has different ways of presenting a digest of the stylistic analysis available on their chosen topics. More research-project-based books still dependent on a qualitative, rather than a quantitative, approach include Stockwell's (2000) book on the poetics of science fiction; McIntyre's (2006) book on style in drama, including a detailed analysis of Alan Bennett's *The Lady in the Van*; Semino (1997), which makes detailed studies of individual poems; Gregoriou (2007), which investigates deviance in detective fiction; and Mandala (2007), which compares dramatic dialogue with ordinary conversation. Further work on the style of particular authors and text-types is forthcoming in the book series 'Advances in Stylistics', including West (forthcoming) on I. A. Richards, Sotirova (forthcoming) on D. H. Lawrence, Ho (forthcoming) on John Fowles, Montoro (forthcoming) on chick-lit and Piazza (forthcoming) on cinematic discourse.

This rather brief survey of some of the qualitative stylistic work which has been published demonstrates its range and variability in terms of scope and topic. It may be that some of the work discussed above will in future be replaced by more quantitative corpus studies, but there remains a place for detailed qualitative analysis in most stylistic research, not least because many of the most interesting aspects of style are not searchable automatically by computer. In addition, short texts, such as poems or individual advertisements, will always lend themselves to qualitative analysis of the following kind. Consider the following short poem:

(3)   *italic*
            ONCE I LIVED IN CAPITALS
            MY LIFE INTENSELY PHALLIC
            but now i'm sadly lowercase
            with the occasional *italic*
                    (Roger McGough)

McGough's poem appears to be a playful comment on the nature of getting old and suggests that, sadly, a reduction in the excitement experienced in life accompanies this. We are likely to see the word 'italic' as referring to some sexual highpoint and the lowercase letters as somehow symbolic of the speaker's now dull life. Clearly, the poem is not a complex one. Nonetheless, a qualitative stylistic analysis can help to determine how this intuitive response to the poem comes about. In this way, a stylistic analysis can help to support an interpretation of the text. The interpretation in effect constitutes a hypothesis that the accompanying stylistic analysis tests. With regard to analytical tools, we will examine the creation of foregrounding effects in the poem via the concepts of deviation and parallelism. Here we suggest that any other stylistician attempting to identify foregrounding via an analysis of linguistic levels (see Chapter 2) would uncover the same foregrounded elements. In this respect, the analysis we present is potentially replicable.

Perhaps the first noticeable element of the language of the poem is its graphology. The text is divided into two pairs of lines. The first two lines are graphologically parallel in that they consist entirely of uppercase letters. The second pair of lines are also graphologically parallel, since they consist entirely of lowercase letters. However, we can also note the presence of graphological deviation, as the common conventions of writing are that we don't write consistently in capitals or consistently in lowercase. Notice too that the poem is not left-justified but centred. This perhaps breaks our prototypical expectations about poetry and therefore constitutes a further graphological deviation. There is, then, a substantial amount of foregrounding in the poem as a result of this deviation and parallelism. The next task is to identify how the foregrounding connects to our interpretation of the poem. Since the poem is short, we can analyse it line by line:

Line 1 'ONCE I LIVED IN CAPITALS'

Living life 'in capitals' suggests living life to the full. This is reinforced by the uppercase letters. The fact that they are literally big and bold is graphologically symbolic. We can also note the polysemy of 'capitals'. In addition to referring to uppercase letters, we might also interpret this to mean capital cities. The appropriateness of this interpretation is that geographical capitals are often thought of as being exciting and vibrant places to live, and this connects with the speaker's implicature of having lived an exciting life.

Line 2 'MY LIFE INTENSELY PHALLIC'

This line indicates more specifically the kind of life that the speaker claims to have lived. 'My life intensely phallic' suggests a life filled with sexual pleasures. The connection between the speaker's suggestion that his life was exciting and the notion that this excitement was sexual comes about because of the graphological parallelism of these first two lines. This pushes us to see a relationship of equivalence between the propositional content of the lines.

Line 3 'but now i'm sadly lowercase'

We can note here that the lowercase letters contrast with the uppercase letters, and that this appears to reflect the fact that the speaker's life is now the opposite of what it used to be. The graphological parallelism of the first and second pairs of lines now sets up a relationship of opposition between them, generated by a conventional assumption of capital letters as the opposite of lowercase letters (see section 3.2.5 for a detailed discussion of categories of opposition). If living life 'in capitals' is leading a busy, exciting life, then being 'lowercase' seems to mean the opposite, and this is reflected in the graphology.

Line 4 'with the occasional *italic*'

The final line contains arguably another piece of sexual innuendo. Despite the fact that the speaker's life is now fairly boring, there is still the occasional high spot. The literal indication of this comes via the graphological deviation inherent in the italicisation of 'italic', creating a graphologically symbolic effect (Short 2000). That we should see this as referring to sexual activity comes about because of the phonological parallelism of 'italic' and 'phallic'. The rhyme pushes us to see the propositional meaning of these two words as being somehow equivalent.

This qualitative analysis uses the concept of foregrounding to identify the source of our initial interpretation of the text, explaining how deviation and parallelism generate particular stylistic effects which push us to interpret the poem in a particular way. We would suggest that anyone else applying foregrounding theory in an analysis of this text would uncover the same kinds of effects as we have noted here, and that in this sense what we have presented is a replicable analysis, albeit of a fairly simple text. Of course, it would be possible to use other stylistic frameworks than foregrounding in the analysis of the poem. Conceptual metaphor, for instance, would seem to be important, in the speaker's conceptualisation of himself as akin to particular kinds of writing. It is also the case that a fuller stylistic analysis could take into account aspects of context that we have not covered here. The point here is that any analysis that did so convincingly would supersede the one we have presented here. This, of course, is a hallmark of objectivity – the willingness to change one's mind if contrary evidence or a better explanation is presented.

Analyses of short texts such as the one we have just seen are a staple of stylistics, and may stand alone or form part of a study bringing together many such analyses, perhaps of parts of a larger corpus which has been excavated automatically to generate short texts to focus upon. In the next section, we will consider the development of computer-aided and computer-driven stylistic research.

7.2.2   Corpus stylistics

In recent years stylistics has profited considerably from the insights offered by corpus linguistics. Indeed, such has been the influence that there is now a developing sub-area of stylistics commonly known as **corpus stylistics**. Corpus linguistics is best viewed as a methodology for the analysis of large quantities of language data, as opposed to being a sub-discipline of linguistics in its own right. Although the origins of corpus linguistics can be traced back to the early years of the twentieth century and the work of the American field linguists (McEnery and Wilson 2001), corpus linguistics only came into its own with the advent of computing, which gave corpus linguists the capacity to store and search large electronic collections of text. Such databases are termed **corpora** (**corpus** is the singular noun). Modern corpora run to many millions of words and cover a wide variety of genres and text-types. Examples include the British National Corpus of 100,000,000 words of written and spoken British English from the 1990s, the Bank of English (stored at the University of Birmingham and the source of the COBUILD series of dictionaries and grammars), and the ICE (International Corpus of English) collection of corpora of international varieties of English.

The advantage of such corpora for stylisticians is that they can provide some measure of what might constitute the norms of language. In this respect, they offer an opportunity to test our intuitions concerning what might be the foregrounded elements of a text. It follows from this that using corpora in stylistic analysis provides another means of achieving the objectivity that stylisticians aim for. Interestingly, while some early stylisticians foresaw the advantages that having access to such large quantities of text could offer, others were dismissive of the value of such statistical information. Freeman (1970), for example, claimed that even if it were possible to ascertain frequency information for particular elements of language, 'they would constitute no revealing insight into either natural language or style' (Freeman 1970: 3). Louw (1993) rightly criticises Freeman for this remarkably short-sighted view, which has since been demonstrated to be erroneous (see, for example, Semino and Short 2004, Stubbs 2005, O'Halloran 2007a, 2007b).

The potential applications of corpus linguistics to stylistics are considerable. Aside from the possibility of discerning frequency information and thus a statistical measure of foregrounding, software for corpus linguistics also makes possible the analysis of complete texts. This has enabled stylisticians to circumvent the problems identified by Leech and Short (1981) concerning how to analyse complete texts in the requisite amount of detail demanded by stylistics, without such analyses being impossibly time-consuming and thus increasingly open to human error.

As an example of what is possible, Semino and Short (2004) report on a large-scale project carried out at Lancaster University to test the model of speech and thought presentation originally outlined in Leech and Short (1981) on a 250,000-word corpus of English writing. The model of speech and thought presentation proposed in Leech and Short (see Chapter 3 for a summary of this) was developed initially through the qualitative analysis of examples drawn from the close reading of texts. Short, Semino and other members of their project team tested this model by constructing a corpus of fiction and non-fiction texts and manually annotating these texts using the categories of discourse presentation presented in Leech and Short's model. As a result of this they found it necessary to modify the model slightly, since the data did not always support the suppositions that Leech and Short had made about how discourse presentation works in English. Semino and Short's corpus work thus refined the original model of speech and thought presentation, as well as providing a statistical measure of which categories were most common. From this, it became possible to state more confidently what constitutes the norm for speech and thought presentation, and thus to identify with greater certainty what constitutes deviation from this norm. Their corpus analysis also revealed more clearly the stylistic effects associated with each category on the cline.

Semino and Short's (2004) study relied on manual annotation of their data, though it is also possible to analyse large quantities of language stylistically without having to do this. Mahlberg (2007), for example, analyses Dickens's *Great Expectations* using the WordSmith Tools software package (Scott 2004) to extract data relating to repeated patterns of usage to determine what she terms their **local textual function**. The patterns that Mahlberg studies are five-word **clusters**: that is, repeated sequences of five words. (Clusters are also known as **n-grams**, where 'n' is simply any number.) Mahlberg identifies twenty-one different five-word clusters, each of which she categorises as belonging to one of the following groups: label clusters (e.g. 'the Old Green Copper Rope-Walk'), speech clusters ('it appeared to me that'), *as if* clusters ('as if he had been'), time and place clusters ('at the end of the') and body-part clusters ('his head on one side'). Her analysis of these patterns provides support for more literary-oriented and intuitive critiques of Dickens's language such as those provided by Brook (1970) and Quirk (1961). For example, on the basis of a qualitative analysis of Chapter 38 of the novel (particularly the pattern 'I saw in this'), Quirk (1961) suggests that Pip's experience causes him to believe that what he sees is unequivocally correct, and that this contrasts with an inherent theme of the novel – namely that seeing does *not* equate to knowing. Mahlberg demonstrates that the *as if* clusters in *Great Expectations* contribute to the theme that Quirk identifies, noting, for example, that the clusters are used when the I-narrator Pip is describing how people look at someone or something (e.g. 'looking dejectedly at me, as if he thought it really might have . . . '). In this way she is able to provide objectively garnered evidence for a previously subjective opinion.

Mahlberg's analysis is primarily what Adolphs (2006: 65) describes as **intra-textual**; that is, it is an analysis that examines a particular piece of language data in order to extrapolate information pertaining specifically to that data. This may be contrasted with **inter-textual** analysis. This latter analytical approach compares the linguistic features of the target text with those of a control text or collection of texts (what corpus linguists would term a **reference corpus**). Corpus-stylistic methods are not just appropriate for the intra-textual analysis of longer texts, of course. While this might be a primary application of the corpus methodology, corpora can also be used to provide supporting evidence for stylistic analyses via inter-textual analysis, often corroborating or disproving the results of qualitative analysis. It can, for instance, be used to discern why a particular linguistic choice is deviant. For example, in Chapter 1 we discussed an extract from a University of Huddersfield staff newsletter, in which the retirement announcement of a member of staff closed with the sentence: 'Stephen intends to spend more time with his wife and caravan.' The unintentionally humorous effect here clearly comes about as a result of the fact that we do not expect to see the word *caravan* turning up in the slot following the phrase *wife and*. As we noted in Chapter 1, on the basis of intuition we are much more likely to expect a word like *children* or *family*. But how are we to know that our intuition is either reliable or shared by other readers? A corpus allows us to check such an intuitive response. Searching for the phrase WIFE AND in the British National Corpus reveals that the most common collocates of this phrase are indeed nouns associated with family. (A **collocate** is a word that typically turns up in close proximity to our target word more than would be expected by chance alone.) Indeed, the only non-family-related word that turns up is *thief*, and a closer inspection reveals that this is part of a film title, *The Cook, the Thief, his Wife and her Lover*. Even so, *thief* refers to a human. *Caravan* is clearly a semantically deviant choice, then, being unrelated to either humans or families. A corpus can thus allow us to check our intuitions and can be particularly useful for analysts investigating a language of which they are a non-native speaker.

Collocational analysis can also reveal the connotations that a particular word may generate. Consider, for example, the following short poem by Roger McGough:

(4)   *Vinegar*

Sometimes
i feel like a priest
in a fish & chip queue
quietly thinking
as the vinegar runs through
how nice it would be
to buy supper for two
          (Roger McGough)

This is not a complex poem interpretatively and it does not need a detailed stylistic analysis to draw out what is perhaps its main theme. The speaker in the poem appears to be ruing his single status and wishing that he was in a relationship. The comparison the speaker makes of himself to a priest seems to be motivated by the fact that Catholic priests typically spend their lives alone, not marrying or entering into an intimate relationship with anyone. Of course, this is a prototypical view and, since the time the poem was written (1967), certain socio-cultural changes that have occurred might affect this interpretation. Nonetheless, it would be easy to dismiss the poem as trivial, were it not for the other connotations that the word *priest* generates. One way of accessing these would simply be to speculate on the basis of intuition. However, a corpus analysis of the **collocates** of *priest* can give us a statistical insight into which connotations are particularly likely to be triggered for the reader.

The statistical significance of collocations can be determined by calculating a **mutual information (MI) score**. This is calculated by comparing the observed frequency with which a particular collocate is associated with the **node word** (in this case, *priest*) with its expected frequency in the corpus as a whole. Most corpus linguistics software packages will carry out this calculation (or a similar one) automatically. For example, Mark Davies's web front-end to the BNC[5] calculates MI scores for collocates and an MI score of 3 or over indicates that the collocation in question is not simply a result of chance alone but is statistically significant.

To return now to the McGough poem, the top ten statistically significant collocates of *priest* in the BNC, in descending order of significance, are *lecherous, maxi, ordained, nun, deacon, Jesuit, celibate, fr, atonement* and *parish*. What this list demonstrates is that *priest* does not have overwhelmingly positive connotations. In fact, the most statistically significant collocate, *lecherous*, has an obvious negative **semantic prosody** which may well cause us to re-evaluate our assessment of the poem as twee and whimsical. A word's semantic prosody is the connotations that it takes on as a result of the meanings of the words that it collocates with. A further statistically significant collocate of *priest* is *celibate*, which again may cause us to re-focus our assessment of the speaker of the poem, suggesting as it does that the comparison with a priest is intended to convey sexual frustration. Of course, these connotations may have been arrived at via introspection, but a corpus analysis provides some measure of objectivity in determining collocates, as well as a statistical calculation of collocational strength. It thus provides an objective means of finding supportive (or non-supportive) evidence for a particular interpretation.

7.2.3   Responses to texts

Concerns about variability in the meaning-potential of texts and how this affects the value of stylistic analysis have arisen from time to time, particularly whilst the parallel debates took place in literary studies as to the location of textual meaning, and whether it made sense to write about textual meaning in the face of theories that placed the reader at the heart of the meaning-making process. Interestingly, though literary studies traditionally privileged the concept of author meaning, and then abandoned it in favour of reader meaning, stylistics has tended to focus on textual meaning, though this has less frequently been the focus for literary studies.[6]

Stylistics has embraced the notion of the reader's contribution to meaning in a number of ways, which reflect on the one hand the view that there is some value in establishing the extent to which there are collective views of textual meaning-potential and on the other hand the view that individuals may have different, and ultimately infinitely variable, experiences of texts. In this section, we will focus particularly on those studies that have collected and analysed the *actual* responses of readers.

The study of readers' responses to literary and other texts has been used in a number of different ways by stylisticians. This technique can be used in studies applying the methods of psychology to the reading process, and has been used with considerable success by, for example, Emmott (1997), who has been concerned with tracking the process by which a reader of narrative fiction will process the participants and events in a story. Her research, then, requires considerable preparation of suitable texts, which have to be invented to allow her to test precisely the kinds of textual feature which produce particular reactions in readers. This kind of empirical testing of reactions to texts is so far difficult to use with independently-occurring texts such as poems and novels, because of the need in experimental conditions to control the possible variables and be sure that the right elements are being tested. (For more on Emmott's work, see the discussion in Chapter 6.)

Other work has used the responses of readers to 'real' texts as some kind of evidence of the meaning potential of such texts. This work originates with a technique known as 'protocol analysis', pioneered by Short and van Peer (1989) and Alderson and Short (1989), in which the analysts (two in each case) were presented with a poem line by line and externalised their thoughts on the meaning of the poem as each line was read. Although not as experimentally controlled as Emmott's work, these experiments did allow for genuine literary texts to be used. Though not a completely natural reading experience, the resulting protocols were at least produced under identical conditions, so they can legitimately be compared with each other. Here is a sample of the kind of (written) responses in Short and van Peer (1989: 29):

> *Flutes and low to the lake falls home.*
>
> MHS The verb! Metaphorical – so it makes a musical (high pitched?) sound and then falls straight down into the lake (cf. the sound patterning and positioning of *low*). *Home* = end; but also anthropomorphic meaning (cf. *his*)?
>
> WVP A verb. Subject = *the fleece of his foam*? *Falls home* is deviant (but cf. *to plunge home*). Makes a musical sound? And grooves? Note vowel parallelism in *coop – comb/flutes – low*; also the rhyme (*home/foam*). Hence this stanza 'describes' a stream thundering down from a height and dropping into the lake. In this dive the water seems to come to a standstill: connotations of rest and peace – *home, flute, low.*

The two analysts (MHS and WVP) seem to notice the same kinds of thing, and describe them in similar ways. Thus, they both notice the musical reference, though the line describes the movement of a waterfall, and they both comment on the vowel sounds in relation to the pitch of the music. The best summary of the findings of these studies is to be found in Short and van Peer (1989: 22):

> Our most striking findings were that:
> a) Our interpretations and strategies for arriving at those interpretations were very similar;
> b) We had made very explicit and very similar evaluative remarks on the text;
> c) These evaluative statements centred on practically identical text locations.

These studies were carried out, of course, by highly-trained stylisticians who shared certain other background features (e.g. gender, age, ethnicity etc.) which could also have produced similar effects. The authors are aware of these possible criticisms and make clear that what they are trying to do is to pilot a technique that might be used elsewhere in order to establish the nature and extent of common ground that readers have in response to texts. This technique has influenced certain other studies, such as Jeffries (2002), which used a visual text with almost no linguistic content to elicit linguistic responses about the meaning of the text. The informants in this case were students with relatively little stylistic training, and the results were used as texts for analysis in their own right, so that stylistic analysis could be used to draw conclusions about the informants' responses that may be unavailable to them consciously. This technique is also influenced by the work of Rob Pope (1994), whose use of **textual intervention** as a pedagogical tool for teaching cultural theory also paves the way for stylistic research using intervention as a way of reflecting on the meaning of texts. Thus, textual intervention is one possible technique of stylistic analysis that could be used by analysts self-consciously or by informants in response to a request to 'paraphrase'. The following short poem (5), for example, could be re-written in a number of ways (6–7):

(5)   *The Front Bedroom*

When the penny dropped
that I was here
only because my mam and dad
had done in the front bedroom
what I had just decided
I would like to do
with Doreen Peasland
behind our barn,
I was disgusted.
                    (Baker 2003: 58)

(6)   I want to have sex with Doreen Peasland,
but it's less appealing now
that I realise my parents
have done it too.

(7)   I have just found out about sex
and have conflicting
views of it, now that I know
my parents must have done it
to have me, though I still fancy
Doreen Peasland.

The many permutations of this kind of re-writing may illuminate the 'base text' by showing what is lost when the language changes. In (6), for example, the loss is one of suspense, which in the base text means that we don't find out what the narrator's reaction is until the main clause in the final line. The rest of the original poem is a subordinate clause, meaning that there is 'deferred gratification' for the reader as s/he waits to find out what the proposition of the sentence will be. In (7) we are caused to reflect on the implicit nature of the meaning in the original, as (7) makes explicit (one reading of) the underlying meaning of the poem. The stylistician may, therefore, use such intervention him/herself, either as a way of discovering the linguistic foci of the text or as a way of explaining her/his analysis. The technique may also be used as a way of discovering the extent of overlap of interpretation and understanding between a group of informants.

What is important about this technique, and the response techniques, whether protocols like Short and van Peer's or more open techniques as used in Jeffries (2002), is that they all produce a legitimate response to the text, and that there is a range of response possible, starting from the most agreed-upon consensual meaning, and shading out to the most individual and varied response, which might be based on personal experience. This recognition, that there is a 'shadow' cast by every text, and that this shadow is darker (i.e. more consensual) the nearer you get to the text itself, is one that is examined in the introduction to Jeffries *et al.* (2007):

> The idea of a text's 'shadow' is taken from terminology employed by crim-inologists and others to describe the great many unreported and unsolved crimes lying behind the ones we know about. How it relates to textual meaning is that it seems to me that there is a very deep shadow close to the text, representing the communal meaning that most readers would agree on, and a lighter and lighter shadow as we get further away from this consensus, including accidental meanings that relate to the individual circumstances of readers and changing meanings that are anachronistic to the text's context of production but happen to resonate with later historical audiences.   (Jeffries *et al.* 2007: xi)

The use of responses to text, then, will depend on the nature of the project being undertaken, though it is certainly worth keeping protocol analysis, textual intervention and other responses in mind as a useful tool for the stylistician.

7.3   Summary and conclusions

Our aim in this chapter has been to return to some of the principles of stylistics outlined initially in Chapter 1, in order to demonstrate the range of theoretical and analytical frameworks available for stylistic analysis. We should make clear, of course, that no one method of analysis is intrinsically better or worse than another. The key to a successful stylistic analysis is to choose the methodology and analytical framework that is appropriate to the text or texts in question. It is also the case that many analyses are substantially improved by the application of numerous analytical methods. Such triangulation can often substantially enhance the evidence in support of a particular hypothesis.

Exercises

Exercise 7.1

It is difficult to set specific exercises to test the reader's ability to plan and carry out research projects, but we will attempt to guide readers here through some different orders of the steps that they might take in progressing from an idea to a project.

Here are some ideas for projects, deliberately written in the kind of (vague) format that often applies to ideas as they occur to us:

- The poetry of Carol Ann Duffy / Simon Armitage / U. A. Fanthorpe (or your choice) is simple to understand without being simplistic. How can we establish the stylistic basis of this effect?
- Jane Austen's novels are easier to follow in terms of plot and characterisation than the Brontës'. How can stylistics help us to work out why?
- Does the popular fiction genre often called 'chicklit' (or 'science fiction' or 'romance' or 'fantasy') have any stylistic characteristics which identify its members?
- What are the distinctive stylistic features of *The Color Purple* (or any other novel) and how are these represented (if at all) in the film version?
- Why does the word 'choice' seem to be so significant in recent social/political discourse? How is it being used?
- How do John Donne's poems differ, stylistically, from his sermons?
- How do the visual elements of film reflect character dialogue?
- Why is it that we often come to feel deeply involved in a narrative as we read?

Choose one or two of the above and work out a project which will attempt to answer the question, remembering that in order to do so, you need to produce a replicable, rigorous method that others will understand and be able to test themselves. You will probably find in most cases that you can only address parts of the question, or only address the question partially – be clear about which of these is true, and in what way. You are likely to have chosen a particular analytical tool or theoretical method to approach your data. Think about why that tool or theory is appropriate to your data and your research question.

Write out your proposed project, re-wording the vague question as given above into a proper research question or series of questions. Describe the project as a whole, being as clear as you can about milestones, timescales and likely outcomes. Try to imagine that you are going to carry out this research and think about what you would do on day one, day two, week three etc. If you find that you are not sure what you would actually have to do, then your project design is not clear enough.

Once you have one clearly designed project, try designing another, completely different one for the same question. So, if your first project uses qualitative analysis, make the second quantitative. If your first was concerned with cognitive questions of readers' meaning, consider the second from a corpus or other empirical point of view.

If you practise project design meticulously, whether or not you intend to carry out the projects, you will find that the process becomes easier, and you are able to apply these skills to future projects more effectively. Learning to focus research questions to the point where they can be investigated stylistically is an important process. Most people begin by being too broad in their scope and vague in their methods.

Further reading

In addition to the specific studies mentioned in this chapter, the following suggestions are recommended as introductory reading for the intending researcher in stylistics. For the qualitative analysis of poetry, Nowottny (1962) and Leech (1969) are early examples, and Verdonk (1993) and Jeffries (1993) provide further guidance on how to carry out the analysis itself. Cluysenaar (1976) is an early introduction to literary stylistics that covers prose and poetry, while Leech and Short (2007) is a classic text that is arguably the best available introduction to the qualitative stylistic analysis of prose fiction. Short (1996) is a very accessible introduction to the linguistic analysis of poems, plays and prose and is especially suitable for those new to the study of language in relation to literature. Short's (1989) *Reading, Analysing and Teaching Literature* contains a number of methodological insights into the practice of stylistics. An excellent introduction to the empirical study of language (and, indeed, other elements of the humanities generally) is *Muses and Measures* (van Peer *et al.* 2007). Wynne (2006) discusses corpus stylistics in general and Adolphs (2006) is a very accessible guide to the kind of electronic text analysis practised by corpus stylisticians. Further corpus-stylistic work can be found in O'Halloran (2007a, 2007b), O'Keefe and McCarthy (2010) and Mahlberg (2010). Finally, Wales (2001) is an indispensable dictionary of stylistic terms.

8 Conclusions and future directions

8.1 Stylistics: an interdiscipline

Throughout this book we have argued for a broad view of stylistics as being concerned with the systematic analysis of style in language in all its forms. This is a wider view of stylistics than some stylisticians might hold; as we have seen, stylistics is often defined more narrowly as the study of literary texts using linguistic techniques. However, as we have also noted at various points throughout this book, the techniques of linguistics are just as applicable in the analysis of non-literary (in the sense of non-fiction) texts as they are in the analysis of prototypically literary works. Furthermore, the problem of defining the concept of literariness (see Chapter 2) lends further weight to the view that stylistics should not be seen as concerned with any one particular text-type. While we cannot dismiss the fact that stylisticians generally have concentrated primarily on the analysis of so-called literary texts, this activity has been motivated by a desire to understand the workings of what is defined socio-culturally as literature rather than by an analytical inability on the part of stylistics to deal with other text-types.

Despite the fact that our broad view of stylistics may not be shared by all practitioners of it, one aspect of our definition of the subject that all stylisticians will be in agreement with concerns its development out of the discipline of linguistics. Stylistics is unremittingly linguistic in orientation. That this is the case can be seen from the fact that stylistics emerged originally out of the discipline of language study, formalised in the early twentieth century as linguistics. Moreover, stylistics proceeds on the *principles* of linguistics. That is, it aims to be objective (notwithstanding the inherent difficulties of achieving objectivity), rigorous, replicable and falsifiable. Thus, stylistics has much more in common with other sub-disciplines of linguistics than it does with sub-areas of traditional literary criticism. Indeed, stylistics has traditionally not had a good relationship with literary criticism specifically because of this difference of opinion between the two disciplines concerning the *methods* of criticism. Nowhere is this difference of opinion more vituperatively expressed than in the articles that form the (in)famous Fowler–Bateson controversy (see Fowler 1971), in which the linguist Roger Fowler and the literary critic F. W. Bateson exchanged metaphorical blows concerning the proper method of studying literature. As we have noted, stylistics has always allied itself with linguistics in its view that objectivity and falsifiability are key to any analysis of the workings of a literary text. Traditional literary criticism, on the other hand, has proceeded according to the belief that literary works can only be discussed subjectively. In an article sub-titled 'a polemic against relativism and fragmentation', West (2008) exposes another inherent problem with English Studies in its traditional sense, namely the lack of concern with the analysis of texts:

> If English is fragmented, then it is so because it is a subject without a soul, and it is a subject without a soul because it lacks a clear object of study and – most scandalously – a clear methodology. What other discipline would delight in these deficits? Do historians not agree, generally, on what they are studying and on the methods that they use? Do mathematicians or astronomers or biologists disagree fundamentally on what their object of study is, or on the methods to study that object? Why is our discipline so fragmented? Why do we shy away from stating explicitly what we are studying, why we are studying it, and how we are going to study it? Why are relativism and fragmentation seen as positive characteristics? A subject without an object of study or a methodology is not a real subject at all, but a playground for amateurs.   (West 2008: 137)

We agree with West's view and it is our contention that literary criticism as a discipline is stagnating because the unfalsifiability of the claims generated by this subjective approach, and the lack of focus on the text, makes critical discussion impossible. It is also our contention that stylistics offers a way out of this impasse.

Leech (2008: 2) describes stylistics as a 'bridge discipline' connecting linguistics and literary studies and explains that 'by undertaking a linguistic *analysis* as part of the interrelation between the two fields of study, we facilitate and anticipate an interpretative *synthesis*' (Leech 2008: 2). On this basis, Leech describes stylistics as an **interdiscipline**: i.e. a discipline in its own right but one which is informed by the insights of other disciplines. This is a view we subscribe to, though with the caveat that there are other disciplines than literary studies that inform stylistics (we have, for example, discussed the contributions of the visual arts and cognitive science to stylistics; there is no reason why history, politics, sociology, etc. should not also have a contribution to make). Indeed, this is in line with developments in linguistics itself, which as a discipline has progressed far beyond its initial and primary concern with the formal elements of language. Leech explains that

> Placing linguistics in a broad humanistic and social science perspective, it no longer seems controversial that when we describe the characteristics of a piece of language, we can (and should) also study its interrelations with those things that lie beyond it but nevertheless give it meaning in the broadest sense. These include the shared knowledge of writer and reader, the social background, and the placing of the text in its cultural and historical context.   (Leech 2008: 3)

To put it succinctly, stylistics is concerned with both form and function, though very much aware of the dangers of interpretative positivism (Simpson 1993).

Finally, as Leech (2008) also notes, stylistics is very much a practical discipline. It has developed and improved its techniques through the application of theoretical frameworks to the practical analysis of texts of all kinds. The success of this approach seems set to continue into the twenty-first century. In this final chapter we will briefly discuss some of the directions that stylistics is currently taking and outline how it might develop in the future.

8.2   New directions in stylistic analysis

The capacity of stylistics for taking insights from other disciplines means that it is a subject that is always expanding and developing. In this section we briefly outline just two of the directions that stylistics is currently taking, as a flavour of what is possible within the area.

8.2.1   Ideology and stylistics

As we have said at various points throughout this book, stylistics is neither theoretically nor in practice limited to studying the language of literature. Having said that, there are many outside the field who consider stylistics and literary stylistics to be identical, and there is, it must be admitted, a great deal more analysis of literary than of other texts. In this section, we will take it as read that non-literary texts (speeches, gas bills, love letters, committee minutes etc.) can be analysed for their stylistic features in just the same way as poems, plays and novels. In such cases, the same kinds of features may be noted, such as the foregrounding of deviation or the use of parallelism to underline a point.

There is also, however, a use of stylistic analysis which may not originally have been envisaged in either literary or non-literary stylistics, but which is increasingly attractive as an option. That is the use of stylistic analysis in order to establish the ideological basis of a text's meaning. The study of ideology in language has a long and respectable history in feminist linguistics (e.g. Cameron 1998), and in critical discourse analysis (e.g. Fairclough 1989). Not all of this study is text-based, of course, and some is more sociological and political than linguistic. However, insofar as there is a linguistic aspect to the work carried out in these fields, it can be called stylistic. Indeed, some of the founders of the critical discourse analysis (CDA) sub-discipline, such as Roger Fowler (see for example Fowler 1991), are also known as stylisticians (e.g. Fowler 1986), and this overlap in technique, if not in aims, is one that has become increasingly evident in recent years.

Simpson (1993) took a large step forward in demonstrating the usefulness of the tools of analysis commonly used by CDA (e.g. modality and transitivity from Hallidayan functional grammar) in tracing the points of view inherent in literary and non-literary texts. This tendency for readers to be 'invited' to view a text world from a particular vantage point is one of the mechanisms by which persuasive, not to say manipulative, texts could influence the ideological outlook of readers, and for this reason, studies combining some of the insights of stylistic analysis with those of CDA are very important. The move towards understanding how readers process text evident in cognitive stylistics, and the development of more ideologically-sensitive tools of analysis, will be vital in this task. Recent examples of the kind of work which seems to combine the text analysis of stylistics with the ideological awareness of CDA include Jeffries (2007b, 2010b) and Davies (2007).

8.2.2   Multimodal analysis

Since stylistics emerged out of linguistics, it is natural that it has traditionally concerned itself with the analysis of language data. However, it is also the case that stylistics has been used predominantly in the analysis of literary texts. Consequently, as literary texts have themselves developed, so too has it become necessary for stylistics to develop new ways of accounting for the effects that such texts can generate. One issue that stylisticians have recently started to grapple with is multimodality. Since a number of different text-types include multimodal elements, a complete analysis of such texts would need to take this into account. Our coverage here of multimodality cannot be comprehensive, so we will instead aim to describe some of the current approaches to the issue that have been applied within stylistics in order to give a sample of work ongoing in this area. We will begin by considering drama, since this is a text-type that is defined in part by its multimodal elements.

Prototypically, dramatic texts are written to be performed and a full stylistic analysis of such texts should be able to account for performance-related effects. That stylisticians of drama have tended not to consider dramatic performances has to do with a methodological problem associated with this, namely that since the-atre performances vary from show to show, the object of analysis is unstable and critical discussion is not viable (Short 1998). This, however, is less of an issue in the stylistic analysis of film drama, since, with the exception of remakes, there is only ever one record of a film performance to be taken into account. McIntyre (2008), for instance, examines a film version of the Shakespeare play, *Richard III*, and presents an analysis that identifies the ways in which the performance emphasises the effects generated by the linguistic elements of the screenplay. The means by which this is achieved is via the application of linguistic analytic frameworks. For example, Brown and Levinson's (1987) politeness theory is predicated on the notion that social distance can be encoded in language and that speakers' linguistic choices can consequently affect social relations. What McIntyre (2008) suggests is that the Brown and Levinson politeness model can also be used to explain literal movement closer to or further away from an interlocutor. In the case of the *Richard III* film that McIntyre analyses, it is noted that:

> In Brown and Levinson's terms, Richard's movement towards the camera (shot 18), and the camera's consequent backing away from him, represents a paralinguistic threat to the viewer's negative face (i.e. his or her desire to be unimpeded). This is because the eye-line vector established between Richard and the camera suggests that Richard is now looking at the viewer (in effect, the camera creates the illusion that the viewer is somehow in the bathroom with Richard). Richard's movement closer to the camera impinges on what we perceive, as a result of what we know the camera to represent, to be our personal space. The position of the camera creates the illusion of there being a direct connection between the discourse world (Werth, 1997) and the text world of which Richard is a part. The illusion of a paralinguistic threat to the audience's negative face further characterizes Richard as a threatening and potentially dangerous character.   (McIntyre 2008: 325)

McIntyre's analysis also makes use of Kress and van Leeuwen's (2006) approach to multimodal texts, which proposes that transitivity analysis (see section 3.2.1) can be applied to visual images in order to determine the syntactic connections between the constituent elements of an image.

The potential for applying linguistic frameworks to the analysis of visual images remains to be fully explored, though it seems that this may be a way forward for tackling multimodal texts. For example, a New Labour political poster from the 2001 UK General Election campaign was set out like a film advert, with the introductory caption 'The Tories present' and the large title 'ECONOMIC DISASTER II' across a photo of an apocalyptic landscape. Above the title are the faces of Michael Portillo, who is said to star as 'Mr Boom', and William Hague, who is introduced as 'Mr Bust'. There is a sub-title, 'Coming to a home, hospital, school near you'. The Labour Party thus used a visual style akin to cinema adverts which has the effect of generating the conceptual metaphor THE CONSERVATIVE PARTY IS A FILM PRODUCTION COMPANY. This in turn gives rise to all the attendant mappings between source and target domain (MPS ARE ACTORS, TORY POLICIES ARE FILM SCRIPTS, etc.) that generate a conception of the Conservative Party as lacking substance and not in touch with the real world. As Forceville (2007: 26) has noted, however, the mappings between source and target domains in a visual metaphor are not triggered in the same way that they are in a verbal metaphor (i.e. by a copula grammatical construction). In multimodal metaphors a different set of mechanisms cues our identification of metaphorical elements. As Forceville explains, at the heart of many of these mechanisms is foregrounding. For example, it is common for the target domain in visual metaphors to deviate from our schematic expectations and to be foregrounded as a consequence. Since foregrounded features invite closer interpretative consideration, we are likely to consider a metaphorical interpretation in order to make sense of the image.

Another example from the 2001 UK General Election campaign, on the other hand, may potentially be analysed using blending theory to explain how the concepts of Thatcherism are seen as intrinsically linked to the policies of the then Conservative Leader, William Hague. The image literally blended together the faces of Margaret Thatcher and William Hague.

It is also becoming possible to use corpus linguistic approaches in the analysis of multimodal discourse, as is reported in Carter and Adolphs (2008) and Dahlmann and Adolphs (2009). The boundaries of stylistics are clearly expanding.

8.3   The future of stylistics

We began this book by noting that stylistics is a subject that is eclectic and open. Evidence of this eclecticism and openness to new ideas can be seen in the wealth of research published in such stylistics journals as *Language and Literature* and the *Journal of Literary Semantics*, and in the presentations made at the annual conference of the Poetics and Linguistics Association, an international association of stylisticians.[1] We therefore end this book on an optimistic note. Stylistics seems set to continue developing in new and exciting ways. In this chapter we have gestured towards new directions in stylistics. Indeed, new frontiers are opening up all the time. If we speculate on what we might expect to see happening within stylistics over the course of the next few years, we would suggest that one area set to expand substantially is corpus stylistics. This approach to stylistic analysis very obviously continues the rich tradition of objectivity and replicability that is the hallmark of stylistics, and, intriguingly, the advent of corpus linguistics software has led stylistics to return to one of its initial concerns: the analysis of authorial style. The ability to analyse large quantities of data has allowed scholars to overcome the methodological problem associated with studying this aspect of style, and recent research in this area is reported by Hoover (2007 and 2008) and Hardy (2007).

Another area of stylistics that is clearly burgeoning is cognitive stylistics. Over the coming years we would expect to see a strengthening of this approach, as cognitive stylisticians empirically test their theoretical claims and in so doing augment the insights that stylistics is able to provide.

We also expect to see a convergence of CDA and stylistics in the field of critical stylistics, where the object of study may be any text-type or genre, but the interpretative component of the study aims to discover the latent ideological assumptions embedded in the text, rather than the aesthetic or other effect as in more traditional stylistic study.

Finally, we might well expect stylistics to develop in terms of the text-types it is able to deal with. In the twenty-first century multimodality is more of an issue than ever before, and stylisticians have already begun to work on the analysis of texts that incorporate substantial multimodal elements, including film and hypertext, among many others. The common factor in all such new work is that it proceeds according to the core principles of stylistics, and in this way stylistics will continue to expand and shed new light on how texts and readers combine to create meaning.

Further reading

The value of stylistics for the analysis of how ideologies are manifested in texts is the subject of Simpson (1993) and Jeffries (2010b), both of which are practical introductions to the topic. Jeffries (2007a and 2007b) demonstrates the application of such techniques in the analysis of political and media texts. Multimodal stylistics is discussed in Boeriis and Nørgaard (2008), McIntyre (2008) and Montoro (2006), and Forceville has published extensively on the application of cognitive metaphor theory in the analysis of visual images (see, for example, Forceville 1996, 2002b, 2005a, 2005b, 2007). The concept of applying transitivity analysis to images is covered in Kress and van Leeuwen (2001). Other relevant works on multimodality are Kress and van Leeuwen (2006), Scollon and Wong-Scollon (2003) and Machin (2007). Affect and emotion are covered in Burke (2008) and Oatley (1992 and 2004). Finally, Lambrou and Stockwell (2007) is a collection of chapters dealing with current issues in contemporary stylistics and represents some of the best current work in the subject.

Answers to exercises

We have not provided answers to all the exercises in this book. Some (such as exercise 1.1) do not require an answer from us, while others (e.g. 3.3) are intended as an opportunity for you to practise a piece of extended stylistic analysis. In the latter cases, lengthy answers from us are not practical, since there are a number of potential analytical perspectives that such texts can be analysed from. A speculative answer from us would not necessarily cover the issues you have investigated. Instead we have concentrated on providing sample answers to those exercises that focus on fairly specific issues. Nonetheless, it should be borne in mind that even here we are not claiming to provide complete answers.

Chapter 2

The commentaries that follow are not comprehensive, but indicate the kinds of statements that can be made about literary style, using the tools of analysis provided by linguistics.

2.1

Keats's famous poem is written in the most common metre of English verse, iambic pentameter, and has a relatively regular, though complex, rhyme scheme. There are three stanzas of eleven lines each, which have the pattern ababcde in the first seven lines and the patterns dcce (first stanza) and cdde (second and third stanzas) in the final four lines. This complexity allows what is in effect a regular use of full rhymes (sun-run; hook-brook-look and so on) to sound musical without becoming monotonous, and thus reflecting the natural world rather than the human-made one. This rhyme scheme is enhanced further by the internal rhymes of the repeated 'more' (lines 8–9) and 'hours' (line 22), in both cases the musical effect being added to by a meaningful one, since the repetition is foregrounded and captures the quantity of late flowers in the one case and the length of time that is spent creating cider in the other.

Phonology contributes a great deal to the effect of this poem, usually by means of a concentration of particular sound types in particular lines. Thus, for example, there are a number of lateral sounds (/l/) in lines 6–8: 'And fill all fruit with ripeness to the core; / To swell the gourd, and plump the hazel shells / With a sweet kernel'. These sounds, involving the centre of the mouth and tongue, might be seen to invoke the fullness that is being described because the articulatory effort in enunciating these lines causes the mouth to feel full of its tongue. Lateral sounds are voiced, and have a resonant effect, which also reflects the 'plump' fruits of autumn. A different effect can be seen in line 11, where the foregrounded use of nasals sets up the humming of the bees: 'For su**mm**er has o'er-bri**mm**'d their cla**mm**y cells'. Remember that spelling is not a good guide to pronunciation in many cases. Thus, the double 'll' and 'mm' spellings here represent only a single sound phonologically. However, there is the potential for a visual effect too, and the double consonants in the spelling may perform the equivalent of sound symbolism in written form.

This example answer to the exercise is not comprehensive and readers may wish to revisit their own answers to the question at this point, and consider the musical and meaningful uses of consonants in lines 15 and 32 (a clue – they're fricatives!). As for the effects of vowel choices in this poem, line 22 makes use of long vowels to evoke the length of time it takes for cider to be strained and pressed. Here is the line, with the phonemic symbols over the relevant vowels:

aʊ   ɑː uː   aʊ   aʊ
Thou watchest the last **oo**zings **hours** by **hours**.

Because diphthongs are roughly equivalent in length to long pure vowels, the occurrence of five long vowels in this line slows it down, emulating as a result the long process of making apples into cider. Line 27 has something of a similar effect, which readers may wish to investigate for themselves.

As well as phonological effects, this poem has a great many lexical, grammatical and morphological features. Keats is not afraid to use the morphological processes of English to produce new uses of words, such as the adjectival derivation of 'moss'd' (line 5) from the noun *moss*, via the verb *to moss*. This underlying verbal sense of the word implies that there may have been someone putting the moss in place on the trees, and this fits well with the general personification of Autumn in this poem. The personification itself is produced by a number of references to Autumn in the second person ('thou', 'thy') and by the use of verbs (line 22: '**Thou watchest**', line 24: '**Think** not of them') which normally require human subjects but in this case have the implied subject of Autumn.

This collocation of Autumn with verbs of human activity is just one aspect of the collocational effects in the poem. Others include the personification of the sun in the phrase 'maturing sun' (line 2), where the verbal adjective 'maturing', which normally precedes a human referent, produces a 'bosom-friend' for the personified Autumn. Readers may like to look for other unusual collocations (one might be 'clammy cells') and consider their effect in the poem.

Returning to morphological foregrounding, Keats also produces new lexical items and these, being deviant, are thus foregrounded in the poem. There are two compound constructions, 'soft-lifted' (line 15) and 'soft-dying' (line 25). These refer to the wind sifting through the grain in the barn and the dusk respectively. By using 'soft-' as an intrinsic modifier to the processes of lifting and dying in this way, Keats characterises the Autumn as a necessarily gentle person, with the implicit contrast to the winter to come. Readers may consider other morphological deviation, such as the deverbal noun 'oozings' (line 22) and the denominal adjective 'wailful' (line 27) and attempt to explain their effects in the context.

The final aspect of Keats's style in this poem that we will consider here is the syntactic structure of the poem. Each of the eleven-line stanzas is syntactically separate. The first is a single sentence, though as it lacks any main clauses, it is effectively a very long minor clause, so-called because there is no over-arching clause structure in the sentence. The function of this long sentence is to address the persona of Autumn, and this function is often known as a 'vocative'. It is like calling someone, to gain their attention. The opening stanza is a description of Autumn which seems timeless as a result of there being no main verb phrase. It is not unambiguously identifiable as a vocative until the beginning of the second stanza, when the second person is used for the first time (line 12: 'Who hath not seen thee oft amid thy store?'). At this point, the reader understands that the poet is addressing the personified Autumn. Each of the remaining two stanzas consists of a line which asks a question and then a ten-line answer to that question, in a single sentence format. The effect of so many long sentences, with minimal main verb phrases and strings of subordinate and often non-finite clauses, is partly to continue the feeling of time standing still, which is one of the ironies of Autumn – that although its very existence indicates time passing, there is also the illusion of stability, as if things could stay that way for ever.

There are, of course, many other stylistic features that could be focused upon in this poem, and the reader may wish to consider how to frame other, more literary and critical responses to the poem as stylistic observations.

The second text is a section of the opening poem of Ted Hughes's *Birthday Letters*, the book which charts his relationship with Sylvia Plath, his wife. In some shorter poems, it makes sense to work through the lines in order, rather than looking at each level in turn. The opening of the extract implies that it is interrupting a longer narrative, using the adverb 'Then' to indicate the rela-tionship between the actions related in the poem and earlier times. In line 2 a broken selectional restriction makes an abstract concept ('absence') into the grammatical object of a verb ('listen') which normally requires an audible form. This indicates the almost tangible nature of the family's absence from the house, and by the lexically negative word 'absence', the reader may be prompted to conjure up a different reality in which the whole family is present rather than absent.

In line 5, the adjectives 'precise and tender' relate to the inlaid corridor, though 'precise' would more normally be expected to modify a process and 'tender' a person. The implication is that these qualities were present in the people who lived there and the actions they took in decorating the house.

Lines 6–10 contain a single sentence with a very long grammatical subject (lines 6–9) and a very short remainder of the clause in line 10. This long subject has an iconic effect, as the delayed verb ('waited') in line 10 is increasingly anticipated by the reader as s/he wades through the list of modified noun phrases that make up the subject. *Wait* itself is a verb which normally takes a human (or animate) subject, so that the house and its contents as listed in lines 6–9 become personified retrospectively when the verb is arrived at. One of the noun phrases making up the subject is 'patient books' (line 7), which also causes a personification, this time of the books. Not only the house, but everything in it is therefore endowed with life and human attributes, and they all wait for the return of the family. The reader may like to consider the effects of other collocations in the poem, such as 'crimson cataract' (line 11) and the compound inventions such as 'snow-loaded' (line 15) and 'brain-life' (line 16).

The appeal of this poem is largely in its collocation, syntax and lexis, the latter being particularly full of the semantic field of colour ('blue', 'dark', 'white', 'crimson'), and there is little formal structure such as regular metre or rhyme scheme. There is also not a great deal of foregrounded phonological patterning, such as alliteration or other sound-symbolic effects. However, some of the lines do seem to have musical effects, and in one case it could be argued that there is some sound-symbolic effect in addition. Lines 3–4 contain a number of long vowels, as follows:

əʊ   ɔ: aɪ eɪ   əʊ

A ghostly trespasser, or my strange gloating

eɪ   əʊ u: aɪ aɪ

In that inlaid corridor, in the snow-blue twilight,

Though there are also some short vowels in these lines, there is a preponderance of long vowels, which perhaps symbolise the 'Oo' of a cartoon ghost, and indicate a level of anxiety in the trespasser that is hinted at in the title ('Robbing myself') and in the use of 'trespasser' in line 3.

Chapter 3

3.1

The transitivity patterns in this passage demonstrate the tension between what Syal's father thought of himself and the reality. His material actions ('handed over', 'place') are modified by adverbs spelling out his lack of confidence ('reluctantly', 'hesitantly') and are anyway subordinate to the main transitivity choices of the passage where Syal herself is the main participant. Thus, she is the Senser in 'I could see', a Mental Perception process which dominates the activities of her father, the Senser too in 'would watch', also a Mental Perception process, and she is the Actor or Senser in most of the main clauses where there are Material Action ('I had followed') or Mental Cognition processes ('I knew'). The modal forms here (mostly 'would') are an indication not of epistemic uncertainty but of repeated or habitual action on the part of the father. However, there is some epistemically strong modality in 'I knew' and 'I could see' which demonstrates on the one hand the strength of Syal's certainty about her father's real identity and at the same time indicates to the reader that her perspective is, after all, only the perspective of an admittedly perceptive child.

3.2

This passage is one where the reader is made aware of the real situation of these boys on different sides of the barbed wire fence at Auschwitz. The discourse presentation here is mostly via direct speech (DS) because that enables the writer to present the naivety of Bruno about not only the geography of Europe but also about the status of Germany. The effect of this apparently well-meaning but misguided young boy's attempt to make friends with Shmuel is made more striking by the indirect thought presentation which is interspersed between the DS ('Bruno replied, remembering something', 'Bruno felt a strong desire', 'Bruno tried to remember'), which helps the reader to understand that he is being torn between his polite, well-mannered upbringing, indicated via his thoughts and feelings, and his ideological indoctrination, indicated through his direct speech.

3.4

There is a lot to comment upon in the language of this poem, but we will focus here upon the effect of negation and the cohesive structure of the poem. The poem is a celebration of the normal sounds and activities of everyday life as though it were a kind of liturgy, reflecting the internal/spiritual life of people who consider themselves non-religious. The use of a negative ('although we cannot pray') itself conjures up the image of an alternative world in which 'we' would in fact be praying, thus pre-empting the theme of the poem which is that people pray despite themselves. Another, morphological, negated form ('faithless') also simultaneously asserts the lack of religion and evokes a possible scenario where faith is indeed present. Again, this is followed by an indication that there is some kind of spiritual 'truth' ('that small familiar pain'), contradicting the factual assertion of atheism ('we are faithless'). Another striking aspect of the poem is the structure, which is highly cohesive lexically, because the religious semantic field ('prayer', 'faithless') pulls into its scope some lexical items which are only indirectly religious ('chanting', 'truth', 'loss') and the result is a strong, lexically-coherent text. By contrast, the reference structure of the poem is far less cohesive. We are introduced to 'we' at the start, but it is not clear, perhaps until later, whether this is inclusive of the reader (you and me) or exclusive (me and someone else), or indeed whether it is a generic pronoun (all of us). This uncertainty is compounded by the introduction of various other characters in the poem, most of whom are indeterminate ('a woman', 'a man', 'someone') and even where they are introduced by the definite article ('the lodger'), it turns out that he too is indeterminate, as we see when we are told where he lives ('a Midland town'). He is, therefore, an exemplar of a lodger – any lodger.

Chapter 4

4.1

In example 22, George's utterance in turn 1 is essentially a string of phrases all meaning 'Good morning'. His choice of slang is representative of his upper-class character. Blackadder's response flouts the maxim of quantity, since it provides more information than is strictly necessary. George *knows* that in English the greeting is 'Good morning', so why does Blackadder tell him? Blackadder's flout of the quantity maxim generates the implicature that what George said was *not* English, and this may be interpreted as a criticism of George's style of speaking – particularly his characteristic excitement.

In example 23, Sloan begins what might be an attempt to opt out of a conversational exchange. Sloan's lawyer then cuts in and answers for his client. His answer is direct and thus a preferred response to the reporter's question. However, having said that his client does not want to make a comment, he then tries to prevent the reporter drawing an inference by making clear what Sloan did *not* implicate. As we have seen, though, attempts to defease implicatures tend to have the opposite effect to that which is desired, namely raising their prominence.

4.2

Example 24 is fairly naturalistic dialogue. We can note that two of the three questions in the dialogue result in a dispreferred response. These responses are foregrounded as a result of deviating from our conventional schematic expectations of the question/answer adjacency pair. For example, Christina's question in turn 1 provokes not an answer from Gerry but a new question. Similarly, Gerry's question in turn 4 results in an answer from Christina that is neither 'yes' nor 'no' but is instead ambiguous. It would seem that the characters are being deliberately unclear with each other and this may reflect the fact that they are both unsure how much to trust the other, having not seen each other for over eighteen months. We might also suggest that there is an element of flirtation to the dialogue, wherein the characters' lack of clarity adds an air of mystique to the fairly fragile relationship that they have.

4.3

The first-person narrator's initial utterance is a face threatening act since it is critical of Tam for dropping litter and hence potentially damaging to his positive face. However, the narrator only begins to mitigate the FTA in his second turn, where he provides a reason ('spoils the countryside') and seeks Tam's agreement

('You know', 'doesn't it?'). That the narrator is able to perform the FTA bald-on-record suggests a fairly close relationship between him and his colleagues and also, perhaps, a degree of institutional power. However, whatever power he has as a supervisor is undermined when Tam attacks his positive face by being directly critical and using taboo language to do so ('That's a load of shite and you know it'). This is what Culpeper (1996) terms positive impoliteness. Note, though, that context plays a large part in determining whether an exchange counts as impolite, since a close relationship may allow for banter that includes surface-level impoliteness. This applies to Tam's next turn too which, at a surface level at least, contains elements of negative impoliteness as a result of being condescending of the first-person narrator's argument.

Chapter 5

5.1

Part of the interpretative process involves accessing any relevant schema we might have that will allow us to make sense of a text. Obviously enough, not all readers possess the same schemas, and even if they do there are likely to be local differences between them that may well result in different reactions to the same text. A reader with no background knowledge of Christianity, for example, would not be affected by the textual triggers for a CHRISTIANITY schema that are to be found in C. S. Lewis's *Chronicles of Narnia*. Consequently, such a reader's reaction to these books would be different from that of a reader who does possess the relevant schema.

5.2

Many readers will easily interpret Lemoni's description of 'a great big spiky rustball' as a fairly primitive description of a mine. Reference to the beach acts as a locale header and confirms the likelihood that this is the case, since our schematic knowledge tells us that mines are likely to wash up on the shore during wartime. Lemoni, however, does not possess the relevant schematic knowledge and is consequently underlexicalised. This accounts for her apparent lack of concern. Corelli, on the other hand, obviously possesses the relevant background knowledge and is duly worried. Note that in this instance, we as readers may well feel closer to Corelli because we share the same schematic knowledge as this character.

5.3

The prevalent conceptual metaphor in the article is POLITICS IS FOOTBALL, and the attendant mappings between source and target domains mean that political parties are characterised as football teams, individual politicians as players, and the *Sun* newspaper (representing the reader) as the referee. The potential effects of the conceptual metaphor are various. Some readers may feel it trivialises politics while others may find that it makes political news easier to comprehend.

5.4

The underlying conceptual metaphor appears to be WORDS ARE WEAPONS. While this is a conventional metaphor (realised, for instance, in phrases such as 'What you said really hurt me'), the actual instantiation of it in the cartoon is novel since what is represented is a politician in danger of receiving a literal injury from an 'incoming' poem. This, then, is one of the mappings; i.e. poems are missiles. This in itself gives rise to a conceptualisation of poets as soldiers. The humour stems from the fact that the cartoon represents the metaphor literally. Furthermore, the idea that poets can really damage politicians, as suggested in the cartoon representation of the conceptual metaphor, is incongruous with our experience of the real world.

Chapter 6

6.1

The major differences between the two texts are that the first situates us much more clearly within the text world, while the second is likely to leave the reader feeling somewhat disoriented. The second uses an *in medias res* ('in the middle of things') effect and it appears that the narrator assumes we know who Peter is and where the little street is located. In contrast, the world-building elements of the first text are in many cases more specific. We know, for instance, that the Empress of Blandings is a pig, and where definite reference is used, qualification often follows: for example, 'the covered shed *where she did her sleeping*'. The function-advancing propositions also differ between the two texts. The Dahl extract includes many more dynamic verb phrases than the Wodehouse example. Consequently, our conceptualisations of the two text worlds of the extracts are likely to differ substantially.

6.2

Initially the deictic terms in the poem provide spatial and temporal indicators of where and when the action in the narrative is taking place ('In May', 'when sea-winds pierced our solitudes', 'in the woods', 'in a damp nook'). The past tense verb phrases locate the action in some past time. However, the proximal spatial deictic *here* ('Here might the redbird come his plumes to cool') acts as a trigger for a spatial shift, since *here* indicates proximity to the centre of the deictic field whose coordinates we have thus far interpreted. At this point in the poem, we are therefore likely to feel suddenly closer to the action being described in the narrative. There are numerous other proximal deictic terms in the poem. For example, 'This charm is wasted on the earth and sky' is likely to have the effect of making the reader feel emotionally close to the 'charm' referred to – i.e. close to the Rhodora. The poem ends with an odd deictic reference which has the effect of seemingly allowing us to conceptualise two deictic fields simultaneously (though in practice we toggle between the two spaces). This is the line 'The self-same Power that brought me there brought you'. 'There' is a distal spatial deictic term which indicates a deictic field distant from the speaker. However, 'brought' indicates movement towards a deictic centre. We might therefore have expected the more conventional *took* – e.g. 'The self-same Power that took me there took you.'

Notes to the text

1 Language and style

1 From the Russian *ostranenie* – 'making strange'.
2 For a discussion of the labelling of this field, and a defence of the term 'stylistics', see Leech (2008: 1–4).
3 For readers not familiar with this term, it refers to linguistic approaches which, for example, describe the grammar or phonology of a language in general terms, without necessarily connecting this description to contextualised examples in particular texts.
4 Note that although this statement appears to ignore the role of the reader in meaning construction, this concern is increasingly present in recent stylistics. See chapters 3–6 for a range of approaches to this topic.
5 In some contexts, such foregrounding may be intentionally humorous, but the reader will have to take on trust that the earnest nature of the remaining text in this article implied a lack of intentionality.
6 See Hoover (2008) and Hoover and Hess (2009) for some examples of authorship studies.
7 For a theoretically informed discussion of the value of linguistic thinking which is not primarily data-based, see Chapman (2006).
8 See, for example, Wynne *et al.*'s (1998) description of analytical practice in analysing discourse presentation in a corpus of written texts.

2 Text and style

1 Nouns are generally categorised as countable nouns (e.g. toy) which may pluralise (toys) and may occur with indefinite articles (a toy) or as mass nouns (e.g. air) which may not pluralise (without changing meaning radically) or occur with indefinite articles (*an air) but may occur with determiners of quantity such as 'some' (some air).
2 For further discussion of internal and external deviation, see Short (1996: 59–61); Leech and Short (2007: 41–5) and Leech (2008:14–18).
3 By rules we mean descriptive rules, not prescriptive ones.
4 Some readers may be wondering why the repetition of backgrounded features is not similar to what has been called parallelism by stylistics. This is because the repetition of backgrounded language is not foregrounded as in the cases of explicit parallelism. The latter are noticeable, whereas the former require detailed (often computer-based) study to discover.
5 See Short (1996: 37–59) for a description of how stylistic deviation works at different levels.
6 Though popular opinion would probably 'place' meaning at the level of the word, there is much evidence from linguistics that meaning is situated throughout the structural levels of language. See Jeffries (1998) for an approach to meaning at all levels of structure.
7 Mimesis is related to the concept of iconicity, used more generally in semiotics to define the direct connection between a sign and its signifier. For discussion of iconicity in stylistics, see Leech (2008: 114–15, 149–50).
8 See, for example, Gill (2002).

9 See, for example, Peace (1999).
10 Readers not familiar with the lexical/grammatical distinction can find it defined in any introductory English grammar, and specifically in Jeffries (2006: 83ff.).
11 The sibilants are a sub-set of fricative consonants (in English, these are /s/, /z/, /ʃ/ and /ʒ/) which are articulated by making a groove in the centre of the tongue, down which the air flows. This results in a more 'whistling' sound, and may therefore be used to represent a particular kind of fricative sound which is more focused than, for example, /f/ or /v/.
12 Note that although sound symbolism is a commonly-used expression for such meaning potential, the relationship between the sound and the meaning is more accurately termed 'indexical' or even at times 'iconic', since it is not completely arbitrary but is somewhat motivated by similarity.
13 This book, as with many in linguistics, illustrates exclusively from English. Most of the points that we make can be applied to other languages, though there are some areas of structural variation, including morphology, where other languages may draw upon a slightly different range of resources to create foregrounding effects.
14 The field of critical discourse analysis uses the concept of naturalisation to explain how ideological concepts may enter the perceived common sense of a social group by repetition and backgrounding. Thus, if an ideology (e.g. women should be thin) is repeatedly assumed, rather than stated, it becomes more difficult to distinguish it from a given 'fact' (e.g. gravity pulls things towards the earth).
15 See Jeffries (1994) for further discussion of the overlap between listing and apposition.
16 Note that although apposition is most common with noun phrases, any two or more structures of the same type may be juxtaposed in a text in such a way that they are implicitly co-referential, and thus appositive.

3 Discourse and context I: Function

1 For more explanation of the mechanisms of cohesion, see Jeffries (2006: 183–7) and for the original explanation, see Halliday and Hasan (1976).
2 You can read more about the pronoun use in this poem, compared with another poem, in Jeffries (2008).
3 Some lexical semanticists (e.g. Cruse 1986, 2004) make finer distinctions between opposites with different conceptual fields, but the ones included here are those most often recognised.
4 This phrase would be considered ungrammatical by some, since 'less' is traditionally used with mass nouns, and 'fewer' with countable nouns like 'emissions'. This appears to be a distinction which is undergoing change at the moment, and 'fewer' is disappearing rapidly.
5 Available at www.visit4info.com/advert/Brains-Performing-Badly-without-Drench-Spring-Water-Drench/67610.

5 Text and cognition I: Text comprehension

1 Cook (1994), Semino (1997), Jeffries (2001) and Semino (2001) produce a range of arguments about the extent to which these uses of schema theory to characterise literary effect can be supported. The interested reader may wish to pursue in particular the 2001 articles, where some of the issues are resolved.
2 Note that although there is no clue in the poem as to the sex of the speaker, we are likely to assume it is a man simply because this is a first-person poem written by a male poet. Our assumption rests largely on the fact that the discourse structure of poems prototypically consists of a speaker addressing a hearer. This simple discourse structure leads us to assume that the speaker and the poet are one and the same. The more complex discourse structure of plays and prose fiction means that we are less likely to make such assumptions when we read these texts.

3 This supposed inadequacy of cognitive metaphor theory is not accepted by all, since the fact of butchery being a highly skilled profession is not part of its popular image, and there is thus no mismatch between the idea of an incompetent surgeon and a butcher in the popular imagination. This challenge to a particular example may therefore undermine the rationale for blending theory in general.

6 Text and cognition II: Text processing

1 Despite his use of these terms, Werth intended his theory to be able to account for all forms of language in use, and so in this chapter it may be assumed that the terms *author*, *text* and *reader* refer also to *speaker*, *discourse* and *hearer*.
2 We use the term 'characters' here to refer also to non-fictional characters. Text world theory uses the more neutral term **enactors**.

7 Methods and issues in stylistic analysis

1 Though see section 1.6 for discussion of the guiding principles of stylistics.
2 Researchers intending to embark on a project involving quantitative research methods should inform themselves about the basic principles of statistical analysis and significance testing. Butler's excellent introduction, *Statistics in Linguistics*, is now out of print, but can be read online at www.uwe.ac.uk/hlss/llas/statistics-in-linguistics/bkindex.shtml. A more recent work, focusing particularly on the use of statistics in humanities research, is Van Peer *et al.* (2007).
3 This principle of stylistics is even now giving way to a more inclusive principle that will soon include multimodal texts with or without linguistic content.
4 This journal is the official publication of the Poetics and Linguistics Association (PALA), which is the organisation bringing together stylisticians from around the world.
5 BYU-BNC; available at: http://corpus.byu.edu/bnc/.
6 The exceptions to this are the study of Old English and Middle English texts, where close analysis of the text itself is the prime focus, and the practice of close reading generally, which came to prominence in the mid-twentieth century and was championed by, among others, I. A. Richards.

8 Conclusions and future directions

1 See www.pala.ac.uk.

References

Adcock, F. (1987) *The Faber Book of 20th Century Women's Poetry*. London: Faber and Faber.

Adolphs, S. (2006) *Introducing Electronic Text Analysis: A Practical Guide for Language and Literary Studies*. London: Routledge.

Alderson, J. C. and Short, M. (1989) 'Reading literature', in Short, M. (ed.) *Reading, Analysing and Teaching Literature*, pp. 72–119. London: Longman.

Archer, D. (2002) 'Can innocent people be guilty? A sociopragmatic analysis of examination transcripts from the Salem Witchcraft Trials', *Journal of Historical Pragmatics* 3(1): 1–31.

Armitage, S. (1999) *Kid*. London: Faber and Faber.

Atkinson, K. (2004) *Case Histories*. London: Black Swan.

Austin, J. L. (1962) *How to Do Things With Words*. Oxford: Oxford University Press.

Baker, A. E. (2003) 'The front bedroom', *Smiths Knoll* 30: 58.

Baker, P. and McEnery, T. (2005) 'A corpus-based approach to discourses of refugees and asylum seekers in UN and newspaper texts', *Language and Politics* 4(2): 197–226.

Bakhtin, M. M. (1981) [1975] 'Discourse in the novel', in *The Dialogic Imagination: Four Essays*, ed. M. Holquist, trans. Caryl Emerson and Michael Holquist. University of Texas Press Slavic Studies 1, pp. 259–422. Austin: University of Texas Press.

Ball, A. (2000) *American Beauty*. London: Channel 4 Books.

Beal, J. (2000) 'From Geordie Ridley to Viz: popular literature in Tyneside English', *Language and Literature* 9(4): 343–59.

Bennett, A. (2000) *The Lady in the Van*. London: Faber and Faber.

Bennison, N. (1993) 'Discourse analysis, pragmatics and the dramatic "character": Tom Stoppard's Professional Foul', *Language and Literature* 2(2): 79–99.

Bernières, L. de (1994) *Captain Corelli's Mandolin*. London: Secker and Warburg.

Biber, D., Johansson, S., Leech, G., Conrad, S. and Finegan, E. (1999) *Longman Grammar of Spoken and Written English*. London: Longman.

Birch, D. (1989) *Language, Literature, and Critical Practice: Ways of Analysing Text*. London: Routledge.

Blake, N. (1989) *The Language of Shakespeare*. Basingstoke: Palgrave.

Boeriis, M. and Nørgaard, N. (2008) 'The multimodal construal of humour and intertextuality in Tele2's Small Bill/Big Bill campaign', in Baldry, A. and Montagna, E. (eds.) *Interdisciplinary Perspectives on Multimodality: Theory and Practice*. Campobasso: Palladino.

Bolinger, D. (1949) 'The sign is not arbitrary', *Boletín del Instituto Caro y Cuervo* 5: 52–62.

Bousfield, D. (2007a) *Impoliteness in Interaction*. Amsterdam: John Benjamins.

(2007b) '"Never a truer word said in jest": a pragmastylistic analysis of impoliteness as banter in Henry IV, Part I', in Lambrou, M. and Stockwell, P. (eds.) *Contemporary Stylistics*, pp. 209–20. London: Continuum.

Boyne, J. (2006) *The Boy in the Striped Pyjamas*. Oxford: David Fickling Books.

Brook, G. L. (1970) *The Language of Dickens*. London: André Deutsch.

Brown, P. and Levinson, S. C. (1987) *Politeness: Some Universals in Language Usage*. Cambridge: Cambridge University Press.

Bühler, K. (1982) 'The deictic field of language and deictic words', in Jarvella, R. and Klein, W. (eds.) *Speech, Place and Action: Studies in Deixis and Related Topics*, pp. 9–30. New York: Wiley.

(1990 [1934]) *Theory of Language: The Representational Function of Language*. (Originally published as *Sprachtheorie*. Translated by Goodwin, D. F.) Amsterdam: John Benjamins.

Burke, M. (2008) *The Oceanic Mind: Charting Emotive Cognition in the Flow of Language and Literature*. Unpublished PhD thesis: University of Amsterdam.

Burnett, P. (ed.) (1986) *The Penguin Book of Caribbean Poetry*. Harmondsworth: Penguin.

Burrows, J. F. (1987). *Computation into Criticism: A Study of Jane Austen's Novels and an Experiment in Method*. Oxford: Clarendon Press.

Burton, D. (1980) *Dialogue and Discourse: A Socio-linguistic Approach to Modern Drama Dialogue and Naturally Occurring Conversation*. London: Routledge and Kegan Paul.

Butt, D., Fahey, R., Feez, S., Spinks, S. and Yallop, C. (2000) *Understanding Functional Grammar: An Explorer's Guide*. 2nd edition. Sydney: National Centre for English Language Teaching and Research.

Cameron, D. (ed.) (1998) *The Feminist Critique of Language: A Reader*. London: Routledge.

Carstairs-McCarthy, A. (1992) *Current Morphology*. London: Routledge.

Carter, R. and Adolphs, S. (2008) 'Linking the verbal and visual: new directions for corpus linguistics', *Language and Computers* 64: 275–91.

and Nash, W. (1983) 'Language and literariness', *Prose Studies* 6(2): 124–41.

(1990) *Seeing through Language: A Guide to Styles of English Writing*. Oxford: Blackwell.

Cauldwell, R. (1999) 'Openings, rhythm and relationships: Philip Larkin reads Mr Bleaney', *Language and Literature* 8(1): 35–48.

Cecconi, E. (2008) 'Legal discourse and linguistic incongruities in Bardell vs. Pickwick: an analysis of address and reference strategies in The Pickwick Papers trial scene'. *Language and Literature* 17(3): 205–19.

Chapman, G., Cleese, J., Gilliam, T., Idle, E., Jones, T. and Palin, M. (1974) *Monty Python and the Holy Grail*. London: Methuen.

(1990) *Monty Python's Flying Circus: Just the Words*, Vol. 2. London: Methuen.

Chapman, S. (2005) *Paul Grice, Philosopher and Linguist*. Basingstoke: Palgrave.

(2006) *Thinking About Language: Theories of English*. Basingstoke: Palgrave.

and Routledge, C. (1999) 'The pragmatics of detection: Paul Auster's City of Glass,' *Language and Literature* 8(3): 241–53.

Clark, R. J. (1999) 'From text to performance: Interpretation or traduction? Trevor Griffiths' Fatherland, as directed by Ken Loach', *Language and Literature* 8(2): 99–123.

Cleese, J. and Booth, C. (1988) *The Complete Fawlty Towers*. London: Methuen.

and Crichton, C. (1988) *A Fish Called Wanda*. London: Mandarin.

Cluysenaar, A. (1976) *Introduction to Literary Stylistics*. London: Batsford.

Coe, J. (2004) *The Rotters' Club*. London: Penguin.

Conan Doyle, A. (2003) [1891] *The Adventures of Sherlock Holmes*. New York: Barnes and Noble.

Cook, G. (1994) *Discourse and Literature: The Interplay of Form and Mind*. Oxford: Oxford University Press.

Cook, S. (1985) *Concrete Poems*. Richmond: The Keepsake Press.

Cooper, M. (1998) 'Implicature, convention and The Taming of the Shrew', in Culpeper, J., Short, M. and Verdonk, P. (eds.) *Exploring the Language of Drama: From Text to Context*, pp. 54–66. London: Routledge.

Crisp, P. (2002) 'Metaphorical propositions', *Language and Literature* 10(1): 5–19.

Cruse, D. A. (1986) *Lexical Semantics*. Cambridge: Cambridge University Press.

(2004) *Meaning in Language: An Introduction to Semantics and Pragmatics*. Oxford: Oxford University Press.

Crystal, D. and Davy, D. (1969) *Investigating English Style*. London: Longman.

Culpeper, J. (1996) 'Towards an anatomy of impoliteness', *Journal of Pragmatics* 25: 349–67.

(1998) '(Im)politeness in dramatic dialogue', in Culpeper, J., Short, M. and Verdonk, P. (eds.) *Exploring the Language of Drama: From Text to Context*, pp. 83–95. London: Routledge.

(2000) 'A cognitive approach to characterization: Katherina in Shakespeare's The Taming of the Shrew', *Language and Literature* 9(4): 291–316.

(2002) 'Computers, language and characterisation: an analysis of six characters in Romeo and Juliet', in Melander-Marttala, U., Ostman, C. and Kyto, M. (eds.) *Conversation in Life and in Literature: Papers from the ASLA Symposium*, pp. 11–30. Uppsala: Universitetstryckeriet.

(2005) 'Impoliteness and entertainment in the television quiz show: The Weakest Link', *Journal of Politeness Research* 1(1): 35–72.

and McIntyre, D. (2010) 'Activity types and characterisation in dramatic discourse', in Schneider, R., Jannidis, F. and Eder, J. (eds.) *Characters in Fictional Worlds: Interdisciplinary Perspectives*. Berlin: De Gruyter.

Cummings, E. E. (1991) *Complete Poems 1904–62*. London: W. W. Norton.

(1964) *73 Poems*. London: Faber and Faber.

Curtis, R., Elton, B., Lloyd, J. and Atkinson, R. (1998) *Blackadder 1485–1917*. London: Michael Joseph.

Dahl, R. (1973 [1945]) *Over to You*. London: Penguin.

Dahlmann, I. and Adolphs, S. (2009) 'Multi-modal spoken corpus analysis and language description: the case of multi-word expressions', in Baker, P. (ed.) *Contemporary Approaches to Corpus Linguistics*. London: Continuum.

Davies, M. (2007) 'The attraction of opposites: the ideological function of conventional and created oppositions in the construction of in-groups and out-groups in news texts', in Jeffries, L., McIntyre, D. and Bousfield, D. (eds.) *Stylistics and Social Cognition*. Amsterdam / New York: Rodopi (PALA Papers).

(2008) *Oppositions in News Discourse: The Ideological Construction of 'Us' and 'Them' in the British Press*. Unpublished PhD thesis: University of Huddersfield.

Dooley, M. (1991) *Explaining Magnetism*. Newcastle upon Tyne: Bloodaxe Books.

(1996) *Kissing a Bone*. Newcastle upon Tyne: Bloodaxe Books.

Douthwaite, J. (2000) *Towards a Linguistic Theory of Foregrounding*. Alessandria: Edizioni dell'Orso.

Doyle, R. (1999) *A Star Called Henry*. Viking.

Duchan, J. F., Bruder, G. A. and Hewitt, L. E. (eds.) (1995) *Deixis in Narrative: A Cognitive Science Perspective*. Hillsdale, NJ: Lawrence Erlbaum.

Duffell, M. J. (2002) 'The Italian line in English after Chaucer', *Language and Literature* 11(4): 291–305.

Duffy, C. A. (1993) *Mean Time*. London: Anvil Press.

Dunn, D. (1985) *Elegies*. London: Faber and Faber.

Eco, U. (1980) *The Name of the Rose*. London: Picador.

Ehrlich, V. (1965 [1955]) *Russian Formalism: History and Doctrine*. The Hague: Mouton.

Emerson, R. W. (1847) *Poems*. Boston: James Munroe.

Emmott, C. (1997) *Narrative Comprehension: A Discourse Perspective*. Oxford: Oxford University Press.

(2002) '"Split selves" in fiction and in medical "life stories": cognitive linguistic theory and narrative practice', in Semino, E. and Culpeper, J. (eds.) *Cognitive Stylistics: Language and Cognition in Text Analysis*, pp. 153–81. Amsterdam: John Benjamins.

(2003a) 'Reading for pleasure: a cognitive poetic analysis of "twists in the tale" and other plot reversals in narrative texts', in Gavins, J. and Steen, G. (eds.) *Cognitive Poetics in Practice*, pp. 145–60. London: Routledge.

(2003b) 'Towards a theory of reading in the age of cognitive science: cross-disciplinary perspectives on narrative from stylistics and psychology', *BELL: Belgian Journal of English Language and Literature* 1: 17–29.

Sanford, A. J., and Dawydiak, E. J. (2007) 'Stylistics meets cognitive science: studying style in fiction and readers' attention from an inter-disciplinary perspective', *Style* 41(2): 204–24.

Enkvist, N. E. (1973) *Linguistic Stylistics*. The Hague: Mouton.

Evans, V. and Green, M. (2006) *Cognitive Linguistics: An Introduction*. Edinburgh: Edinburgh University Press.

Fairclough, N. (1989) *Language and Power*. London: Longman.

(1992) *Discourse and Social Change*. Cambridge: Polity Press.

Fanthorpe, U. A. (1978) *Side Effects*. Liskeard: Peterloo Poets.

Fauconnier, G. (1985) *Mental Spaces*. Cambridge, Mass.: MIT Press.

and Turner, M. (2002) *The Way We Think: Conceptual Blending and the Mind's Hidden Complexities*. New York: Basic Books.

Faulkner, W. (1987 [1929]) *The Sound and the Fury*. New York: Vintage.

Fenton, J. (1980) *A German Requiem: A Poem*. Edinburgh: Salamander.

Fielding, H. (1999) *Bridget Jones's Diary*. London: Penguin.

Fish, S. (1981 [1973]) 'What is stylistics and why are they saying such terrible things about it?', in Freeman, D. C. (ed.) *Essays in Modern Stylistics*, pp. 53–78. London: Methuen.

Fitzmaurice, S. (2000) 'Tentativeness and insistence in the expression of politeness in Margaret Cavendish's Sociable Letters', *Language and Literature* 9(1): 7–24.

Fleming, I. (1985 [1958]) *Dr No*. London: Triad/Panther.

Fludernik, M. (1993) *The Fictions of Language and the Languages of Fiction: The Linguistic Representation of Speech and Consciousness*. London: Routledge.

Forceville, C. (1996) *Pictorial Metaphor in Advertising*. London: Routledge.

(2002a) 'The conspiracy in The Comfort of Strangers: narration in the novel and the film', *Language and Literature* 11(2): 119–35.

(2002b) 'The identification of target and source in pictorial metaphors', *Journal of Pragmatics* 34(1): 1–14.

(2005a) 'Visual representations of the Idealized Cognitive Model of anger in the Asterix album La Zizanie', *Journal of Pragmatics* 37(1): 69–88.

(2005b) 'Cognitive linguistics and multimodal metaphor', in Sachs-Hombach, K. (ed.) *Bildwissenschaft: Zwischen Reflektion und Anwendung*, pp. 264–84. Cologne: Von Halem.

(2007) 'Multimodal metaphor in ten Dutch TV commercials', *The Public Journal of Semiotics* 1(1): 19–51.

Fowler, R. (ed.) (1966) *Essays on Style and Language*. London: Routledge & Kegan Paul.

(1971) *The Languages of Literature*. London: Routledge & Kegan Paul.

(ed.) (1975) *Style and Structure in Literature: Essays in the New Stylistics*. Oxford: Blackwell.

(1977) *Linguistics and the Novel*. London: Methuen.

(1986) *Linguistic Criticism*. Oxford: Blackwell.

(1991) *Language in the News*. London: Routledge.

(1995) *The Language of George Orwell*. Basingstoke: Palgrave.

France, L. (ed.) (1993) *Sixty Women Poets*. Newcastle upon Tyne: Bloodaxe Books.

Fraser Gupta, A. (2000) 'Marketing the voice of authenticity: a comparison of Ming Cher and Rex Shelley', *Language and Literature* 9(2): 150–69.

Freeman, D. C. (ed.) (1970) *Linguistics and Literary Style*. New York: Holt, Rinehart and Winston.

Freeman, M. H. (2005) 'The poem as complex blend: conceptual mappings of metaphor in Sylvia Plath's "The Applicant"', *Language and Literature* 14(1): 25–44.

Galbraith, M. (1995) 'Deictic shift theory and the poetics of involvement in narrative', in Duchan, J. F., Bruder, G. A. and Hewitt, L. E. (eds.) *Deixis in Narrative: A Cognitive Science Perspective*, pp. 19–59. Hillsdale, NJ: Lawrence Erlbaum.

Gavins, J. (2003) 'Too much blague? An exploration of the text worlds of Donald Barthelme's Snow White', in Gavins, J. and Steen, G. (ed.) *Cognitive Poetics in Practice*, pp. 129–44. London: Routledge.

(2007) *Text World Theory: An Introduction*. Edinburgh: Edinburgh University Press.

and Steen, G. (eds.) (2003) *Cognitive Poetics in Practice*. London: Routledge.

Genette, G. (1994 [1976]) *Mimologics*. Lincoln: University of Nebraska Press.

Gibbs, R. (1994) *The Poetics of Mind: Figurative Thought, Language, and Understanding.* Cambridge: Cambridge University Press.

Gill, D. (2002) *The Amateur Yorksherman.* Bradford: Redbeck Press.

Goatly, A. (2007) *Washing the Brain: Metaphor and Hidden Ideology.* Amsterdam: John Benjamins.

Goodblatt, C. (2000) 'In other words: breaking the monologue in Whitman, Williams and Hughes', *Language and Literature* 9(1): 25–41.

Gregoriou, C. (2006) *The Poetics of Deviance in Contemporary American Crime Fiction.* Basingstoke: Palgrave.

(2007) *Deviance in Contemporary Crime Fiction.* London: Palgrave.

Grice, H. P. (1975) 'Logic and conversation', in Cole, P. and Morgan, J. L. (eds.) *Syntax and Semantics 3: Speech Acts*, pp. 41–58. New York: Academic.

Haddon, M. (2007) *A Spot of Bother.* London: Vintage.

Halliday, M. A. K. (1985) *An Introduction to Functional Grammar.* London: Edward Arnold.

Halliday, M. A. K. (1994) *An Introduction to Functional Grammar.* 2nd edition. London: Edward Arnold.

and Hasan, R. (1976) *Cohesion in English.* London: Longman.

and Matthiessen, C. (2004) *An Introduction to Functional Grammar.* 3rd edition. London: Arnold.

Hardy, D. E. (2003) *Narrating Knowledge in Flannery O'Connor's Fiction.* Columbia: University of South Carolina Press.

(2004) 'Collocational analysis as a stylistic discovery procedure: the case of Flannery O'Connor's Eyes', *Style* 38(4): 410–27.

(2005) 'Towards a stylistic typology of narrative gaps: knowledge gapping in Flannery O'Connor's fiction', *Language and Literature* 14: 363–75.

(2007) *The Body in Flannery O'Connor's Fiction: Computational Technique and Linguistic Voice.* Columbia: University of South Carolina Press.

Hardy, T. (1987 [1886]) *The Mayor of Casterbridge.* Oxford: Oxford University Press.

Harris, S. (1984) 'Questions as a mode of control in magistrates' courts', *International Journal of the Sociology of Language* 49: 5–27.

Harrison, T. (1975) *Palladas: Poems.* London: Anvil Press.

(1984) *Selected Poems.* Harmondsworth: Penguin.

Harvey, K. (2000) 'Describing camp talk: language/pragmatics/politics', *Language and Literature* 9(3): 240–60.

Havránek, B. (1964 [1932]) 'The functional differentiation of standard language', in Garvin, P. (ed.) *A Prague School Reader on Esthetics, Literary Structure, and Style*, pp. 3–16. Washington, DC: Georgetown University Press.

Heywood, J., Semino, E. and Short, M. (2002). 'Linguistic metaphor identification in two extracts from novels', *Language and Literature* 11(1): 35–54.

Hidalgo-Downing, L. (2000) 'Negation in discourse: A text world approach to Joseph Heller's Catch-22', *Language and Literature* 9(3): 215–39.

Hinton, L., Nichols, J. and Ohala, J. (eds.) (1994) *Sound Symbolism.* Cambridge: Cambridge University Press.

Ho, Y. (forthcoming) *Corpus Stylistics in Principle and Practice.* London: Continuum.

Hogenraad, R., McKenzie, D. and van Peer, W. (1997) 'On fact making in empirical studies of literature', *SPIEL (Siegener Periodicum zur Internationalen Empirischen Literaturwissenschaft)* 16: 169–74.

Hoover, D. (2004a) 'Altered texts, altered worlds, altered styles', *Language and Literature* 13(2): 99–118.

(2004b) 'Testing Burrows's Delta', *Literary and Linguistic Computing* 19(4): 453–75.

(2007) 'Corpus stylistics, stylometry, and the styles of Henry James', *Style* 41(2): 174–203.

(2008) 'Word frequency, statistical stylistics, and authorship attribution', in Archer, D. (ed.) *What's in a Word-list? Investigating Word Frequency and Keyword Extraction*, pp. 35–52. Aldershot: Ashgate.

and Hess, S. (2009) 'An exercise in non-ideal authorship attribution: The Mysterious Maria Ward', *Literary and Linguistic Computing* 24: 467–89.

Ivanchenko, A. (2007) 'An "interactive" approach to interpreting overlapping dialogue in Caryl Churchill's *Top Girls* (Act 1)', *Language and Literature* 16(1): 74–89.

Jakobson, R. (1960) 'Closing statement: linguistics and poetics', in Sebeok, T. A. (ed.) *Style in Language*, pp. 350–77. Cambridge, MA: MIT Press.

Jeffries, L. (1993) *The Language of Twentieth Century Poetry*. Basingstoke: Macmillan.

(1994) 'Language in common: apposition in contemporary poetry by women', in Wales, K. (ed.) *Feminist Linguistics in Literary Criticism*, pp. 21–50. London: Boydell and Brewer.

(1998) *Meaning in English*. Basingstoke: Macmillan.

(2000) 'Point of view and the reader in the poetry of Carol Ann Duffy', in Jeffries, L. and Sansom, P. (eds.) *Contemporary Poems: Some Critical Approaches*, pp. 54–68. Huddersfield: Smith-Doorstop.

(2001) 'Schema theory and White Asparagus: cultural multilingualism among readers of texts', *Language and Literature* 10(4): 325–43.

(2002) 'Meaning negotiated: an investigation into reader and author meaning', in Csábi, S. and Zerkowitz, J. (eds.) *Textual Secrets: The Message of the Medium*, pp. 247–61, Budapest: Eötvös Loránd University.

(2006) *Discovering Language: The Structure of Modern English*. Basingstoke: Palgrave.

(2007a) 'Journalistic constructions of Blair's "apology" for the intelligence leading to the Iraq War', in Johnson, S. and Ensslin, A. (eds.) *Language in the Media, Representations, Identities, Ideologies*, pp. 48–69. London: Continuum.

(2007b) *Textual Construction of the Female Body*. Basingstoke: Palgrave Macmillan.

(2008) 'The role of style in reader-involvement: deictic shifting in contemporary poems', *Journal of Literary Semantics* 37(1): 69–85.

(2010a) *Opposition in Discourse*. London: Continuum.

(2010b) *Critical Stylistics*. Basingstoke: Palgrave.

McIntyre, D. and Bousfield, D. (eds.) (2007) *Stylistics and Social Cognition*. Amsterdam: Rodopi.

Kress, G. and Van Leeuwen, T. (2001) *Multimodal Discourse: The Modes and Media of Contemporary Communication*. London: Arnold.

(2006) *Reading Images: The Grammar of Visual Design*. 2nd edition. London: Routledge.

Lachenicht, G. (1980) 'Aggravating language: a study of abusive and insulting language', *International Journal of Human Communication* 13(4): 607–88.

Lahey, E. (2003) 'Seeing the forest for the trees in Al Purdy's "Trees at the Arctic Circle"', *BELL: Belgian Journal of English Language and Literature* 1: 73–83.

Lakoff, G. (1993) 'The contemporary theory of metaphor', in Ortony, A. (ed.) *Metaphor and Thought*, pp. 202–51. Cambridge: Cambridge University Press.

and Johnson, M. (1980) *Metaphors We Live By*. Chicago: Chicago University Press.

and Turner, M. (1989) *More Than Cool Reason: A Field Guide To Poetic Metaphor*. Chicago: Chicago University Press.

Lambrou, M. (2003) 'Collaborative oral narratives of general experience: when an interview becomes a conversation', *Language and Literature* 12(2): 153–74.

and Stockwell, P. (eds.) (2007) *Contemporary Stylistics*. London: Continuum.

Larkin, P. (1964) *The Whitsun Weddings*. London: Faber and Faber.

Leech, G. N. (1966) *English in Advertising*. London: Longman.

(1969) *A Linguistic Guide to English Poetry*. London: Longman.

(1970) 'The linguistic and the literary', *Times Literary Supplement*, 23 July: 805–6.

(2008) *Language in Literature: Style and Foregrounding*. London: Pearson Education.

and Short, M. (1981) *Style in Fiction: A Linguistic Introduction to English Fictional Prose*. London: Longman.

(2007) *Style in Fiction: A Linguistic Introduction to English Fictional Prose*. 2nd edition. London: Pearson Education.

Lester, G. A. (1996) *The Language of Old and Middle English Poetry*. Basingstoke: Palgrave.

Levin, S. R. (1962) *Linguistic Structures in Poetry*. The Hague: Mouton.

(1965) 'Internal and external deviation in poetry', *Word* 21: 225–37.

Levinson, S. C. (1983) *Pragmatics*. Cambridge: Cambridge University Press.

Lorde, A. (1997) *The Collected Poems of Audre Lord*. New York: W. W. Norton.

Louw, B. (1993) 'Irony in the text or insincerity in the writer? The diagnostic potential of semantic prosodies', in Baker, M., Francis, G. and Tognini-Bonelli, E. (eds.) *Text and Technology: In Honour of John Sinclair*, pp. 157–76. Amsterdam: John Benjamins.

Machin, D. (2007) *Introduction to Multimodal Analysis*. Oxford: Oxford University Press.

MacKay, R. (1996) 'Mything the point: a critique of objective stylistics', *Language and Communication* 16(1): 81–93.

MacNeice, L. (1964) *Selected Poems of Louis MacNeice*. Ed. W. H. Auden. London: Faber and Faber.

Mahlberg, M. (2007) 'A corpus stylistic perspective on Dickens' Great Expectations', in Lambrou, M. and Stockwell, P. (eds.) *Contemporary Stylistics*, pp. 19–31. London: Continuum.

(2010) *Corpus Stylistics and Dickens' Fiction*. Abingdon: Routledge.

Malmkjær, K. (2004) 'Translational stylistics: Dulcken's translations of Hans Christian Andersen', *Language and Literature* 13(1): 13–24.

Mandala, S. (2007) *Twentieth Century Dramatic Dialogue as Ordinary Talk: Speaking Between the Lines*. London: Ashgate.

Marvell, A. (1681) *Miscellaneous Poems*. Ed. Mary Marvell. Facsimile edition: Scolar Press, 1969.

Masefield, J. (1984 [1935]) *The Box of Delights*. London: Fontana.

Matthews, P. H. (1991) *Morphology*. 2nd edition. Cambridge: Cambridge University Press.

McCall Smith, A. (1998) *The No. 1 Ladies' Detective Agency*. London: Abacus.

(2005) *The Sunday Philosophy Club*. London: Abacus.

(2007) *Blues Shoes and Happiness*. London: Abacus.

McEnery, T. and Wilson, A. (2001) *Corpus Linguistics*. 2nd edition. Edinburgh: Edinburgh University Press.

McGough, R. (1979) *Holiday on Death Row*. Cape.

McGuckian, M. (1984) *Venus and the Rain*. Loughcrew: The Gallery Press.

(1997) *Selected Poems: 1978–1994*. Oldcastle, Co. Meath: Gallery Books.

McGuinness, F. (1998) *Dancing at Lughnasa: Screenplay*. London: Faber and Faber.

McIntyre, D. (2004) 'Point of view in drama: a socio-pragmatic analysis of Dennis Potter's *Brimstone and Treacle*', *Language and Literature* 13(2): 139–60.

(2005) 'Logic, reality and mind style in Alan Bennett's *The Lady in the Van*', *Journal of Literary Semantics* 34(1): 21–40.

(2006) *Point of View in Plays: A Cognitive Stylistic Approach to Viewpoint in Drama and Other Text-types*. Amsterdam: John Benjamins.

(2007) 'Deixis, cognition and the construction of viewpoint', in Lambrou, M. and Stockwell, P. (eds.) *Contemporary Stylistics*, pp. 118–30. London: Continuum.

(2008) 'Integrating multimodal analysis and the stylistics of drama: a multimodal perspective on Ian McKellen's *Richard III*', *Language and Literature* 17(4): 309–34.

Bellard-Thomson, C., Heywood, J., McEnery, A., Semino, E. and Short, M. (2004) 'Investigating the presentation of speech, writing and thought in spoken British English: a corpus-based approach', *ICAME Journal* 28: 49–76.

McMurtry, L. (1985) *Lonesome Dove*. New York: Simon & Schuster.

Meek, J. (2005) *The People's Act of Love*. London: Canongate.

Melrose, R. (2006) 'Sites and parasites of meaning: Browning's "My Last Duchess"', *Language and Literature* 15(2): 123–40.

Miall, D. (1998) 'The hypertextual moment', *English Studies in Canada* 24: 157–74.

Mills, M. (1998) *The Restraint of Beasts*. London: Harper Perennial.

Minsky, M. (1975) 'A framework for representing knowledge', in Winston, P. E. (ed.) *The Psychology of Computer Vision*, pp. 221–77. New York: McGraw-Hill.

Montgomery, M. (1999) 'Speaking sincerely: public reactions to the death of Diana', *Language and Literature* 8(1): 5–33.

(2005) 'The discourse of war after 9/11', *Language and Literature* 14(2): 149–80.

Montoro, R. (2006) 'Analysing literature through films', in Watson, G. and Zyngier, S. (eds.) *Literature and Stylistics for Language Learners: Theory and Practice*, pp. 48–59. Basingstoke: Palgrave.

(forthcoming) *Cappuccino Fiction*. London: Continuum.

Morrison, B. and Motion, A. (1982) *The Penguin Book of Contemporary British Poetry.* Harmondsworth: Penguin.

Mukařovsky, J. (1964) [1958] 'Standard language and poetic language', in Garvin, P. (ed.) *A Prague School Reader on Esthetics, Literary Structure, and Style,* pp. 17–30. Washington, DC: Georgetown University Press.

Mullany, L. (2004) '"Become the man that women desire": gender identity and dominant discourses in email advertising language', *Language and Literature* 13(4): 291–305.

Murphy, J. (1980) *Peace at Last.* Harmondsworth: Penguin.

Nahajec, L. (2009) 'Negation and the creation of implicit meaning in poetry', *Language and Literature* 18(2): 109–27.

Nash, W. (1985) *The Language of Humour.* London: Longman.

Nicholson, P. (1990) 'If it happens', in Parrott, E. O. (ed.) *How to Be Well Versed in Poetry.* London: Viking.

Nørgaard, N. (2007) '"Disordered collarettes and uncovered tables": negative polarity as a stylistic device in Joyce's "Two Gallants"', *Journal of Literary Semantics* 36: 35–52.

Notting Hill (1999) Universal Pictures. Director: Roger Michell. Writer: Richard Curtis.

Nowottny, W. (1962) *The Language Poets Use.* London: Athlone Press.

Oatley, K. (1992) *Best Laid Schemes: The Psychology of Emotions.* Cambridge: Cambridge University Press.

——— (2004) *Emotions: A Brief History.* Malden, MA: Blackwell.

O'Brien, S. (ed.) (1998) *The Firebox.* London: Picador.

O'Halloran, K. (2007a) 'The subconscious in James Joyce's "Eveline": a corpus stylistic analysis which chews on the "Fish hook"', *Language and Literature* 16(3): 227–44.

——— (2007b) 'Corpus-assisted literary evaluation', *Corpora* 2(1): 33–63.

Ohmann, R. (1970) 'Generative grammars and the concept of literary style', in Freeman, D. C. (ed.) *Linguistics and Literary Style,* pp. 258–78. New York: Holt, Rinehart and Winston.

O'Keefe, A. and McCarthy, M. (eds.) (2010) *The Routledge Handbook of Corpus Linguistics.* Abingdon: Routledge.

Peace, D. (1999) *1974.* London: Serpent's Tail.

Pearce, M. (2001) '"Getting behind the image": personality politics in a Labour party election broadcast', *Language and Literature* 10(3): 211–28.

Person, R. F., Jr (1999) *Structure and Meaning in Conversation and Literature.* Lanham: University Press of America.

Piazza, R. (forthcoming) *Let Cinema Speak.* London: Continuum.

Place, M. (1995) *In a Rare Time of Rain.* London: Jonathan Cape.

Plath, S. (1965) *Ariel.* London: Faber and Faber.

Pope, R. (1994) *Textual Intervention.* London: Routledge.

Potter, D. (1996) *Pennies From Heaven.* London: Faber and Faber.

Quirk, R. (1961) 'Some observations on the language of Dickens', *A Review of English Literature* 2(3): 19–28.

Rash, F. (2000) 'Language-use as a theme in German-language Swiss literature', *Language and Literature* 9(4): 317–41.

Richards, I. A. (2001 [1924]) *Principles of Literary Criticism.* London: Routledge.

Ronen, R. (1994) *Possible Worlds in Literary Theory*. Cambridge: Cambridge University Press.

Rubin, E. (1915) *Synsoplevede Figuere*. Copenhagen: Gyldendalsde Boghandel.

Rumelhart, D. E. (1980) 'Schemata: the building blocks of cognition', in Spiro, R. J., Bruce, B. C. and Brewer, W. F. (eds.) *Theoretical Issues in Reading Comprehension*, pp. 38–58. Hillsdale, NJ: Erlbaum.

Rumens, C. (1995) *Best China Sky*. Newcastle upon Tyne: Bloodaxe Books.

Ryan, M. L. (1991) *Possible Worlds, Artificial Intelligence and Narrative Theory*. Indianapolis: Indiana University Press.

Ryder, M. E. (2003) 'I met myself coming and going: Co(?)-referential noun phrases and point of view in time travel stories', *Language and Literature* 12(3): 213–32.

Sacks, H. (1995) *Lectures on Conversation*, vols. 1 and 2. Oxford: Blackwell.

Sanford, A., Sturt, P., Moxey, L., Morrow, L. and Emmott, C. (2004) 'Production and comprehension measures in assessing plural object formation', in Carreiras, M. and Clifton, C. (eds.) *The On-line Study of Sentence Comprehension: Eyetracking, ERPs and Beyond*, pp. 151–66. London: Taylor and Francis.

Saussure, F. de (1959 [1916]) *Course in General Linguistics*. New York: McGraw-Hill.

Schank, R. C. (1982) *Dynamic Memory: A Theory of Reminding and Learning in Computers and People*. Cambridge: Cambridge University Press.

and Abelson, R. (1977) *Scripts, Plans, Goals and Understanding*. Hillsdale, NJ: Lawrence Erlbaum Associates.

Schegloff, E. A. and Sacks, H. (1974) 'Opening up closings', in Turner, R. (ed.) *Ethnomethodology: Selected Readings*, pp. 233–64. Harmondsworth: Penguin.

Schram, D. and Steen, G. (eds.) (2001) *The Psychology and Sociology of Literature*. Amsterdam: John Benjamins.

Scollon, R. and Wong-Scollon, S. (2003) *Discourse in Place: Language in the Material World*. London: Routledge.

Scott, M. (2004) *WordSmith Tools*. Oxford: Oxford University Press.

Seargeant, P. (2007) 'Discursive diversity in the textual articulation of epidemic disease in Early Modern England', *Language and Literature* 16(4): 323–44.

Searle, J. R. (1969) *Speech Acts: An Essay in the Philosophy of Language*. Cambridge: Cambridge University Press.

(1979) *Expression and Meaning: Studies in the Theory of Speech Acts*. Cambridge: Cambridge University Press.

Sebeok, T. A. (ed.) (1960) *Style in Language*. Cambridge, MA: MIT Press.

Segal, E. (1995) 'Narrative comprehension and the role of deictic shift theory', in Duchan, J. F., Bruder, G. A. and Hewitt, L. E. (eds.) *Deixis in Narrative: A Cognitive Science Perspective*, pp. 3–17. Hillsdale, NJ: Lawrence Erlbaum.

Semino, E. (1997) *Language and World Creation in Poems and Other Texts*. London: Longman.

(2001) 'On readings, literariness and schema theory: a reply to Jeffries', *Language and Literature* 10(4): 345–55.

(2002) 'Stylistics and linguistic variation in poetry', *Journal of English Linguistics* 30(1): 28–50.

(2008) *Metaphor in Discourse*. Cambridge: Cambridge University Press.

and Culpeper, J. (eds.) (2002) *Cognitive Stylistics: Language and Cognition in Text Analysis*. Amsterdam: John Benjamins.

and Short, M. (2004) *Corpus Stylistics: Speech, Writing and Thought Presentation in a Corpus of English Writing*. London: Routledge.

Heywood, J. and Short, M. (2004) 'Methodological problems in the analysis of a corpus of conversations about cancer', *Journal of Pragmatics* 36(7): 1271–94.

Short, M. (1981) 'Discourse analysis and the analysis of drama', *Applied Linguistics* 11(2): 180–202.

(ed.) (1989) *Reading, Analysing and Teaching Literature*. London: Longman.

(1995) 'Discourse analysis and power relationships in The Ebony Tower by John Fowles', in Verdonk, P. and Weber, J. J. (eds.) *Twentieth-century Fiction: From Text to Context*, pp. 45–62. London: Routledge.

(1996) *Exploring the Language of Poems, Plays and Prose*. London: Longman.

(1998) 'From dramatic text to dramatic performance', in Culpeper, J., Short, M. and Verdonk, P. (eds.) *Exploring the Language of Drama: From Text to Context*, pp. 6–18. London: Routledge.

(2000) 'Graphological deviation, style variation and point of view in Marabou Stork Nightmares by Irvine Welsh', *Journal of Literary Studies/Tydskrif vir Literatuur Wetenskap* 15(3/4): 305–23.

(2007) 'How to make a drama out of a speech act: the speech act of apology in the film A Fish Called Wanda', in Hoover, D. and Lattig, S. (eds.) *Stylistics: Prospect and Retrospect*, pp. 169–89. Amsterdam: Rodopi.

and van Peer, W. (1989) 'Accident! Stylisticians evaluate: aims and methods of stylistic analysis', in Short, M. (ed.) *Reading, Analysing and Teaching Literature*, pp. 22–71. London: Longman.

and van Peer, W. (1999) 'A reply to Mackay', *Language and Literature* 8(3): 269–75.

and Wen Zhong, H. U. (1997) 'Analyzing the changing character and sophistication of TV advertisements in the People's Republic of China', *Text* 17(4): 491–515.

Freeman, D., van Peer, W. and Simpson, P. (1998) 'Stylistics, criticism and myth-representation again: squaring the circle with Ray Mackay's subjective solution for all problems', *Language and Literature* 7(1): 40–50.

Silkin, J. (ed.) (1979) *The Penguin Book of First World War Poetry*. Harmondsworth: Penguin.

Simpson, P. (1993) *Language, Ideology and Point of View*. London: Routledge.

(1996) *Language through Literature: An Introduction*. London: Routledge.

(2004) *On the Discourse of Satire*. Amsterdam: John Benjamins.

and Montgomery, M. (1995) 'Language, literature and film: the stylistics of Bernard MacLaverty's Cal', in Verdonk, P. and Weber, J. J. (eds.) *Twentieth-century Fiction: From Text to Context*. London: Routledge.

Sinclair, J. (2004) *Trust the Text: Language, Corpus and Discourse*. London: Routledge.

Somacarrera, P. (2000) '"Barometer Couple": balance and parallelism in Margaret Atwood's Power Politics', *Language and Literature* 9(2): 135–49.

Sopcák, P. (2007) '"Creation from nothing": a foregrounding study of James Joyce's drafts for Ulysses', *Language and Literature* 16(2): 183–96.

Sotirova, V. (forthcoming) *D. H. Lawrence and Narrative Viewpoint*. London: Continuum.

Spencer-Oatey, H. (2002) 'Managing rapport in talk: using rapport sensitive incidents to explore the motivational concerns underlying politeness', *Journal of Pragmatics* 34: 529–45.

Steen, G. J. (1994) *Understanding Metaphor in Literature: An Empirical Approach.* London: Longman.

(2007) *Finding Metaphor in Grammar and Usage.* Amsterdam: John Benjamins.

Steffensen, M. S. and Joag-Dev, C. (1984) 'Cultural knowledge and reading', in Alderson, J. C. and Urquhart, A. H. (eds.) *Reading in a Foreign Language*, pp. 48–64. London: Longman.

Stockwell, P. (2000) *The Poetics of Science Fiction*. Harlow/London: Longman.

(2002a) *Cognitive Poetics: An Introduction*. London: Routledge.

(2002b) 'Miltonic texture and the feeling of reading', in Semino, E. and Culpeper, J. (eds.) *Cognitive Stylistics: Language and Cognition in Text Analysis*, pp. 73–94. Amsterdam: John Benjamins.

(2003) 'Surreal figures', in Gavins, J. and Steen, G. (eds.) *Cognitive Poetics in Practice*, pp. 13–26. London: Routledge.

Stubbs, M. (2005) 'Conrad in the computer: examples of quantitative stylistic methods', *Language and Literature* 14(1): 5–24.

Syal, M. (1997) *Anita and me*. London: Flamingo.

Tarantino, Q. (1994) *Reservoir Dogs*. London: Faber and Faber.

Thomas, D. (2003) *Collected Poems*. Ed. Walford Davies and Ralph Maud. London: Phoenix.

Thomas, J. (1995) *Meaning in Interaction: An Introduction to Pragmatics*. London: Longman.

Todd, L. (1989) *The Language of Irish Literature*. Basingstoke: Palgrave.

Toolan, M. (1988) *Language in Literature: An Introduction to Stylistics*. London: Hodder Arnold.

(1996) 'Stylistics and its discontents; or, getting off the Fish "hook"', in Weber, J-J. (ed.) *The Stylistics Reader*, pp. 117–35. London: Hodder Arnold.

Tsur, R. (1992) *Towards a Theory of Cognitive Poetics*. Amsterdam: Elsevier.

Turner, M. (1987) *Death is the Mother of Beauty: Mind, Metaphor, Criticism*. Chicago: University of Chicago Press.

Ungerer, F. and Schmid, H. J. (1996) *An Introduction to Cognitive Linguistics*. London: Longman.

Van Peer, W. (1980) *The Stylistic Theory of Foregrounding: A Theoretical and Empirical Investigation*. Unpublished PhD thesis: Lancaster University.

(1986) *Stylistics and Psychology: Investigations of Foregrounding*. London: Croom Helm.

(1993) 'Typographic foregrounding', *Language and Literature*, 2(1): 49–61.

(ed.) (2007) *Language and Literature*, Special Issue: *Foregrounding*, 16(2): 99–224.

Hakemulder, J. and Zyngier, S. (2007) *Muses and Measures: Empirical Research Methods for the Humanities*. Cambridge: Cambridge Scholars Publishing.

Mentjes, A. and Auracher, J. (in press) 'Does reading literature make you happy?', in Martindale, C., Dorfman, L., Petrov, V. and Leontiev, D. (eds.) *New Directions in Aesthetics, Creativity, and the Psychology of Art*. Amityville, NY: Baywood Publ. Co.

Venn, J. (1880) 'On the diagrammatic and mechanical representation of propositions and reasonings', *The London, Edinburgh, and Dublin Philosophical Magazine and Journal of Science* 9: 1–18.

Verdonk, P. (ed.) (1993) *Twentieth-century Poetry: From Text to Context*. London: Routledge.

Verne, J. (1994 [1873]) *Around the World in Eighty Days*. Ware: Wordsworth.

Wales, K. (1989) *A Dictionary of Stylistics*. 1st edition. London: Longman.

(2001) *A Dictionary of Stylistics*. 2nd edition. London: Longman.

Wallhead, C. (2003) 'Metaphors for the self in A. S. Byatt's the Biographer's Tale', *Language and Literature* 12(4): 291–308.

Werth, P. (1994) 'Extended metaphor: a text world account', *Language and Literature* 3(2): 79–103.

(1995) 'How to build a world (in a lot less than six days and using only what's in your head)', in Green, K. (ed.) *New Essays on Deixis: Discourse, Narrative, Literature*, pp. 49–80. Amsterdam: Rodopi.

(1997) 'Remote worlds: the conceptual representation of linguistic would', in Nutys, J. and Pederson, E. (eds.) *Language and Conceptualization*, pp. 84–115. Cambridge: Cambridge University Press.

(1999) *Text Worlds: Representing Conceptual Space in Discourse*. London: Longman.

(2007 [1995]) '"World enough, and time": deictic space and the interpretation of prose', in Carter, R. and Stockwell, P. (eds.) *The Language and Literature Reader*, pp. 155–66. Abingdon: Routledge.

West, D. (2007) 'I. A. Richards' Theory of Metaphor: between protocognitivism and post-structuralism', in Jeffries, L., McIntyre, D. and Bousfield, D. (eds.) *Stylistics and Social Cognition*. Amsterdam: Rodopi.

(2008) 'Changing English: a polemic against diversity and fragmentation', *Changing English: An International Journal of English Teaching* 15(2): 137–43.

(forthcoming) *I. A. Richards: Towards a Cognitive Stylistics*. London: Continuum.

Wodehouse, P. G. (1980 [1969]) *A Pelican at Blandings*. London: Penguin.

(1991) *The Mating Season*. London: Random House.

Wordsworth, W. (1971) *The Prelude: A Parallel Text*. Ed. J. Maxwell. London: Penguin.

Wynne, M. (2006) 'Stylistics: corpus approaches', in Brown, K. (ed.) *Encyclopedia of Language and Linguistics*, 2nd edition, Vol. 12, pp. 223–6. Oxford: Elsevier.

Short, M. and Semino, E. (1998) 'A corpus-based investigation of speech, thought and writing presentation in English narrative texts', in Renouf, A. (ed.) *Explorations in Corpus Linguistics*, pp. 231–45. Amsterdam: Rodopi.

Index